Photomedicine

Volume I

Editors

Ehud Ben-Hur, Ph.D.
Department of Radiobiology
Nuclear Research Center-Negev
Beer-Sheva, Israel

Ionel Rosenthal, Ph.D.
Head
Division of Food Technology
Agricultural Research Organization, Volcani Center
Bet Dagan, Israel

CRC Press, Inc.
Boca Raton, Florida

Library of Congress-in-Publication Data

Photomedicine.

Includes bibliographies and index.
1. Phototherapy.   2. Photochemotherapy.   3. Light--
Physiological effect.   I. Ben-Hur, Ehud.   II. Rosenthal,
Ionel.   [DNLM: 1. Phototherapy.   WB 480 P5745]
RM837.P48   1987   615.8′3   86-34293
ISBN-0-8493-4673-8 (set)

Direct all inquiries to CRC Press, Inc., 2000 Corporate Blvd., N.W., Boca Raton, Florida, 33431.

© 1987 by CRC Press, Inc.

International Standard Book Number 0-8493-4674-6 (v. 1)
International Standard Book Number 0-8493-4675-4 (v. 2)
International Standard Book Number 0-8493-4676-2 (v. 3)
International Standard Book Number 0-8493-4673-8 (set)

Library of Congress Card Number 86-34293
Printed in the United States

INTRODUCTION

Go outside and play in the sun. It's good for you.

My mother

The use of sunlight and drugs for the treatment of skin diseases has been documented for over 3400 years; for an even longer time, the reddening, blistering, and tanning effects of sunlight have probably been known. With the discovery of lasers a new dimension was added in the study and application of light in medical therapy. Ophthalmologists adopted the laser in the clinic as a photocoagulator for the treatment of detached retina, and the use of laser as a scalpel for noncontact, noninvasive, and even subcellular surgery is at an earlier state of acceptance. In addition to surgical uses, new, promising ideas are continuing to emerge. Thus, laser can be used to diagnose and treat malignant tumors using photoradiation therapy. This renewed interest, stimulated by the mutual interplay of both scientific and technological innovations, is characterized by a multidisciplinary approach involving physicists, chemists, biochemists, and physicians.

Our objective has been to collect in these three volumes the most up-to-date assessment of our understanding of light in medicine. Since *Photomedicine* was defined as an informative guide to practical applications rather than an esoteric study of medical discipline, the level of medical rigor was reasonably relaxed.

Given limitations on length, the chapters are not intended to be all embracing reviews of the field, but rather to present an overview of key ideas and directions with the objective of delineating the most promising and exciting problems. We hope that the text is sufficiently introductory to stimulate the curiosity and interest of a neophyte, and to simultaneously provide the specialist with a rather short, but current summary of the status of this field. Most important, we hope that the volumes will further highlight this rapidly developing science and spur current and new researchers and ideas.

Ehud Ben-Hur
Ionel Rosenthal

THE EDITORS

Ehud Ben-Hur, Ph.D., was born in Israel in 1940. After graduation from the Hebrew University of Jerusalem in 1965, he went on to study biochemistry at the Technion, Israel Institute of Technology at Haifa, where he obtained his M.Sc. and doctorate degrees. He then joined the Biology Department of Brookhaven National Laboratory as Research Associate where he completed postdoctoral work on the radiobiology of cultured mammalian cells under the auspices of Dr. M. M. Elkind. Upon returning to Israel in 1973, he first joined the Department of Cellular Biochemistry at the Hebrew University and then the Nuclear Research Center-Negev, in 1975, where he is currently engaged in studies of biological effects of ionizing and nonionizing radiations.

The main thrust of his research activity in the past was related to radiation-induced damage in DNA and its repair. During the last few years he has become interested in photodynamic therapy of cancer and is actively involved with Dr. I. Rosenthal in developing new and improved photosensitizers for this purpose.

Dr. Ben-Hur is affiliated with the Department of Radiation Biology, Colorado State University. He is also affiliated with Ben-Gurion University, Beer-Sheva, Israel, where he teaches photobiology. Dr. Ben-Hur has published over 80 papers in scientific journals, is a member of the American Society for Photobiology and the Radiation Research Societies of both the U.S. and Israel, and is on the Editorial Board of the *International Journal of Radiation Biology.*

Dr. Ben-Hur is married with two children and lives most of the time in Beer-Sheva.

Ionel Rosenthal, Ph.D., received his degree in Chemical Engineering from the Polytechnic Institute in Bucharest (Romania) and Ph.D. degree from the Freinberg Graduate School of the Weizmann Institute of Science, Rehovoth, Israel. Dr. Rosenthal has had a very colorful professional career which has included Plant Engineer at "Mahteshim" Chemical Co. and Senior Scientist at the Department of Organic Chemistry at the Weizmann Institute of Science and at the Department of Organic Chemistry, Nuclear Research Center-Negev. Currently he is Principal Scientist at the Department of Food Science, Agricultural Research Organization, Bet-Dagan, and Professor in the Department of Agricultural Biochemistry at the Faculty of Agriculture of the Hebrew University, Jerusalem.

His scientific interests in organic photobiochemistry and food chemistry (and its spin-off: cookery) have resulted in more than 100 research publications in these areas.

ACKNOWLEDGMENTS

The editors wish to acknowledge their indebtedness to the authors for their ready response to our request to contribute, and for their kindness and understanding in accepting their editorial efforts.

CONTRIBUTORS

Esther Azizi, M.D.
Senior Dermatologist
Department of Dermatology
Sheba Medical Center
Tel-Hashomer, Israel

Roger W. Barnes, B.S.
Assistant to the Director
Office of Device Evaluation
U.S. Food and Drug Administration
Silver Springs, Maryland

Ehud Ben-Hur, Ph.D.
Department of Radiobiology
Nuclear Research Center-Negev
Beer-Sheva, Israel

Jeffrey D. Bernhard, M.D.
Director, Division of Dermatology
Director, Phototherapy Center
Assistant Professor
Department of Medicine
University of Massachusetts Medical
  Center
Worcester, Massachusetts

Homer S. Black, Ph.D.
Director
Photobiology Laboratory
Veterans Administration Medical
  Center
Baylor College of Medicine
Houston, Texas

Larry E. Bockstahler
Division of Life Sciences
Optical Radiation Branch
U.S. Food and Drug Administration
Rockville, Maryland

S. G. Bown
Department of Surgery
University College London
London, England

John A. S. Carruth
Senior Lecturer in Otolaryngology
Southampton University Hospitals
Southampton, England

James E. Cleaver, Ph.D.
Professor
Laboratory of Radiobiology and
  Environmental Health
University of California
San Francisco, California

Farrington Daniels, Jr., M.D., M.P.H.
Emeritus Professor of Medicine
The New York Hospital-Cornell Medical
  Center
New York, New York

John H. Epstein, M.D.
Clinical Professor of Dermatology
University of California Medical School
San Francisco, California

I. Farine, M.D.
Professor and Head
Orthopedic Department
Sheba Medical Center
Tel-Hashomer, Israel

Richard P. Felten
Department of Health and Human
  Services
Division of Life Sciences
U.S. Food and Drug Administration
Rockville, Maryland

Anna Flint, Ph.D.
Department of Dermatology
Sheba Medical Center
Tel-Hashomer, Israel

Orna Geyer, M.D.
Department of Ophthalmology
Tel Aviv Medical Center
Tel Aviv, Israel

Barbara A. Gilchrest, M.D.
Professor and Chairman
Department of Dermatology
Boston University School of Medicine
Boston, Massachusetts

Philip C. Hanawalt, Ph.D.
Professor and Chairman
Department of Biological Sciences
Stanford University
Stanford, California

M. Heim, M.D.
Department of Rehabilitation
Sheba Medical Center
Tel-Hashomer, Israel

Kiki B. Hellman, Ph.D.
Senior Scientist
Division of Life Sciences
U.S. Food and Drug Administration
Rockville, Maryland

Victoria M. Hitchins, Ph.D.
Division of Life Sciences
Optical Radiation Branch
U.S. Food and Drug Administration
Rockville, Maryland

H. Horoszowski, M.D.
Head
Department of Orthopedy
Sheba Medical Center
Tel-Hashomer, Israel

Elizabeth D. Jacobson, Ph.D.
Acting Director
Office of Science and Technology
Center for Devices and Radiological
 Health
U.S. Food and Drug Administration
Rockville, Maryland

W. Patrick Jeeves, Ph.D.
Department of Medical Physics
Ontario Cancer Treatment and
 Research Foundation
Hamilton, Ontario, Canada

Anthony Lamanna
Division of Life Sciences
Optical Radiation Branch
U.S. Food and Drug Administration
Rockville, Maryland

Robert J. Landry, Ph.D.
Electrooptics Branch
U.S. Food and Drug Administration
Rockville, Maryland

Moshe Lazar, M.D.
Department of Ophthalmology
Ichilov Hospital
Tel-Aviv, Israel

Sidney Lerman, Ph.D.
Professor
Department of Opthalmology
Emory University
Atlanta, Georgia

Jerome I. Levine, Ph.D.
Division of Life Sciences
Optical Radiation Branch
U.S. Food and Drug Administration
Rockville, Maryland

Julia G. Levy, Ph.D.
Professor
Department of Microbiology
University of British Columbia
Vancouver, Canada

C. David Lytle, Ph.D.
Division of Life Sciences
Optical Radiation Branch
U.S. Food and Drug Administration
Rockville, Maryland

I. A. Magnus, M.D., F.R.C.P.
Professor Emeritus
Photobiology Department
Institute of Dermatology
London, England

Micheline M. Mathews-Roth, M.D.
Associate Professor of Medicine
Channing Laboratory
Harvard Medical School
Boston, Massachusetts

Daphne Mew, Ph.D.
Faculty of Medicine
Foothill Hospital
University of Calgary
Calgary, Alberta, Canada

K. Mohan, Ph.D.
Science & Technology
U.S. Food and Drug Administration
Rockville, Maryland

Warwick L. Morison, M.D.
Associate Professor of Dermatology
Johns Hopkins Medical Institutions
Baltimore, Maryland

D. Phillips
Royal Institution
London, England

Maureen B. Poh-Fitzpatrick, M.D.
Associate Professor of Dermatology
Columbia University
New York, New York

Michael K. Reusch, M.D.
Department of Dermatology
Stanford University Medical School
Stanford, California

Ionel Rosenthal, Ph.D.
Head
Division of Food Technology
Agricultural Research Organization,
 Volcani Center
Bet Dagan, Israel

Stephen M. Sykes
Division of Life Sciences
Optical Radiation Branch
U.S. Food and Drug Administration
Rockville, Maryland

Morris Waxler
Office of Science and Technology
Center for Devices and Radiological
 Health
U.S. Food and Drug Administration
Rockville, Maryland

Abraham Werner, Ph.D.
Chief Physicist
Department of Oncology
Sheba Medical Center
Tel-Hashomer, Israel

Brian C. Wilson, Ph.D.
Department of Medical Physics
Ontario Cancer Treatment and
 Research Foundation
Hamilton, Ontario, Canada

Bruce U. Wintroub
Department of Dermatology
University of California
San Francisco, California

TABLE OF CONTENTS

Volume I

Volume II

Volume III

Chapter 1

BASICS OF PHOTOCHEMISTRY

Ionel Rosenthal

TABLE OF CONTENTS

I. PHOTOCHEMICAL TERMS

The science of photochemistry is concerned with the chemical and physical effects associated with electronic excitation of the chemical compounds. The promoter of excitation, for most practical purposes, is electromagnetic radiation in the UV and visible region of the spectrum (Table 1). Electromagnetic radiation can be regarded as having a dual nature.

• The light propagation phenomena such as reflection, refraction, interference, diffraction, and polarization can be explained in terms of a wave propagation. The wave is composed of oscillating electric and magnetic fields operating in planes which are perpendicular to each other and to the direction of propagation. The time variable strength of the resulting vector could be described by a sinusoidal function (Figure 1). The wave of radiation is characterized by wavelength (λ) which is the distance between identical positions on successive waves, or by frequency (v) which is the number of waves that pass a fixed point per second. These two parameters are related in Equation 1:

$$v = \frac{c}{\lambda} \tag{1}$$

where c is the speed of electromagnetic radiation in vacuum (2.9979×10^8 m/sec). The wavelength of radiation determines the color of the light.

• At the same time, the phenomena of absorption or emission of radiation must occur only in discrete units called quanta or photons which have energies E as given by Equation 2:

$$E = hv = \frac{hc}{\lambda} \tag{2}$$

where h is a universal constant called Planck's constant (6.6256×10^{-34} J sec). It results that the energy absorbed or emitted by a molecule is inversely proportional to the wavelength of radiation. The energy of one "mole" of light, *viz.,* an Einstein, is given by Equation 3:

$$E = N \frac{hc}{\lambda} \tag{3}$$

where N is Avogadro's constant (6.022×10^{23}).

The first law of photochemistry — the Grotthuss-Draper law — requires that the radiant energy must be absorbed in order to induce a photochemical or photobiological reaction. The energies which can be absorbed by a particular molecule can be determined from the wavelengths in the absorption spectrum. The absorption spectrum of each molecule is, in turn, determined by the kind and arrangement of its component atoms. The first law of photochemistry is true for conventional light sources, but may require modifications for polyphotonic processes initiated by intense light sources such as lasers.

The second fundamental law, which is a result of the quantum theory, was proposed by Stark and Einstein and states that if a molecule absorbs radiation, then only one is excited for each quantum of radiation absorbed. The Stark-Einstein law implies that the efficiency of a photochemical process can be defined by its quantum yield (ϕ) which is the ratio of molecules undergoing a particular change and the number of quanta absorbed. In most photochemical reactions, the quantum yield will range from zero to

Table 1
THE DISTRIBUTION OF THE ELECTROMAGNETIC
SPECTRUM

Radiation	Wavelength	Absorption or emission of radiation involves
Gamma rays	0.0005—0.14 nm	Nuclear transition
X-rays	0.01—10 nm	Transitions of inner atomic electrons
Vacuum UV	1—200 nm	Transitions of outer atomic electrons
UV	200—400 nm	Transitions of outer atomic electrons
Visible	400—800 nm	Transitions of outer atomic electrons
Near IR	0.8—1.5 μm	Molecular vibrations
IR	1.5—5.6 μm	Molecular vibrations
Far IR	5.6—1000 μm	Molecular rotations
Micro- and radiowaves	1000 μm—550 m	Oscillations of mobile or free electrons

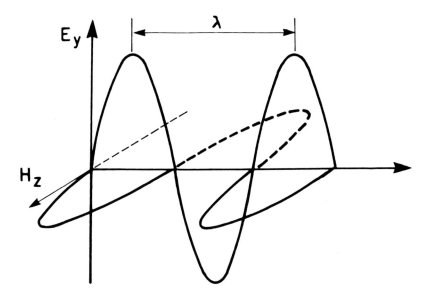

FIGURE 1.   The electric (Ey) and magnetic (Hz) vectors of an electromagnetic light wave.

unity. However, in a chain reaction, where the absorption of one photon initiates the reaction, the value of the quantum yield may be several powers of ten. The determination of the quantum yield of a process will depend on the accurate determination of the number of molecules reacting or formed, and the number of photons absorbed. While the first quantity can be obtained by chemical analyses, a measure of the number of photons absorbed is best achieved by comparison with a reaction system, the quantum yield of which has been determined accurately using a photosensitive instrumental technique. Such a reaction system is known as an actinometer.

The intensity of an absorption band follows the empirical Beer-Lambert law, which states that the fraction of light transmitted through an absorbing system is as presented in Equation 4 and, in the log form, in Equation 5:

$$\frac{I_t}{I_o} = 10^{-\varepsilon cd} \qquad (4)$$

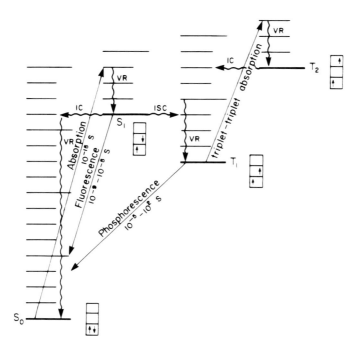

FIGURE 2. Energy level (Jablonski) diagram indicating the principal light-induced molecular photophysical processes. VR = vibrational relaxation, 10^{-10} sec; IC = internal conversion, 10^{-10} sec; ISC = intersystem crossing, 10^{-6} sec.

$$\log \frac{I_o}{I_t} = \xi cd \qquad (5)$$

where I_t and I_o are transmitted and incident light intensities, c is the concentration of the absorber, and d is the depth of absorber through which the light has passed. ξ is a constant of proportionality known as the extinction coefficient and is dependent on the wavelength and occasionally on concentration. The product ξcd is also named the optical density (OD) of the system.

When a molecule absorbs energy, the process is referred to as excitation. It is possible to represent the various physical processes involved in the photochemical excitation in the Jablonski diagram (Figure 2). The molecule is raised from its ground state of minimum energy to an excited state of higher energy. In the UV and visible region of the electromagnetic spectrum, this involves excitation to electronic energy levels. In the IR region, the excitation occurs between rotational levels at the lower energies of the far IR, while increase in the vibrational energy occurs in the near and medium IR region. While it is generally true that electronic excited states are the precursors of a photochemical change and, as such, are of primary importance in photobiology, they are inevitably accompanied by some increase in vibrational and rotational energy.

The electronic structure of the absorbing molecule changes as the result of excitation. This change is visualized in simple molecule orbital terms as a change in the occupation pattern of a set of orbitals. The combination of two atomic orbitals of different atoms by overlap along the internuclear axis results in the formation of two molecular orbitals — a bonding orbital (either σ or π), and an antibonding orbital (σ^* or π^*). In addition, the nonbonding electrons, if present as at an oxygen atom, occupy a nonbonding orbital n which by its nature does not possess an antibonding counterpart. Two electrons are assigned to each molecular orbital so that their spins are paired. In general, a molecule in its ground state has all of its electrons spin-paired (a notable exception is molecular oxygen, the ground state of which is a triplet). The absorption of a quanta of radiation in the UV-visible range by a molecule leads to electronic excitation of the absorber. That is the promotion of an electron from one molecular orbital to another, unoccupied, of higher energy, e.g., $\sigma \to \sigma^*$, $n \to \sigma$, $\pi \to \pi^*$, and n $\to \pi^*$. In general, excitation of an electron to the σ^* orbital requires an amount of energy corresponding to wavelengths below 200 nm, which are not readily accessible to conventional irradiation apparatus and are of little relevance to photobiology. The alternative excitation processes ($\pi - \pi^*$ and $n - \pi^*$) are responsible for the bulk of photochemical reactions, since the wavelengths associated with these two excitations are located in the accessible regions of the UV and visible part of electromagnetic spectrum.

The initial electronic excitation occurs without change in the orbital spin; i.e., the molecule, although in the excited state, still preserves the "singlet" multiplicity. The multiplicity, M, of a system is defined by Equation 6:

$$M = 2S + 1 \qquad (6)$$

where S is the total spin of the system. Thus, in a spin-paired system, $S = 0$ and $M = 1$ (singlet), while for a spin-parallel system, $S = 1$ and $M = 3$ (triplet). The excited singlet state is very short-lived and it may decay to the original ground state by conversion to heat or spontaneous photon emission (fluorescence). Alternatively, the molecule in this state could be destabilized to initiate a chemical reaction or could convert to a triplet state in a process which involves a spin flip of one of the electrons in the highest occupied molecular orbital. In this process, named intersystem crossing, the system becomes spin-parallel. Since transitions between states of different multiplicities are "forbidden" because they involve a spin inversion, the reversal from the excited triplet state to the ground singlet state is slow, and the molecule in the triplet state is long-lived. A triplet state always has a lower energy than the corresponding singlet state because of the repulsive nature of the spin-spin interaction between electrons of the same spin. The spontaneous radiation emission from the triplet state is known as phosphorescence. Because of its long lifetime, the triplet-state molecule is the most important in the initiation of chemical and biochemical reactions in vivo and in vitro. Reactions may also originate from excited singlets, but their much shorter lifetime most often limits their importance. The triplet molecule may react directly, inter- or intramolecularly, or may dispose of its energy by energy transfer to a vicinal suitable system. The concept of energy transfer can be represented in a general form by Equation 7:

$$^3D^* + {}^1A \to {}^1D + {}^3A^* \qquad (7)$$

where D and A are the donor and acceptor, respectively, in the triplet and singlet states. Excitation of a ground-state molecule by energy transfer from another excited species is termed sensitization, and the deactivation of the excited species is termed quenching. The energy-transfer processes play an important role in photobiology. Thus, the photosensitization creates the possibility of generating an excited molecule indirectly, rather than by its irradiation. Furthermore, the excited states of many organic molecules are quenched by molecular oxygen in a diffusion-controlled manner. Consequently, photochemical reactions are often drastically altered by the presence of molecular oxygen.

II. THE PRINCIPLE OF LASING

The laser (*L*ight *A*mplification by *S*timulated *E*mission of *R*adiation) is a device by which interaction of a photon with an excited species induces emission of a photon from this species. As the name implies, the operation of a laser depends on a stimulated emission of radiation. Stimulated emission is rarely important in photochemical processes in which thermal equilibrium is established. However, in a nonequilibrium situation, when the spontaneous emission in the system is suppressed in some way, the excited state becomes more populated than the ground st..te ("population inversion"). At this stage, the absorption of a photon of the transition frequency will trigger an emission which will predominate over absorption, and a net emission will result. The lasing system consists of an emitting material set between a pair of parallel mirrors, one of which is partially transparent. The mirrors are separated by an integral number of half of the emission wavelength. As a result, the light reflected from a mirror will be in phase with the incident wave, by a process called constructive interference. The population inversion essential to laser action is achieved by excitation to an excited state which is higher in energy than the lasing state. The excitation is most often achieved by photochemical techniques. When a population inversion has been generated in the emitting material, spontaneous emission provides a few photons, which on collision with molecules of the exciting lasing material stimulate it to emit in phase with the incident photons. Thus a light wave builds up in intensity as it travels back and forth between the mirrors, and this cascade reaction destroys the population inversion in a very short interval of time (1 μsec) producing a burst of radiation which escapes through the partially transmitting mirror. Since the cavity is tuned only for axial radiation, all off-axis radiation escapes after few reflections without reaching the lasing stage. Subsequently the laser beam exhibits a very accurate parallelism and can be focused to a spot of very small dimensions (of the order of a wavelength), thus generating very high radiation densities ($>10^9$ W/cm^2) for short laser pulses. In addition, the cavity is tuned to one particular frequency, and the light of any other frequency is removed by destructive interference. Subsequently, the emerging light exhibits a very high monochromaticity and coherence; i.e., the emitted light waves are all in phase.

III. QUANTUM LIGHT UNITS OF MEASURE

Many different terms and units have been, and still are being used in the literature to describe light. Several slightly different values can be found in the literature for conversion factors. The origin for discrepancies could not always be traced. The conversion factors between various units of energy of electromagnetic radiation are as follows:

$$1 \text{ J} = 10^7 \text{ erg} = 6.25 \times 10^{18} \text{ eV} = 2.38 \times 10^{-4} \text{ kcal}$$

The intensity of light is expressed in units of energy per unit of cross section. Most commonly, W/cm^2 or related energy units are employed. When using this term, the wavelength region must be specified. Alternatively, Einstein/sec/cm^2 is also used for radiant energy in a mole of photons.

The intensity of a source of visible light can also be measured in candle power. The candela (candle) is 1/60 of the luminous intensity of 1 cm^2 of a full radiator at the freezing temperature of platinum (2046 K). More recently, candela was defined as the luminous intensity of a source emitting monochromatic radiation with a frequency of 540×10^{12} Hz and a radiant intensity of 1/683 W per steradian. This corresponds to about 54.5 candle power to 1 W at 556 nm, which is the wavelength of maximum visibility. The total visible energy emitted by a source per unit time is called the total luminous flux from the source. The unit of flux, the lumen, is the flux emitted in a unit solid angle (steradian) by a point source of 1 cd. Thus, 1 cd intensity emits 4π lm. The density of the luminous flux on a surface is called illumination. It is the quotient of the flux by the area of the surface when the latter is uniformly illuminated. The footcandle corresponds to the illumination of 1 lm incident per square foot; alternatively, the lux equals 1 lm/m². Finally, solar radiation is customarily measured in *Langleys* (Ly) per minute. The Langley is 1 cal/cm².

The conversion factors between the various light-intensity units are as follows:

$$1 \text{ W/cm}^{-2} = 9.29 \times 10^2 \text{W/ft}^{-2} = 8.36 \times 10^{-9}\lambda \text{ (nm) einstein/sec/cm}^{-2}$$

$$= 5.8 \times 10^5 \text{fc (at 556 nm)} = 6.28 \times 10^6 \text{lx (at 556 nm)}$$

REFERENCES

1. Seliger, H. H. and McElroy, W. D., *Light: Physical and Biological Action*, Academic Press, New York, 1965.
2. Calvert, J. G. and Pitts, J. N., Jr., *Photochemistry*, John Wiley & Sons, New York, 1967.
3. Cundall, R. B. and Gilbert, A., *Photochemistry*, Thomas Nelson & Sons, 1970.
4. Wayne, R. P., *Photochemistry*, Elsevier, New York, 1970.
5. De Puy, C. H. and Chapman, O. L., *Molecular Reactions and Photochemistry*, Prentice-Hall, Englewood Cliffs, N.J., 1972.
6. Murov, S. L., *Handbook of Photochemistry*, Marcel Dekker, New York, 1973.
7. Arnold, D. R., Baird, N. C., Bolton, J. R., Brand, J. C. D., Jacobs, P. W. M., de Mayo, P., and Ware, W. R., *Photochemistry*, Academic Press, New York, 1974.
8. Coxon, J. M. and Halton, B., *Organic Photochemistry*, Cambridge University Press, London, 1974.
9. Daniels, F., *Direct Use of the Sun's Energy*, Yale University Press, New Haven, Conn., 1974.
10. Clayton, R. K., *Light and Living Matter*, Vol. 1, McGraw Hill, New York, 1977.
11. Turro, N. J., *Modern Molecular Photochemistry*, W. A. Benjamin, New York, 1978.
12. Phillips, R., *Sources and Applications of Ultraviolet Radiation*, Academic Press, London, 1983.
13. Rabek, J. F., *Experimental Methods in Photochemistry and Photophysics*, John Wiley & Sons, New York, 1982.

Chapter 2

MOLECULAR AND CELLULAR PHOTOBIOLOGY

Ehud Ben-Hur

TABLE OF CONTENTS

I. INTRODUCTION

Life evolved on earth under continuous exposure to electromagnetic radiation from the sun, ranging from the far ultraviolet (UVC) to the visible part of the spectrum. UV light can damage many cellular structures, mainly nucleic acids. This results in lowered cell viability and hereditary changes in surviving cells. Thus, the evolving primitive cells were under a selective pressure to protect themselves from the deleterious effects of the UV light of the sun and to develop mechanisms that deal with the damage produced in critical targets, e.g., DNA. Today we have a fairly good, although incomplete, knowledge of the important photodamage in DNA, RNA, proteins, and membranes. We also know the general outlines of most of the repair mechanisms that have been developed to deal with UV-induced damage in DNA. This information is more detailed for prokaryotes than for mammalian cells but new data are being continuously added in this intensively studied field.

Because of the vast scope of the subject matter, it is impossible to give an in-depth state-of-the-art description of molecular and cellular photobiology in one chapter. Rather, what was attempted is to give the reader a general view of this topic with pertinent examples where appropriate. For those wishing to explore this fascinating field further, an extensive list of references is provided.

The first part of this chapter is devoted to the introduction of photodamage and its biological effects. Later parts deal with the biochemical responses to DNA damage, mainly in terms of repair mechanisms, and the way these responses are reflected at the cellular level.

II. MOLECULAR PHOTODAMAGE IN CELLS

A. Photochemistry of Nucleic Acids

Because DNA and RNA have the strongest absorption in the UV of all cellular components, they are also the most sensitive to photochemical changes. The four heterocyclic bases serve as the chromophores, with λ_{max} about 260 nm. The pyrimidines undergo photochemical reactions $\sim$10 times more readily than purines. The following is a list of the photoproducts according to prevalence and importance. In general, those produced in DNA are more important than those produced in RNA because of the unique position of the former in the chain of information transfer within the cell.

1. Cyclobutane-Type Pyrimidine Dimers

The isolation and identification of a cyclobutane-type thymine dimer (Thy <> Thy) from UV-irradiated frozen solution of thymine[1] opened the way for modern molecular photobiology. Thy <> Thy has four isomeric forms, of which two exist in optically active forms[2,3] (Figure 1). In UV-irradiated DNA, dimerization of adjacent pyrimidines is the predominant photochemical reaction. This gives rise to thymine-cytosine and cytosine-cytosine (Thy <> Cyt, Cyt <> Cyt) dimers, in addition to Thy <> Thy, all of which are in *cis-syn* configuration. The photochemical reactivity of DNA depends upon the primary base composition and sequence and DNA secondary structure and its environment during irradiation.[4] For example, the rate of Thy <> Thy formation in denatured DNA is twice that of DNA irradiated in the native state. Also, because of the greater freedom of movement of the bases in denatured DNA, the *trans-syn* isomer is also produced.[5]

Pyr <> Pyr formation in DNA proceeds as follows. Absorption of a photon excites a pyrimidine base from its ground state (S_o) to a singlet excited state (S_1). In the new electronic configuration the van der Waals' radius of the base is reduced, allowing an

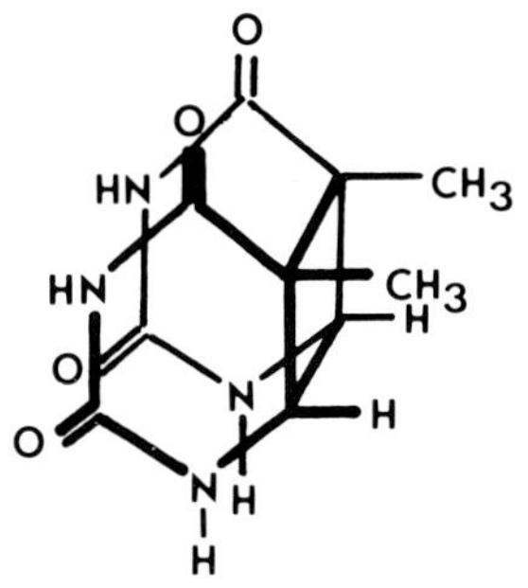

(MESO)
CIS – SYN

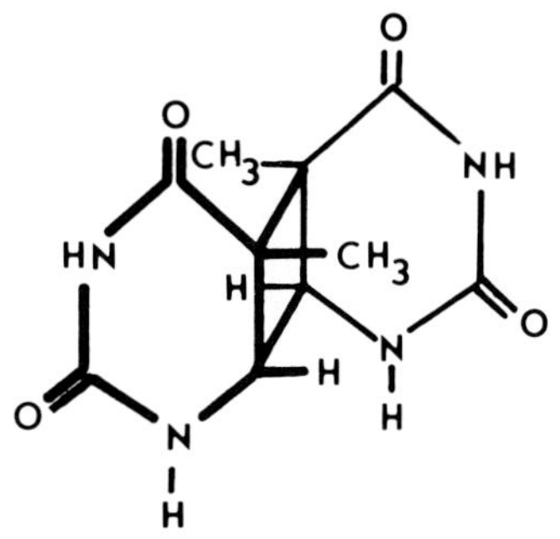

(d, l)
TRANS – SYN

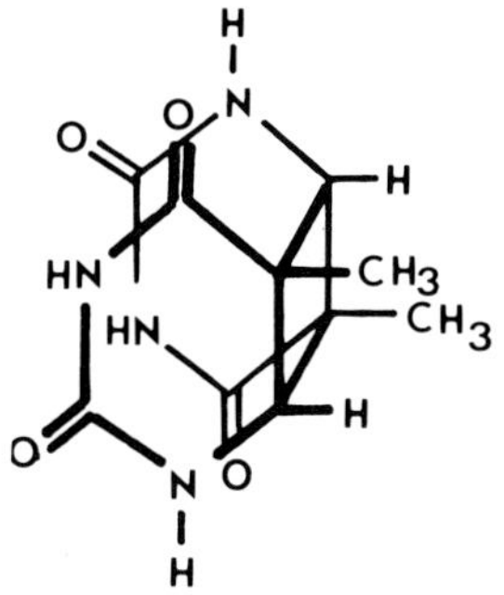

(d, l)
CIS – ANTI

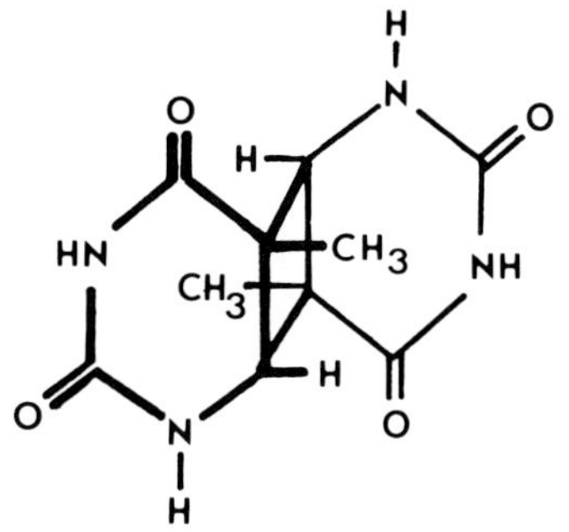

(MESO)
TRANS – ANTI

FIGURE 1. Thy <> Thy isomers.

adjacent pyrimidine to move closer and share the excitation energy. This "excimer" can undergo intersystem crossing into the more stable triplet state (T_1) from which a Pyr <> Pyr may arise.

$$\mathrm{Pyr}_{S_0} \xrightarrow{h\nu} \mathrm{Pyr}_{S_1} + \mathrm{Pyr}_{S_0} \rightarrow [\mathrm{Pyr} \cdot \mathrm{Pyr}]_{S_1} \xrightarrow{isc} [\mathrm{Pyr} \cdot \mathrm{Pyr}]_{T_1} \rightarrow \mathrm{Pyr} <> \mathrm{Pyr}$$

DNA undergoes a change from a B conformation to A when its degree of hydration is reduced. Because Pyr <> Pyr yield is drastically reduced and a new photoproduct is formed upon UV irradiation of DNA in the dry state,[6] it was assumed that DNA photochemistry is modified by its conformation. More recent data have shown that the degree of hydration rather than the conformational state is the critical factor in determining which of the photoproducts will form in native DNA.[7]

The absolute yield of Pyr <> Pyr is twofold greater in DNA irradiated (254 nm) in vitro than in vivo.[8] This "shielding" effect is not due to cytoplasmic absorption, although in mammalian cells this may be a contributing factor. Rather, it reflects the dense packing of DNA in cells, as opposed to its more linear, extended form in solution. The ratios of the different Pyr <> Pyr formed in vivo depend on the base content of the DNA. In *E. coli* there are 1 Cyt <> Cyt:5 Cyt <> Thy:10 Thy <> Thy and the yield per genome molecular weight per unit fluence is 2.3 Pyr <> Pyr/10^8 daltons/J/m^2 at 254 nm. At longer wavelengths relatively more Cyt-containing dimers are formed, although the total yield decreases above 265 nm. The presence of Pyr <> Pyr produces some distortion in DNA structure, as evidenced by a lowered melting tem-

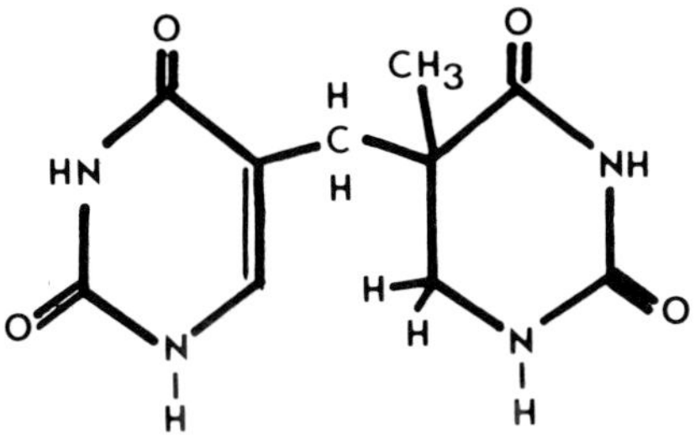

FIGURE 2.   Molecular structure of Thy (α-5)hThy.

perature[9] and increased reactivity to formaldehyde.[10] Melting of DNA (4.3 A-T bp are broken per dimer[9]) would reduce the twisting of one strand around its complement and should therefore affect the superhelicity of the entire molecule. By measuring the untwisting in negatively supercoiled DNA it was estimated that the unwinding angle per dimer is −14°.[11] Alterations in superhelicity can affect the binding of proteins to DNA and the processes of transcription, recombination, and replication.[12] In torsionally stressed superhelical DNA, unwinding by dimers will affect the helix structure in more distant regions and thus UV radiation could affect cellular function at a distance from the lesions themselves.[13]

Pyr <> Pyr are nonrandomly distributed in DNA.[10,14] Although this observation was contested,[15,16] it was later shown to be real and that dimerization occurs preferentially in long thymine tracts.[17] However, at the biological dose-range, the probability of forming a dimer "cluster" in DNA of moderate A-T content is rather low, and whether or not this phenomenon has a biological significance remains to be seen.

Detecting the presence and amount of Pyr <> Pyr in DNA can be achieved in two ways: (1) by breaking down the nucleic acid to individual components, separating them by some type of chromatographic procedure, and detecting their presence by absorbance or radioactivity measurements; and (2) by detecting the dimer *in situ* using a specific property (e.g., immunological reaction, the susceptibility to an enzyme). Some of these methods are very sensitive and can detect one dimer per 10^9 daltons DNA. These approaches are also used to detect other photoproducts. For a detailed description see Reference 4.

2. 5-Thyminyl-5,6-Dihydrothymine

When DNA is irradiated in the dry state,[6,18] at subzero temperatures[19] or in bacterial spores,[18] Pyr <> Pyr formation is greatly reduced and a new thymine-derived photoproduct appears. This was identified as 5-thyminyl-5,6-dihydrothymine, Thy(α-5)hThy (Figure 2).[20] It is usually referred to as "spore photoproduct" and was thought to be responsible for spore death following UV irradiation. However, recently another photoproduct was isolated from spores and identified as 6-4'-(pyrimidine-2'-one)-thymine (see next section).[21] Its contribution to the biological effects of UV on bacterial spores has yet to be determined.

The absence of water is necessary for Thy(α-5)hThy formation, which is consistent with the free-radical mechanism proposed.[20] Therefore, this photoproduct is biologically significant only for bacteria exposed to UV under extreme conditions of cold and dryness (e.g., in outer space).

3. Pyrimidine Adducts

A minor photoproduct (about 10% of the total) containing thymine was first isolated from DNA by Varghese and Wang.[22] This was identified as the acid-stable prod-

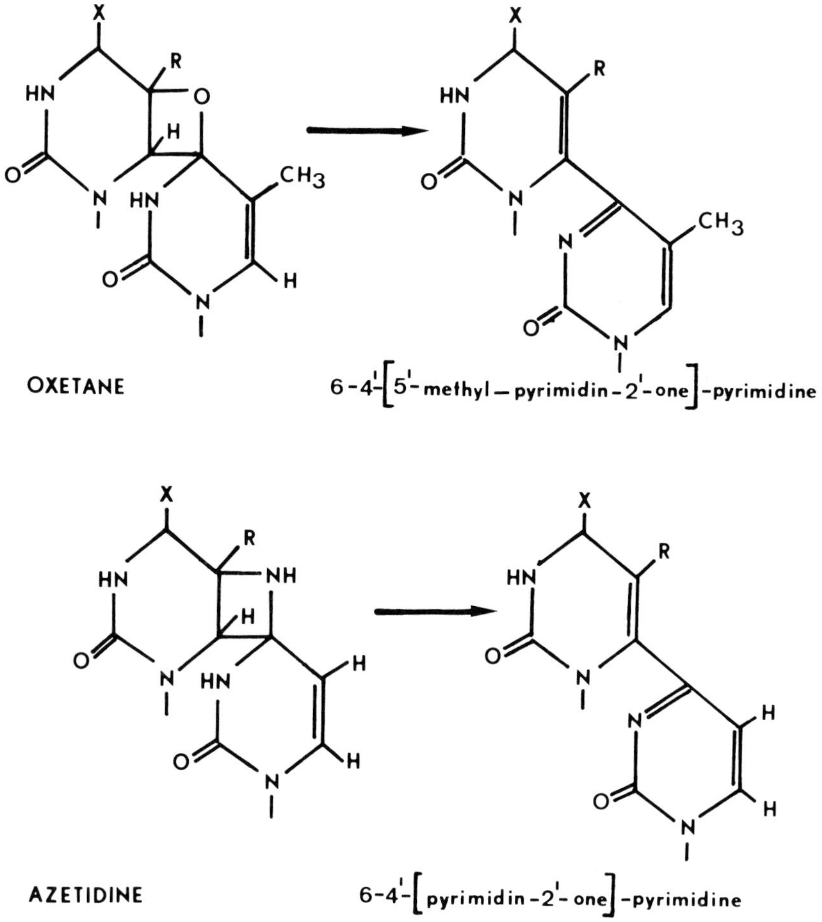

FIGURE 3.   Molecular structure of pyrimidine adducts isolated from irradiated DNA. When X is C=O then R is CH₃; X is NH₂ when R is H.

uct 6-4′-(pyrimidine-2′-one)-thymine (Thy(6-4)Pyo) resulting from dehydration of the Thy-Thy adduct containing an oxetane ring[23] (Figure 3). Similar adducts are formed via an azetidine ring between Thy-Cyt, and Cyt-Cyt.

The action spectrum for Pyr-Pyr adduct formation is essentially the same as that for Pyr <> Pyr in *Escherichia coli* DNA,[24] with a maximum at 265 nm. The quantum yield for Cyt-Thy (0.0015) is about half that of Cyt <> Thy (0.0024) and an order of magnitude lower than that for Thy <> Thy formation (0.019). The relative rates of formation of Cyt-Thy and Pyr<> Pyr depend strongly on the percent of Ade + Thy in DNA in an opposite manner. Cyt-Thy adducts formation increases with decreasing Thy contents of the DNA and with increasing dehydration. Also in contrast to Pyr <> Pyr, the formation of Pyr adducts is greater in native than in denatured DNA.[24]

The mechanism of Pyr-Pyr adducts formation does not involve the excited triplet state. It could involve phototautomerization in the G·C bp, serving as traps for singlet excitation energy, with subsequent addition of the imino double bond of the excited Cyt tautomer to the 5,6-double bond of a neighboring Thy.[4]

The most striking feature of Pyr adducts is the absorbance maximum at 315 nm. As a result, they can be eliminated from DNA by irradiation at λ = 310 to 340 nm, which has no effect on Pyr <> Pyr. The quantum yield for Cyt-Thy adduct photolysis is

0.003, close to the value (0.0015) for its formation. This is in contrast to the two to three orders of magnitude which separate the forward and reverse reaction involving Pyr <> Pyr.

Because of its low yield, the biological effects of Pyr adducts were neglected until recently, when a role in mutagenesis was proposed for this photoproduct (see Section III).

4. Deoxycytidine Photohydration

Upon excitation by UV light, dCyt in DNA and Cyt and Ura in RNA can add a water molecule to the 5,6-double bond, resulting in the formation of 6-hydroxy-5,6-dihydro-pyrimidine. In DNA, photohydration of dCyd is ∿5 times more efficient in the denatured than in the native state.[4] This is because the bases are more accessible to water in single-stranded DNA. The ratio of Thy <> Thy to photohydrate decreases with increasing exposure to UV. At high fluences the former has reached a photostationary state. The photohydrate formation, on the other hand, is not photoreversible. At 5 kJ/m² of 254-nm light there are 6 Thy <> Thy per photohydrate in native DNA. This value is probably higher in the biological dose-range. Photohydrates undergo dehydration at high temperatures and low pH. The half-life of dCyd hydrate in native DNA under physiological conditions is close to 1 hr.[25] This is sufficient not to ignore it as a lesion of possible biological importance. It is further emphasized by studies with the RNA bacteriophage R17, where uridine photohydrates were shown to be the major lethal lesion irrespective of Pyr <> Pyr formation.[26]

5. Other Pyrimidine Photoproducts

Yamane et al.[27] reported the isolation of 5,6-dihydrothymine from heavily irradiated DNA. Since identification of this product depends solely on the basis of chromatographic mobility of radioactive samples, and since there has been no other report of its formation, further discussion is not warranted at this time.

Ring-saturated thymine photoproducts (thymine glycols) of the 5,6-dihydroxy dihydrothymine-type ($ho^{5,6}hdT$) are produced in DNA of human cells upon UV irradiation under aerobic conditions.[28] Their yield per Thy <> Thy is very low at 260 to 280 nm (0.06) but increases dramatically at longer wavelengths, reaching 0.73 at 313 nm. Thus, ring-saturated thymine lesions represent minor lesions relative to pyrimidine dimers in the far UV but major lesions in the near UV.

6. Purine Photodamage

The quantum yields for photochemical alteration of the purines Ade and Gua are tenfold less than those for pyrimidines. Because of this, Pur photochemistry was not considered as important biologically and there are only a few studies concerning Pur photodamage in DNA. Using circular dichroism measurements, the quantum yield for UV-induced structural change in poly A and poly dA was estimated to be 3×10^{-4} and 2.5×10^{-3} mol/Einstein, respectively.[29] In DNA, an efficient photoalkylation of Pur occurs when irradiation is in the presence of alcohols, with a concomitant decrease in Pyr <> Pyr formation.[30] The biological significance of the above reactions is not known.

Recently, a photoadduct of Ade-Thy was isolated from UV-irradiated DNA.[31] It is formed in both denatured and native calf thymus DNA with respective quantum yields of 5×10^{-5} and 1×10^{5} mol/Einstein. The overall yield of Ade-Thy in a particular DNA will depend on how frequently T-A doublets occur within its sequence. Evidently, this adduct is a minor photoproduct. However, its biological significance will be determined not only by its abundance but also by its susceptibility to the cellular DNA repair mechanisms (see Section V) and the functional importance of the target sites. In the latter respect, the sequence T-A-T-A is a conserved feature of many promoters. Because this sequence is self-complementary, Thy-Ade photoadduct could be formed at the same site on both strands of a DNA duplex. Such an event would cause a permanent loss of genetic information.

7. UV-Induced Changes in the Secondary Structure of DNA

UV-induced damage in DNA can be detected by changes in the secondary structure of the DNA double helix. Base damage has an indirect effect by disrupting hydrogen bonding and leading to partial denaturation. Chain breaks and cross-links have a direct effect on DNA structure since they influence the length of the strands and their separability.

UV-induced chain breaks occur in DNA about 300 times less frequently than Pyr <> Pyr. At 254 nm, the presence of oxygen has little effect on the yield of single-strand breaks. At longer wavelengths, oxygen has an enhancing effect,[32] and at the same time there is a decrease in the ratio of Pyr dimers to strand breaks. These breaks may therefore acquire biological importance in the near-UV region.

The mechanism by which DNA chain breaks are induced by UV is not known. Since scavengers of hydroxyl radicals decrease the rate of strand breakage, OH· is probably involved.

Reliable estimates for the yield of DNA cross-links are not available because the production of strand breaks interferes with their measurement. At 280 nm, cross-links are formed at approximately the same yield as DNA strand breaks.[33] The chemical nature of the cross-links is not known. Because the action spectrum resembles the absorbance of Thy and because the yield is increased in Thy-rich DNA, Thy is probably involved. Pyr <> Pyr isomers other than *cis-syn* (Figure 1) and Thy-Cyt adduct are not involved since additional irradiation at 240 nm, which reverses Pyr dimers, and at 313 nm, which alters Thy(6-4)Pyo does not decrease the amount of DNA cross-links.[34]

8. Cross-Linking of DNA to Protein

Evidence for the cross-linking of DNA to protein was first discovered in UV-irradiated mammalian cells[35] as reduced extractability of DNA. This effect of UV was reversed by proteolytic digestion of the extract. Other lines of evidence imply that covalent bonds exist between nucleotide moieties of DNA and amino acid residues of proteins. However, the exact chemical nature of the photoproducts has not been established. A cysteine-Thy adduct has been isolated in UV-irradiated model systems[36] and DNA in vitro and in vivo[37] with 0.5 to 0.3 the efficiency with which Pyr <> Pyr are produced. Other amino acids, most notably tyrosine, although not as reactive as cysteine, also react with DNA and RNA upon UV irradiation (for review see Reference 38). It is expected that chromatin proteins, e.g., histones, will be particularly susceptible to UV-induced cross-linking to DNA. However, a detailed characterization of the cross-linked proteins has yet to be made.

The biological significance of DNA to protein cross-linking under normal conditions of exposure to UV is not known. It appears to be important when bacteria are exposed at subzero temperatures, since enhanced cell killing at low temperatures is accompanied by increased yield of cross-linking and reduced formation of Pyr <> Pyr.

B. DNA as the Primary Target to UV Light

Nucleic acids contain the genetic information necessary for the various cellular functions. Loss or alteration of a single nucleotide in an essential gene may cause the death of a cell. In contrast, damage to a few protein molecules or other cell substances would have little or no effect. In addition, in the far UV, nucleic acids are the most important absorbers of light energy. Because of this, it can be predicted that killing and mutation in most cells at 240 to 280 nm is due to absorption in nucleic acids.

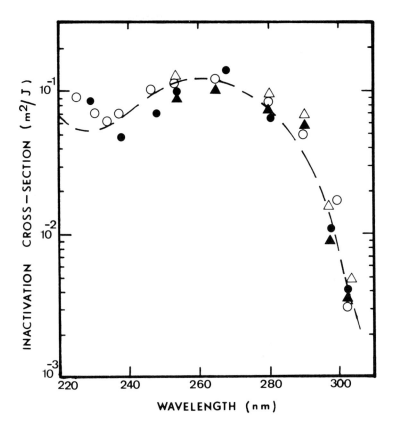

FIGURE 4.   Action spectra for killing of *E. coli* (•) and *S. aureus* (O), Chinese hamster cells (△), and induction of Pyr <> Pyr in Chinese hamster cells (▲). The dashed curve shows the relative absorption of DNA, normalized to its value at 260 nm. The data for Chinese hamster cells were normalized relative to 265 nm.[39,53]

This prediction is borne out by action spectra (an action spectrum is the relative response of a system to different wavelengths) obtained before DNA was known to be genetic material. Thus, the action spectra for killing of the bacteria *E. coli* and *Staphylococcus aureus* and of mammalian cells correspond closely to the absorption spectra of the nucleic acids and not to those of the aromatic amino acids of proteins (Figure 4). In addition, a close correspondence also exists between the above and action spectrum of Pyr dimers formation. These spectra were confirmed, for both killing and mutation, by many workers.

Because three of the four bases are the same, absorption spectra of DNA and RNA are very similar; therefore, action spectra do not permit differentiation. Moreover, both DNA and RNA are photoreactivable, although animal cells may not contain an RNA photolyase (see Section V). Nevertheless, because in most biological systems DNA is the primary genetic material, *a priori* DNA must be the main target to far-UV effects on cells. This interpretation is strengthened by experiments in which the effects of UV on transforming principles were studied. These are DNA molecules containing several genes from one organism, which are capable of infecting another organism and combining with its genome, thus transferring to the infected organism heritable genetic changes represented by the genes in the transforming principle. Inactivation of the transforming activity of such DNA in vitro by UV is caused primarily (∿90%) by Pyr <> Pyr.[40] Furthermore, the UV-induced lesions in transforming DNA can kill the host cell into whose genome it is integrated.[41] Another line of evidence implicating DNA as the target is the use of uracil derivatives substituted by a halogen at the 5-position. The 5-chloro, -bromo, and -iodo derivatives are analogs of Thy and are incorporated into DNA. As a result, the organism becomes more sensitive to UVC and UVB.[42] The 5-fluorouracil analog is incorporated into RNA without affecting the response to UV.

Of course, some biological systems do not possess DNA (e.g., mature erythrocytes). In others, RNA serves as the carrier of the genetic information (all plant viruses and many animal viruses). In these systems RNA is expected to be the primary target. In mammalian cells some contribution to the UV response of protein cross-linked to DNA may be envisaged. This has yet to be determined. A notable exception among microorganisms is the highly UV-resistant bacterium *Micrococcus radiodurans*. Because of its highly efficient repair of UV-induced damage in DNA (see Section V), protein damage becomes important for cell killing.

C. Photosensitization

While the phenomena that are called photosensitization are manifold, a general definition is "the action of a component (photosensitizer) of a system that causes another component of the system to react to light". The photosensitizer serves as the chromophore, absorbing the light, and upon excitation transfering the energy to an acceptor molecule. For details see Chapter 1.

Photosensitization of biological systems to visible light involves various dyes and usually requires molecular oxygen. These are the so-called photodynamic reactions. In general, photosensitized oxidations proceed via the triplet state of the sensitizer. In type I photooxidation reactions, the triplet sensitizer molecule can react directly with a substrate molecule by an electron transfer process to give a semireduced form of the sensitizer, $S^{\cdot-}$, and a semioxidized form of the substrate, $A^{\cdot+}$, both of which are free radicals. The semioxidized substrate can react with molecular oxygen to give a fully oxidized product. Other reactions can also be involved.[43] The semireduced form of the sensitizer can also react with oxygen to produce ground-state sensitizer and $O_2^{\cdot-}$. The superoxide radical can in turn oxidize another molecule in the system.

The type II process involves the interaction of triplet photosensitizer with ground-state oxygen, giving ground-state sensitizer and a highly reactive, singlet-state of oxygen, $^1O_2$:

$$^3S + \, ^3O_2 \rightarrow S_o + \, ^1O_2$$

$$^1O_2 + A \rightarrow A_{ox}$$

$^1O_2$ can react with a wide variety of substrates to give a fully oxidized form, A_{ox}. This process is common in many biologically important photosensitization reactions involving sensitizers such as acridines, porphyrins, xanthenes, and thiazines.

While the potential substrates in the cell for photooxidation are varied, the actual target molecules depend mainly on the localization of the photosensitizer within the cell. Thus, porphyrins concentrate in the lysosomes. Subsequent illumination causes damage to the lysosomal membranes and rupture of the lysosomes.[44] Other sensitizers, such as rose bengal, accumulate selectively in the plasma membrane of cells while acridines accumulate in chromosomes. Illumination in the latter case produces chromosome breakage. Guanine residues are selectively destroyed in DNA under these conditions, but cross-linking of DNA and proteins, and DNA strand breakage, also occur.[45]

Some photosensitization reactions do not involve molecular oxygen. The most important biologically are the furocoumarins. These naturally occurring photosensitizers intercalate between the DNA bases and form covalent bonds with the pyrimidines upon exposure to near UV.[46] They are discussed extensively in Volume II, Chapter 1.

Sensitized photochemical formation of Pyr <> Pyr has been described using either triplet photosensitizers such as acetone and acetophenone[47] or heavy metals (Ag, Cu, Hg, Au).[34] In the first case, the energy from the triplet state of the photosensitizer is directly transferred to thymine or cytosine. Heavy metals exert their effect by modifying the excited states of DNA. While contributing to our understanding of how Pyr <> Pyr are formed and what are their biological effects, photosensitized production of dimers is not known to occur under normal conditions.

D. Near-UV and Visible Light-Induced Damage

Because absorbance of light at $\lambda > 300$ nm by the cellular components falls rapidly with increased wavelength, near UV and visible light are far less effective compared to far UV in producing photochemical changes in the cell. As a result, to produce an equivalent number of Pyr <> Pyr in DNA at 313 nm and 365 nm, about 100 and 5×10^5 more energy is required, respectively, compared to 254 nm.[48,49] At $\lambda > 400$ nm, no dimers are produced even after a fluence of 10^8 J/m².[50] Interestingly, in mammalian cells the dimer yield was found to increase significantly with the irradiation temperature (at 313 nm). At 37°C it is almost twice the yield obtained at 0°C.[49] This is more pronounced for Cyt <> Thy than for Thy <> Thy. Whether or not this effect is wavelength dependent has not been determined. This phenomenon is probably due to changes in DNA local structure and/or temperature effects on the conformation of chromatin proteins containing aromatic amino acids. The latter are known to photosensitize Pyr dimerization.[51]

In addition to Pyr <> Pyr, near UV induces single-strand breaks in DNA at a rate close to that for dimers.[50] Production of breaks depends on the presence of oxygen and is inhibited by radical scavengers, suggesting the involvement of free radicals. The chemical nature of the breaks has not been defined but is likely to be similar to that produced by ionizing radiation. The rate of breaks induction relative to that of Pyr <> Pyr increases from 254 to 405 nm. Thus, the ratio of dimers to that of breaks is 800, 21, 1, and 0.1 at 254, 313, 365, and 405 nm, respectively.

At wavelengths >436 nm, DNA-protein cross-linkage can be observed in mammalian cells exposed in culture medium under physiological conditions for many hours.[52] This photodamage is enhanced by oxygen and is not decreased by adding catalase to the medium. Thus, unlike strand breaks, H_2O_2 is not involved. The photochemistry involved and the biological significance of visible light-induced DNA-protein cross-links remain to be determined.

Absorption of DNA at $\lambda > 320$ nm is extremely low and difficult to measure. Because of this, DNA photodamage by UVA and visible light is probably mediated by endogenous photosensitizers. Compounds that are likely candidates are the rare base 4-thiouridine, present in specific transfer RNA molecules in bacteria, and riboflavin and nicotinamide adenine dinucleotide (NAD) in mammalian cells.[197] The damage induced by these photosensitizers (mostly strand breaks) depends on the presence of oxygen, which may become rate limiting at high fluence rates. This may explain why lethality in *E. coli* after exposure to 365-nm light increases as the fluence rate is decreased below 750 Wm⁻², a deviation from the reciprocity law.[198] This law states that the effect of radiation is the function of the total radiant energy, and is independent of intensity and time.

Recently, attention is being paid to membrane damage induced by near UV in both prokaryotes[54] and eukaryotes.[55] The evidence for this damage is inferred indirectly from permeability changes and needs to be defined chemically. It strongly depends on the presence of oxygen during exposure and is not produced by far UV. Although membrane damage was claimed to be biologically important, this has not been sufficiently substantiated. In addition, there are no action spectra available.

III. BIOLOGICAL EFFECTS OF UV LIGHT

A. Cell Killing

In a dividing population of cells the term "killing" usually refers to the loss of the ability of the cell to divide. What is actually measured is the surviving fraction, i.e., the fraction of cells able to divide and give rise to a macroscopic colony. It should be stressed that many of the cells that are scored as having been killed in this assay may remain physiologically active in other respects for long periods. This is because the UV-induced impairment of the functional integrity of DNA (see Section IV) is immediately expressed as inhibition of DNA replication and cell division, effects from which the cell may not recover, depending on the UV fluence. Other cellular functions are not immediately affected or only affected at higher fluences.

Inactivation data are usually expressed in the form of "survival curves". These are plots of fractional survival, N/N_o, vs. fluence, F, on the abscissa; N_o being the initial number of cells, and N the number of surviving cells after the fluence. The statistical nature of radiation absorption and inactivation, coupled to the all-or-none behavior of individual photons, led to a statistical formulation known as "target theory", which helped elucidate the nature of radiation action in biological systems.[39] Using this approach it can be shown that inactivation can follow one-hit, multihit, or multitarget kinetics. Survival in the former case can be expressed as:

$$N/N_o = e^{-\sigma F}$$

or

$$\ln \frac{N}{N_o} = -\sigma F$$

where σ is the inactivation cross-section, the relative probability that an incident photon will inactivate. This expression represents an exponential inactivation, yielding a straight-line curve when the surviving fraction on a logarithmic scale is plotted against the fluence on a linear scale (Figure 5). For one-hit kinetics, at 37% survival there is an average of one hit per cell. The 37% survival fluence is designated as F_{37} and is equal to the inactivation cross-section.

Survival curves of UV-irradiated cells seldom display exponential kinetics. Usually, an exponential portion is preceded by a shoulder (Figure 5). Such kinetics are formalistically due to multitarget inactivation, expressed by:

$$N/N_o = 1 - (1 - e^{-\sigma F})^n$$

where n is the number of targets that have to be hit in order to inactivate a cell. At high fluences this can be written as:

$$N/N_o = ne^{-\sigma F}$$

When this expression is extrapolated back to zero fluence, the surviving fraction is equal to the number of targets, n, which is also called the extrapolation number. The fluence on the exponential part of the survival curve required to reduce survival by 37% is designated as F_o, in analogy with F_{37} for one-hit kinetics.

Because cellular repair of UV-induced DNA damage has a profound effect on cell survival (see Sections V and VI), target theory has been successful in describing the

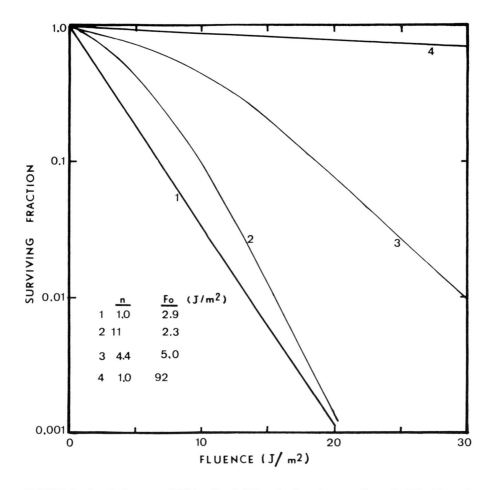

FIGURE 5. Survival curves of UV-irradiated (254-nm) cultured mammalian cells. Fibroblasts obtained from humans (1),[56] bovine (2),[56] and Chinese hamster (3).[57] Curve 4 is for Chinese hamster
cells exposed to 265-nm light from a pulsed laser (23 J/m²/15 nsec pulse).[58] 1 and 4 are single-hit
curves while 2 and 3 are multitarget survival curves.

survival behavior of simple systems only. In more complex systems, such as the mammalian cell, kinetics of inactivation which fit some target theory kinetics should not be
taken to imply a specific biophysical mechanism. This reservation is less serious in
repair-deficient mutants.

The lesions leading to the lethal effects of far UV are photoproducts in DNA, mainly
Pyr <> Pyr. The evidence for this in bacteria comes mainly from the ability of the
photoreactivating enzyme (see Section V) to reverse 50 to 90% of the lethal effect. This
enzyme specifically monomerizes Pyr <> Pyr. In mammalian cells, the evidence is less
conclusive since they contain very low levels of this enzyme. Nevertheless, studies using
cells deficient in DNA repair suggest an important role for dimers in UV-induced lethality of human cells (see Chapter 2, Volume II). In the near-UV region, the role of
Pyr <> Pyr in cell killing is reduced progressively with longer wavelengths. Concomitantly the importance of DNA strand breakage increases.[50] This is inferred mainly
from the similarity between the oxygen dependence of cell killing and DNA strand
breakage. Such a photodynamic effect is mediated via an endogenous photosensitizer,
which has not been identified so far. Candidates for the chromophores that could be
involved are many. A recently published action spectrum in the visible for the induc-

tion of DNA strand breaks in human fibroblasts is similar to the absorption spectrum for riboflavin, a known photosensitizing agent, suggesting this molecule as the absorbing chromophore.[59]

The mechanism by which DNA damage kills a cell is complex and is not completely understood. It will be further discussed in the following sections. The efficiency of a specific lesion in causing lethality varies from one organism to another. Thus, although a typical bacteria, e.g., *E. coli*, is about twice as resistant as a mammalian cell to far UV, because the genome of the latter is $\sim 10^3$ times larger, ~ 300 times more Pyr $<>$ Pyr are produced by a lethal hit (F_{37}) in mammalian cell than in a bacterium. Since DNA repair in mammalian cells is not more efficient than that operating in bacteria it appears that the former can tolerate large numbers of modified bases without losing their proliferative ability. Exactly how this is accomplished is not known, but it should be noted that most of the DNA in a mammalian cell is not required for storing information.

In addition to cell killing in dividing cells discussed earlier, also known as mitotic death, mammalian cells can suffer interphase death after a very large UV fluence. Interphase death is characterized by the development of nuclear pyknosis. Morphologically, this resembles nuclear pyknosis induced in lymphatic cells by low doses of ionizing radiation. The mechanisms, however, are different, in that respiratory metabolism is not required for the development of UV-induced degeneration.[60]

An additional insight into the mechanism of UV-induced cell killing may be obtained by using synchronized cells. Such studies reveal that mammalian cells are most resistant in mitosis (M), resistance decreases as cells move into G_1 and S phase and reaches a minimum in mid S. It then increases as cells progress out of S and into G_2 phase.[61,62] These changes in sensitivity of cell lethality are correlated with enhanced formation of Pyr $<>$ Pyr as cells progress from M into G_1 and S phase.[62] This cycle dependence of photoproduct formation is most probably due to changes in the target geometry and consequent changes in the specific absorption of UV by DNA. However, the cycle dependence of UV killing is only partly explicable by changes in dimer yield. Some of it could be due to cycle-related formation of DNA-protein cross-links[63] and to change in DNA repair capacity through the cell-cycle (see Section V).

B. Mutagenicity
1. General Considerations

The mutagenic potential of UV light in microorganisms has been known for many years. Research on mutation induction accelerated after World War II, but the modern period of study of UV mutagenesis began after the discovery in 1964 of DNA repair (see Section V). Most of our knowledge comes from studies with prokaryotes. However, during the last decade appropriate mammalian cell systems have been developed and information from them is rapidly accumulating.

Since mutations arise as a result of changes in the DNA bases, it is not surprising that the action spectrum for UV-induced mutagenesis mimics the absorption spectrum for DNA. Alterations in DNA that lead to mutations are of two types: (1) Substitution of one base pair by another. This can be due to *transition* in which a purine base is replaced by another purine, or *transversion*, i.e., the replacement of a purine by a pyrimidine or vice versa. (2) *Frame shift* mutation is the deletion or insertion of a base pair, altering the continuity of genetic code. This results in either a *nonsense* codon (a triplet of nucleotides that does not code for an amino acid), which terminates the growing polypeptide chain, or incorrect amino acids would be inserted into the enzyme, making it inactive *(missense)*.

The types of mutations that have been studied have been those that are easily assayed. In bacteria, most studies have followed the acquisition of resistance to killing

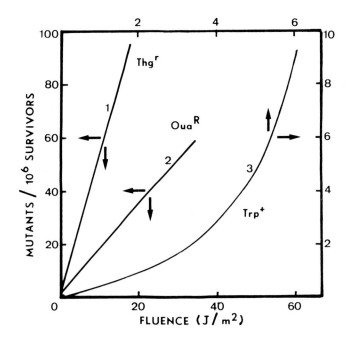

FIGURE 6.   UV (254 nm)-induced mutagenesis in *E. coli* B/r Hcr (curve 3) measured as reversion to tryptophan independence (trp⁻ → trp⁺),[50] and in Chinese hamster cells (curves 1 and 2) assayed as induced resistance to 6-thioguanine (Thg^r) and ouabain (Oua^r).[64] Note the tenfold difference in scale for bacteria and mammalian cells.

by antibiotics and the reversion to prototrophy (an auxotroph requires an amino acid for growth but a prototropic revertant does not). In mammalian cells the most widely used genetic markers have been (1) the acquisition of 6-thioguanine resistance (Thg^r) due to loss of hypoxanthine-guanine phosphoribosyltransferase (HGPRT) activity, and (2) the induced resistance to ouabain (Oua^r) which involves alteration of the plasma membrane Na⁺/K⁺ ATPase.

An important point to consider when studying mutagenesis is the time needed to express the new phenotype. This time is in a wide range of a few hours in bacteria to a few days in mammalian cells. During that time the cells divide and the premutational lesions in DNA are fixed and then expressed in the daughter cells. Therefore, transfer into the selection medium must be done only at the end of the expression time. When comparing the mutagenic response of two cell lines that differ in their sensitivity to killing by UV, the problem is whether to compare it at equal fluence or at equal survival. Although in most studies the former approach is used, it is not certain that this is most appropriate.

2. Fluence-Response Curves

In bacteria, the mutant frequency response curve after UV irradiation is bending upward, following fluence-square kinetics (Figure 6). This suggests a two-event process, which is supported by other findings. The fluence response in mammalian cells is linear (Figure 6) and therefore the mechanism of mutagenesis is probably not the same as that in bacteria. Also, at low fluences mammalian cells are more sensitive to the mutagenic effect of UV than bacteria. This is actually more pronounced than apparent from Figure 6, since the bacterial strain shown is deficient in excision repair (see Section V) and therefore more susceptible to UV mutagenesis. It is also evident from

Figure 6 that the amount of mutagenic response depends on the genetic locus under study. One reason for this is that target theory dictates that to hit a locus requires fewer photons as its size increases. In addition, inactivation of a function that is not essential for growth, as is Thg^r, would be accomplished by various types of genetic lesions. Oua^r on the other hand involves an essential function and would therefore show mutagenic response only to specific types of changes in DNA (e.g., specific base substitutions) that do not inactivate this function.

3. The Premutational Lesion

Most far UV-induced mutations probably result from the formation of Pyr <> Pyr in bacterial DNA. The strongest evidence for this comes from studies involving photoreactivation. With the *E. coli* mutant strain lacking the enzyme for splitting of Pyr <> Pyr, no photoreactivation of UV-induced mutation lesions was seen, while such photoreactivation did occur with the parental strain possessing this enzyme.[65] However, as will be discussed later, this evidence is not conclusive.

In the case of suppressor mutations for reversion of auxotrophic bacteria, the mutagenic process appears to require two types of DNA-damaging events, an induction/ indexing signal and a premutational photoproduct that targets the mutation. While the first of these could be any lesion that disrupts DNA synthesis to stimulate SOS induction or index-critical overlapping daughter-strand gaps[66] (see Section V), the targeting photoproduct could be unique. Using acetophenone as a triplet photosensitizer to change the ratio of Pyr <> Pyr to Thy <> Cyt, it was shown that for class 2 suppressor mutations (those resulting from $G \cdot C \rightarrow A \cdot T$ transitions) any type of dimer could serve as an induction/indexing signal, but only Thy <> Cyt is a premutational lesion at the target site.[67] Targeted mutagenesis was also shown to occur in mammalian cells, probed with SV40 DNA, through a base pair substitution pathway.[199]

Pyrimidine adducts of the type Pyr(6-4)Pyo can also be mutagenic. This was deduced from a correlation between the UV-induced distribution of nonsense mutations hotspots along the *lac I* gene of *E. coli* and that of UV-induced DNA damage.[68] The correlation is better for Pyr(6-4)Pyo than for Pyr <> Pyr. Using the same system, it was also shown that each of these hotspots occur at a site in the potential hairpin loop of quasi-palindromic sequences.[69] These observations suggest an important role for DNA structure in determining the fate of UV-induced premutational lesions. This is not surprising, since secondary structure has been predicted to play a role in a number of processes, including the initiation of DNA replication and the regulation of transcription.

Currently, there is no information with regard to the mutagenicity of other photolesions in DNA, except strand breaks. These do not appear to be mutagenic.[50]

4. The Mutation Process

Mutagenesis due to photodamage in DNA does not arise simply by the introduction of errors when the lesions are being replicated. This was realized when it was discovered by the pioneering work of Weigle[70] that irradiation of bacteriophages is not sufficient to induce mutation. Irradiation of both the bacterial virus and the host cell is necessary for mutagenesis of the virus. This so-called "Weigle mutagenesis" does not occur when the host cells are *rec A*$^-$ or *lex A*$^-$,[66] in which SOS repair is deficient (see Section V). Such bacteria are not mutagenized by UV, indicating that active participation of the SOS system is required to convert premutational lesions into actual mutations. This system is induced by the inhibitory effect of UV on DNA replication under conditions which allow RNA and protein synthesis. The activity that is induced facilitates DNA synthesis on a damaged template, inserting bases opposite Pyr <> Pyr nonrandomly.[71] A bias toward specific error could result because the chemical nature of Pyr <> Pyr in template DNA is significantly different due to changes in tautomeric configurations. This could result in cytosine bonded in a dimer pairing with adenine. Alternatively, insertion of adenine residues at a noninstructive dimer may be an inherent characteristic of DNA polymerase in transdimer synthesis. The final result is a *de facto* bias for G·C to A·T transitions at cytosine-containing pyrimidine dimers. Modulation of this process can be effected by DNA structural isomers that may transiently form during DNA replication, just when mutations are being fixed by the error-prone repair.[69] Expression of the induced mutations occurs after the DNA containing a fixed mutation is replicated.

The requirement for two events for the mutagenic response in bacteria complicates the interpretation of photoreactivation experiments as an indication of the role of Pyr <> Pyr as premutational lesions. Exposure to UV light followed shortly by photoreactivation removes most of the damage that induces the SOS functions. Under these conditions the SOS functions might never be induced, resulting in drastic reduction in the yield of mutations. Therefore, photoreactivation phenomena may not reflect removal of premutagenic lesions, but rather reflect reversal of the signals necessary to induce the genes required for mutation fixation.

The information regarding the mutation process in mammalian cells is scant. Unlike bacteria, mutagenesis of UV-irradiated viruses can be expressed in unirradiated human cells. The yield of viral mutants can be increased by twofold when the host cells are irradiated 24 hr prior to infection.[72] This, and the linear fluence-response of mutation induction (Figure 6), suggest that mutagenesis in mammalian cells does not require the induction of an error-prone DNA repair. Further evidence for this comes from experiments in which inhibition of protein synthesis in Chinese hamster cells failed to affect UV mutagenesis.[73] Changes in postirradiation DNA synthesis, however, do affect the yield of mutants.[73] This finding can be explained by the fact that imbalanced nucleotide pools produced by UV facilitate errors of replication of damaged DNA,[74] due to decreased fidelity of DNA synthesis by eukaryotic DNA polymerases α and β.[75]

A functional DNA excision repair is important in determining the mutagenic response in both bacteria and mammalian cells. Thus, Chinese hamster[76] and human fibroblasts[77] that are deficient in the initial step of excision are hypermutable as compared with normal fibroblasts. This is most pronounced when comparison is made at the same fluence, although a significant difference remains when cells are compared at equitoxic fluences. Presumably, removal of premutational lesions by excision repair before they can be fixed is the cause of lowered mutability in normal cells.

As for cell killing, the mutagenic response of mammalian cells to UV is cell-cycle dependent. However, the exact age-response structure for mutagenesis has not been defined and is somewhat more difficult to interpret. It will depend, for example, on the time during S that the genetic locus under study is replicated. A detailed action spectrum for mutagenesis in mammalian cells is available for the range 235 to 313 nm.[79] It is similar to that of cell killing and Pyr <> Pyr production, suggesting DNA as the target for UV-induced mutagenesis. Using continuous spectrum near UV with various cutoffs at the shorter wavelengths it was shown that mutagenicity falls off rapidly with increased wavelength at 290 nm.[78] On the basis of induced dimers, at $\lambda > 310$ nm, 50 to 60 times as many mutants were induced per dimer than by $\lambda > 290$ nm UV; the latter appeared approximately as mutagenic as 254 nm. These results suggest that UVA induces mutagenic lesions other than Pyr <> Pyr.

C. Oncogenic Transformation

The in vitro transformation of normal mammalian cells into cells that are able to form tumors is a model system for studying carcinogenesis in a quantitative manner. The first, and still most widely used such system is 10T^1/$_2$ cells derived from a C3H mouse embryo, introduced in 1973 by the late Charles Heidelberger. These are fibroblasts that demonstrate contact inhibited growth in monolayer culture. Morphologically transformed cells are identified as a colony that overgrows the confluent sheet of cells. Two types of such colonies produce fibrosarcomas when inoculated into appropriately prepared C3H mice. The transformation of a cell by an initiator like UV light can be expressed as a frequency per surviving cell. The first fluence-response curve published for mouse cells exposed to 254 nm[80] showed a linear increase in transformation frequency, up to 7.5 J/m². No further increase was observed at higher fluences. Surprisingly, the yield of transformants is tenfold higher than that of mutation induction to Thg^r. This must be due to a tenfold larger target for the former process and suggests that a hit in any one of several genes can initiate the transformation process. Such assumption is consistent with the recent observations that there exist in mammalian cells several oncogenic genes that are involved in the transformation of a normal cell into a cancer cell.

Evidence that UV-induced transformation is due to damage in DNA, mainly Pyr <> Pyr, comes from two kinds of experiments. First, the action spectra for neoplastic transformation, production of Pyr <> Pyr, and lethality between 240 and 313 nm in Syrian hamster cells, were essentially the same.[81] These spectra correspond also to the absorption spectrum of DNA. Second, UV-irradiated thyroid cells of the fish *Poecilia formosa*, when injected into isogeneic recipients, give rise to thyroid tumors. If the UV light is followed, but not preceded, by photoreactivation, the yield of thyroid tumors is markedly decreased. Because of the specificity of photoreactivation to Pyr <> Pyr, these data are strong evidence that production of dimers in DNA can give rise to tumors.

Whether or not oncogenic transformation in rodent cells is mediated via an inducible, SOS-like process is not known. Such a process does not appear to operate in the plateau phase (G$_o$), where enhanced transformation during split fluence UV irradiation is due to plateau-phase holding (see Section VI.B) rather than to the influence of fractionation per se.[82] Since transformation is cell-cycle dependent, it remains to be seen if it can be potentiated by split fluence in other phases of the cell cycle.

In contrast to rodent cells which readily undergo spontaneous as well as UV-induced malignant transformation in culture, cells from normal human donors are difficult to transform by carcinogenic agents. A small fraction of transformed progeny can be obtained in human cells by infection with simian virus 40 (SV40). This fraction can be greatly enhanced by prior exposure to UV.[84] Since this UV-enhanced transformation is not observed in repair-deficient human cells (XP), it is probably mediated by cellular DNA repair functions. XP patients are highly susceptible to cancer caused by UV light (see Chapter 2, Volume II). Viruses similar to SV40, therefore, do not play a major role in carcinogenesis of XP patients. Because of the above, it is not clear what, if any, relationship exists between transformation in vitro and UV-induced carcinogenesis in man. This is said in spite of the apparent relationship between the two processes in mice.[95] For further discussion see Chapter 4.

D. Chromosomal Damage

Morphologically, an early manifestation of DNA damage, such as that caused by exposure to UV light, is the appearance of cells containing chromosome and chromatid breaks and rearrangements. It is therefore not surprising that the action spectrum of the frequency of chromatid aberrations per cell is similar to the absorption spectrum for DNA,[85] and that Pyr <> Pyr are implicated as the main initiating lesions for both chromosomal aberrations and sister-chromatid exchanges.[85-88] For the latter, about 2 × 10⁴ Pyr <> Pyr have to be introduced in Chinese hamster cells for each additional exchange, and an even larger number of dimers are necessary to produce a chromosomal aberration. One of the reasons for the substantial number of dimers is that only those dimers that are not removed by excision repair can participate in producing aberrations. Thus, repair-deficient cells from XP patients are more susceptible than normal cells to the clastogenic effect of UV-mimetic agents.[89]

Further evidence for the role of repair processes comes from studies employing inhibitors of repair. The most widely used, although its mode of action is not clear, is caffeine.[90] When added after UV irradiation, the most striking effect of caffeine was the appearance of a high incidence of cells with multiple aberrations or "shattered chromosomes", also called pulverized chromosomes.[91] A probable explanation is the prevention by caffeine of the G_2 arrest produced by UV. As a result, cells enter mitosis before repair is completed, the damaged chromosomes are shattered, and the cells die. Indeed, there is a pronounced enhancement of UV-induced cell killing by caffeine.

Most recently, new observations indicate that some of the UV-induced chromosome aberrations are produced indirectly.[92] In the case of sister-chromatid exchanges it is 25%. The evidence comes from fusing UV-irradiated mouse cells with unirradiated Chinese hamster cells. The results suggest that unirradiated chromosomes in heterokaryons are damaged by a stable, nondiffusible cytoplasmic component contributed by the irradiated cell.[93] This active factor could be a nucleolytic enzyme released by radiation-induced rupture of lysosomes.[94]

IV. BIOCHEMICAL RESPONSES TO UV LIGHT

A. Inhibition of DNA Synthesis

An immediate and pronounced biochemical response to UV light-irradiation is inhibition of DNA synthesis. This is to be expected if DNA is the main target to UV in the cell. Damage in DNA is likely to interfere with the ability of the DNA to serve as a template for its replication, as well as for RNA synthesis.

In vitro, the residual replications detected when UV-irradiated templates are used proceed semiconservatively and result in the production of pieces of duplex DNA approximately the same size as the average distance between Pyr <> Pyr.[96] This is taken as evidence that dimers are blocks to the progression of the replication fork. In the case of the single-stranded ϕx174 phage DNA as a substrate, Pyr <> Pyr act as an absolute block for chain elongation by DNA polymerase I and III.[97] Nucleotide turnover due to idling by DNA polymerase (i.e., incorporation and subsequent excision of nucleotides opposite the dimer, by the $3' \rightarrow 5'$ "proofreading" exonuclease) prevent replication past the dimer and the potentially mutagenic event that should result. Mammalian DNA polymerase-α that is devoid of exonuclease activity is only partially inhibited by UV irradiation of the template, accompanied by an increased incorporation of noncomplementary nucleotides.

In repair-proficient bacteria, UV fluences below 20 J/m² induce short, fluence-dependent delays in DNA replication. Larger fluences do not cause further delay, but the rate of DNA replication is decreased.[98] The immediate stoppage of DNA synthesis after a small UV fluence is controlled by the *rec A* gene product (see Section V.D).[99] Presumably, it enhances the efficiency of repair by allowing the excision enzymes to act on the damaged DNA without interference with DNA replication. Dimers are not permanent blocks to the replication of bacterial DNA. The replication fork can skip past a dimer and continue its normal operation, leaving a single-strand gap behind (see Section V.C).

DNA replication is also depressed in UV-irradiated mammalian cells, but the mechanism is not as clear as it is in bacteria. To begin with, the mammalian chromosome is much larger and its organization more complex than that in bacteria. Its replication proceeds by a hierarchical mechanism in which individual replicating units (replicons) are replicated bidirectionally from central origins and grouped into clusters of ten or more that initiate replication synchronously. Adjacent clusters replicate independently, but are under some higher control that regulates the time in S phase in which replication takes place. Replication forks from adjacent origins approach one another until termination occurs. The size of an individual replicon varies over a wide range (10 to 100 μm). In human cells, the average rate of DNA chain growth is 0.5 to 1.0 μm/min at each fork.

Following exposure to low, noncytotoxic fluences (1 J/m², producing less than one Pyr <> Pyr per replicon) initiation of DNA synthesis in new replicons is inhibited. This effect is exerted at the replicon-cluster level. Higher fluences inhibit DNA synthesis in operating replicons presumably because the elongation of nascent strands is blocked when the replication fork arrives at a dimer. The net result is inhibition of chain elongation.[100] This effect is more pronounced in XP cells which are unable to remove Pyr <> Pyr ahead of DNA growing points. Dimers, however, are not permanent blocks to replication and are bypassed sooner or later. After fluences 10 J/m², reinitiation beyond a dimer does not occur for at least 1 hr.[101] Indeed, in frog cells, Pyr <> Pyr can act as blocks to nascent DNA synthesis even 24 hr after UV irradiation.[102]

Cells recover their capacity to replicate DNA as time passes after irradiation. The rate at which cells recover their ability to synthesize more and larger-size DNA is a function of both replicon size and of excision-repair capacity.[103] Cells with small replicons recover more rapidly than cells with large replicons, and excision repair-deficient cells recovered less rapidly than excision-competent cells. Recovery of replicon initiation rate after a low fluence occurs within several hours.[100] In part, this recovery is due to completion of excision repair and reinitiation of replication in previously suppressed replicon clusters. However, since recovery is faster than the actual rate of dimer excision, it probably depends on more factors.

B. Inhibition of RNA Synthesis

The major effect of UV photoproducts in bacterial DNA on RNA synthesis is to cause premature termination of RNA chain growth and release of the growing RNA chains and RNA polymerase at the site of DNA photodamage.[104] As a consequence, the rate of transcription is depressed and, on a given transcription unit, the expression of promoter-distal genes appears to be more sensitive to irradiation than that of promoter-proximal genes. Promoter binding and RNA chain initiation steps are relatively insensitive to UV light.

The probability of causing a UV lesion within a transcription unit is directly proportional to its length, making it possible to use UV fluence response to measure the distance between a gene and its promoter. In human cells for example, the synthesis of low molecular weight nuclear RNAs C and D (less than 200 nucleotides long) is highly sensitive to UV because their transcription units are as long as 5 kb.[105] The RNA chains transcribed in UV-irradiated cells are reduced in size. This effect is fluence dependent. The ability of mammalian cells to synthesize full-length RNA transcripts is restored during postirradiation incubation of both primate[106] and murine[107] cells. In the latter, Pyr <> Pyr are not excised and recovery therefore is likely to take place due to the synthesis of DNA daughter strands by a postreplication repair process. In human cells, RNA synthesis recovers quite rapidly after UV irradiation.[108] This recovery is too rapid to be accounted for by excision repair, and, since it occurs in the absence of DNA synthesis, it can neither be explained by postreplication repair. Presumably, for recovery to occur, the transcription machinery is altered in such a way that Pyr <> Pyr no longer cause termination of growing RNA chains and RNA polymerase is able to proceed past the lesions. It should be pointed out that in nondividing human fibroblasts, the lethal action of UV light is due to inhibition of required protein synthesis by preventing RNA transcription.[109] Under these conditions, recovery appeared to depend on the excision-repair capacity of the cells.

C. Effects on Protein and Inducible Enzymes Synthesis

The protein-synthesizing machinery is composed of mRNA, tRNA, ribosomes, and various enzymes and co-factors. RNA in the first three components can be photodamaged by UV light, leading to inhibition of protein synthesis.[110] However, because of target size and multiplicity of the components, inhibition of protein synthesis immediately after UV irradiation requires considerably higher fluences than for inhibition of DNA and RNA syntheses. This is the case for cells growing in culture.[111] The situation in vivo, however, is more complicated. Thus in granular cells of human skin (differentiated epidermal cells) protein synthesis was markedly inhibited within 1 to 3 hr after a mild erythemal dose of UV light.[112]

Some enzyme proteins are not synthesized continuously but only when the need arises, as a result of an inducing signal (inducible enzymes). The induction process usually requires that the appropriate mRNA be first synthesized (transcriptionally controlled induction). In such a case, exposure to UV would be expected to inhibit mRNA synthesis, resulting in reduced amounts of enzyme. Such inhibition of induced enzyme synthesis occurs in human cells following exposure to UV fluences in the biological range (3 to 10 J/m^2). In hepatoma cells, inhibition of tyrosine aminotransferase is inhibited by UV due to inhibition of transcription while pre-existing cytoplasmic mRNA is not inactivated nor its translation inhibited.[113] In human breast carcinoma cells, induction of ornithine decarboxylase is similarly inhibited by low UV fluences. The cells are able to recover from this inhibition by a process that depends on excision repair of DNA damage.[114] These effects of UV on inducible enzyme synthesis should be taken into consideration when searching for a UV-induced DNA repair pathway in mammalian cells (see Section V).

It should be noted that the opposite can also occur. Many genes in mammalian cells are quiescent and can be converted into the fully expressed state by gene activation followed by activation of transcription. Exposure to low UV doses was shown to induce metallothionein-I gene activation in mouse cells.[195] The process is associated with extensive demethylation of the DNA region containing the gene. The extent of methylation of cytosine is thought to regulate gene activity, and exposure to UV can produce demethylation of the repaired sites of DNA.[196] This provides a model for UV carcinogenesis unrelated to point mutagenesis. According to this model, under appropriate conditions UV or chemical carcinogens might activate known cellular oncogenes by causing demethylation. The activated oncogenes then cause transformation of the normal cell into a cancer cell.

V. REPAIR OF DNA PHOTODAMAGE

The fact that organisms have the potential of counteracting the damage caused by solar radiation was recognized only a few decades ago. The idea that cells might be able to prevent radiation-induced damage by repair mechanisms first arose due to observations that cell survival depended on postradiation treatment of the cell. Because of the central role of DNA in both the life of the cell and as a target for UV light, it is no surprise that these mechanisms evolved primarily to repair DNA damage. The elucidation of repair pathways and the enzymes mediating them is critical to our understanding of the effects of sunlight on man.

A. Photoreactivation

The phenomenon of biological recovery when UV-irradiated cells are subsequently exposed to longer wavelength light was first recognized in fungi.[115] Photoreactivation is an enzymatic repair process that occurs in almost all organisms, from bacteria to man.[116] Rupert[117,118] was the first to show that the photoreactivating enzyme (the exact term is DNA photolyase) repairs DNA in a light-dependent reaction. The enzyme is highly specific to Pyr <> Pyr (*cis-syn*).[5,119] It first binds to the dimer-containing region of DNA, forming an enzyme-substrate complex. The complex can absorb light of wavelengths 300 to 600 nm; the dimer is monomerized,[120] yielding repaired DNA and releasing the enzyme for further repair.

$$\text{Pyr} <> \text{Pyr} + \text{E} \rightarrow (\text{Pyr} <> \text{Pyr} \cdot \text{E}) \xrightarrow{h\nu} 2 \text{ Pyr} + \text{E}$$

In eukaryotes, this scheme may involve an additional step, requiring an activating dose of light to produce an activated enzyme-substrate complex.[121]

Photoreactivation is an efficient and economical repair pathway, using the external visible photon as an energy source. It is an error-free, nonmutagenic repair that involves no intermediate structural changes in DNA. Because of its simplicity it is the best characterized repair process. In bacteria, the number of enzyme molecules per cell is small (five to ten in *E. coli*). This number is higher in eukaryotes in order to compensate for a lowered efficiency and a larger amount of DNA per cell.[121] The enzymatic activity is mediated by rather different proteins in the range of 35 to 130 k mol wt. The wavelength of maximum efficiency varies from 365 to 435 nm, and so does the wavelength range over which the various enzymes are active. The short wavelength extent, 300 nm, is probably limited by the ability of these wavelengths to produce dimers directly in DNA. The long wavelength edge varies from about 450 nm for the *E. coli* and yeast enzymes to 600 nm for human[122] and marsupial[123] enzymes. These differences are probably due to the presence of various prosthetic groups serving as chromophores to the various DNA photolyases. Thus, in baker's yeast, the enzyme is a flavoprotein, containing flavin adenine dinucleotide (oxidized) as a prosthetic group.[124] In *Streptomyces griseus* the chromophore appears to be a 5-deazaflavin derivative.[125] However, there is another class of photoreactivating enzymes that appear to lack an intrinsic chromophore (judged from the absence of absorption of the purified enzyme in the visible or near-UV region). During the complex formation of these enzymes with irradiated DNA, a charge-transfer type of absorption band is induced, thus providing the opportunity to absorb photoreactivating light.

The amount of DNA photolyase per cell depends not only on the species of the organism but also on the growth phase and the medium in which the cells are grown. For complex organisms, it may vary with the organ and the animal age or developmental stage.[126] All these results point to cellular regulation of the enzyme levels by unknown effectors, necessitating a careful control of experimental variables when measuring biological or biochemical photoreactivation. In vivo, photoreactivation (monomerization of Pyr <> Pyr) was found to occur in the dermis but not in epidermis of neonatal mouse skin. No photoreactivation could be detected in the skin of adult mice.[127] In human skin, after suberythemal doses, photoreactivation is highly efficient, leading to the disappearance of one half of the dimers in 1.3 min.[128] Thus, during *normal* sunlight exposure, photoreactivation may be the major repair path. The importance of this repair pathway is emphasized by the low levels of DNA photolyase in cells from XP patients.[129] The molecular cause of the lowered photoreactivating enzyme activity in XP patients is not known. It could be a mutation in the structural gene for the enzyme or a mutation in a control region leading to a reduced rate of enzyme production. In any case, the defect appears to be inherited in a simple Mendelian pattern where the heterozygote XP parents are *Pp* and the XP children are *pp*.

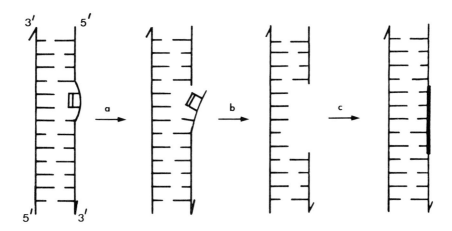

FIGURE 7. Schematic representation of excision repair of Pyr <> Pyr in DNA. (a) UV-irradiated DNA containing a dimer is attacked by an endonuclease specific for such damage, or merely recognizing the distortion in the double helix, to produce a nick adjacent to the dimer; (b) an exonuclease removes the dimer together with a few additional nucleotides on the 3′ side; (c) DNA polymerase inserts the missing nucleotides using the opposing DNA strand as a template (repair synthesis), followed by DNA ligase which joins the newly synthesized DNA piece to the pre-existing strand. The arrows indicate the direction at which the strands are synthesized.

B. Excision Repair

Excision repair is the main pathway by which photodamage in DNA is repaired in the dark. The existence of this repair was discovered in *E. coli* over 20 years ago[6,130,131] and has since been shown to occur in all organisms that were studied. Figure 7 shows the major elements of excision repair, but the details, not all of them known, vary among organisms. The first step is recognition of the damage (Pyr <> Pyr or other photoproducts) or the distortion it causes in the DNA double helix. This is usually performed by a UV-specific endonuclease which then cleaves the phosphodiester backbone 5′ to the dimer. The incision event can be more complicated, involving two steps, as in *Micrococcus luteus* and phage T4.[132,133] In these organisms the UV endonuclease has two activities, an *N*-glycosylase activity that cleaves the *N*-glycosyl bond between the 5′ pyrimidine of a dimer and the corresponding sugar, and an apyrimidinic (AP) endonuclease activity that cleaves a phosphodiester bond 3′ to the newly created AP site.

Incision is followed by excision of the dimer and adjacent nucleotides. In vitro, this step can be performed by various exonucleases (phosphodiesterases that require a terminus to initiate hydrolysis), including the 5′ → 3′ exonucleolytic activity of DNA polymerases I and III of *E. coli*. In *E. coli*, however, most excision is probably mediated by the *uvr ABC* enzyme which cuts the DNA strand on both sides of a Pyr <> Pyr (or other bulky adducts in DNA).[134] In human cells, two exonucleases whose substrate specificities suggest repair roles are DNAse VII and VIII. These enzymes release the dimer and a short oligonucleotide, generating a gap of about 10 nucleotides in length (for a recent review of enzymes involved in repair see Reference 135).

The step of reinserting the excised nucleotides is carried out by various DNA polymerases. In *E. coli*, pol I and III are able to do this, at least in vitro, in coordination with excision because of their associated 5′ → 3′ exonuclease capabilities. However, despite the lack of DNA polymerase-associated exonuclease activity in mammalian cells, it is not certain the excision resynthesis is without coordination in eukaryotic systems. Coordinated repair is indicated by findings that Pyr <> Pyr excision is stimulated by the four deoxynucleoside triphosphates and Mg^{2+} in sonicated human cells[135] and that DNA polymerase-β is stimulated by the incision of AP DNA by a $5' \rightarrow 3'$-exonuclease-AP endonuclease combination from human lymphoblasts.[137] Also, the UV excision-repair system appears to involve a complex of protein subunits in the order of 1 million daltons,[138] which is probably composed of a few enzymatic activities working in concert. Of the best-characterized mammalian polymerases, α, β, and γ, the latter is mitochondrial DNA polymerase, and has no role in nuclear functions such as replication or repair. Pol α has primarily a replicative role but can be involved, together with pol β, in DNA repair synthesis. The latter is primarily a repair enzyme. The fraction of repair mediated by each of the two polymerases is dependent on the DNA-damaging agent and on the amount of damage.[139] Pol α participation increases with increasing DNA damage. The maximal level of its involvement is $\sim$80% following UV radiation (12 J/m^2).

The final integrity of repaired strands is restored by a single enzyme species in bacteria. When nucleotide juxtaposition has been achieved by the repair polymerase, polynucleotide ligase restores strand continuity.[140] In mammalian cells, there are two distinct forms of the enzyme activities.[141] Both activities require Mg^{2+} and ATP as cofactors; however, DNA ligase I is more stable to heat and has a broader pH optimum than DNA ligase II.

The use of UV-sensitive mutants which are deficient in various repair enzymes has allowed a detailed description of the excision-repair pathway in bacteria. Excision-repair deficient mutants are designated *uvr*. Because incision is the rate-limiting step in excision, the deficiency in *uvr* mutants is usually in the incising endonuclease. Unfortunately, very few UV-sensitive mutants were isolated from mammalian cells. In humans, excision-repair deficiency was observed in XP patients[142] which is analogous to the *uvr* mutation in bacteria (see Chapter 2, Volume II).

Excision repair can be measured by following the various steps of its pathway. Because the process is coordinated, incision breaks are present only transiently and do not accumulate. However, by using inhibitors of the polymerization and/or ligation steps, breaks can be accumulated and the rate of excision measured at any time after UV irradiation.[143] The reason only the rate of excision can be measured and not its total amount is that the inhibition of late steps has a feedback effect on incision. The first inhibitor employed was hydroxyurea,[144] which inhibits the enzyme ribonucleotide reductase, thus preventing the synthesis of precursors for DNA replication. Additional inhibitors now in use are arabinosyl cytosine and aphidicolin, which are specific for pol α, and dideoxythymidine, a pol β specific inhibitor.

The excision step can be measured by determining the reduced dimer content of the DNA with time after UV exposure. Using this approach, it can be shown that human cells remove all the dimers from DNA within 24 hr, both in vitro[145] and in vivo[145] following 10 J/m^2 of 254 nm or 2 minimal erythema doses (MED) of UVB, respectively. Excision becomes progressively saturated after higher fluences. About 30 nucleotides are removed per Pyr <> Pyr dimer excised[147] but there are no clues as to why the cell removes so many nucleotides. One hypothesis that is consistent with the measurements maintains that excision is terminated when a specific base sequence is encountered.[148]

Insertion of new nucleotides into the excision gap is termed DNA repair synthesis. It was first measured by supplying cells undergoing repair with bromodeoxyuridine, an analog which is heavier than thymidine, and measuring the density shift of the DNA.[149] Bromodeoxyuridine incorporated into DNA during repair replication can be subsequently photolyzed with 313 m light, resulting in DNA strand breaks which are easily quantitated.[150] This is an extremely sensitive method. For some as yet unexplained reason it yields an estimate of average patch size which is about twice as large as that estimated from the density-shift method. Another often-used method is termed unscheduled DNA synthesis (UDS) in which cells are tested for their ability to incorporate radioactive precursors into DNA in response to UV at times of the cell cycle other than the normal synthetic period.[151] Quantitation is made by means of autoradiography. Its main disadvantage is that it does not measure repair synthesis in S-phase cells.

The completion of excision repair by DNA ligase cannot be measured directly in the cell because intermediate structures for ligation do not accumulate. Interestingly, DNA ligase is the only enzyme participating in repair which was shown to be induced *de novo* in UV-irradiated cells.[152] The activity of this enzyme is further regulated in irradiated mammalian cells by synthesis of the polymer poly (ADP-ribose).[153] Thus, it appears important for the cell that very few breaks are present in DNA at any time during repair.

DNA in mammalian chromatin is organized as nucleosomes consisting of a core region and a linker region. The core region is composed of the inner histones around which is wrapped ∿145 bp of DNA. The cores are joined together by shorter stretches of linker DNA. In this arrangement, the nucleosomes appear in electron micrographs like beads on a string. During excision repair, gap filling (and presumably dimer excision) occurs initially faster in the linker regions.[154] In time, however, nucleosomal rearrangement leads to homogeneous distribution of excision in all the chromatin regions. Since induction of Pyr <> Pyr does not occur preferentially in linker regions, it appears that structural constraints placed upon DNA in chromatin also place constraints upon the excision-repair process. Presumably, the DNA in the core regions is less accessible to repair enzymes.

Another important parameter that appears to affect the rate of excision repair is age. Although this is still controversial, a negative correlation was obtained between the age of an individual and the capacity of his peripheral leukocytes to perform UV-induced repair synthesis.[155] A significant decline in DNA repair after 14 months of age was also observed in UV-irradiated rat hepatocytes.[200] Moreover, there is a positive correlation between the ability of fibroblasts to perform UDS and the life span of the species.[156] However, more extensive studies reveal unexplained deviations from this rule.[157] Probably, alternative repair systems, especially postreplication repair, must also be considered.

The repair pathway discussed so far is strictly termed nucleotide excision repair, to distinguish it from base excision repair. The latter pathway operates to remove a damaged base by means of DNA glycosylase.[176] This enzyme, which is specific for various damaged bases, catalyzes hydrolysis of the glycosidic bond linking the base to the sugar in DNA. This is followed by an AP endonuclease that incises the AP site. The rest of the scheme is excision resynthesis as in nucleotide excision repair. Most glycosylases are specific for alkylated bases and only one in *M. luteus*, mentioned earlier, recognizes Pyr <> Pyr and initiates excision after UV irradiation. It is quite likely that there are glycosylases specific for photoproducts other than dimers but none has been described so far.

C. Postreplication Repair

When growing cells are exposed to UV, there is a certain probability that the DNA replication fork will encounter a dimer before it is excised. Bacteria handle such dimers by a bypass-recombinational mechanism,[158] also called postreplication repair since the actual repair occurs after replication of the damaged DNA. Figure 8 shows an outline of the main features of this repair. In the course of DNA replication, the polymerase leaves a gap opposite the dimer. Subsequently, a recombinational mechanism yields a new configuration of the strands so that the dimer-containing region is annealed to a

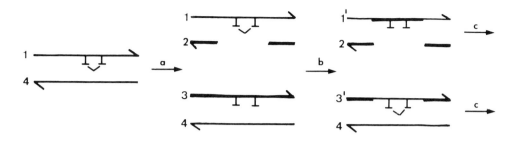

FIGURE 8. A scheme showing postreplication repair in bacteria. (a) DNA containing a Pyr <> Pyr undergoes replication to yield two types of daughter duplexes. Arrows on strands indicate polarity of DNA. (b) By recombination, dimer in strand 1 is transferred to strand 3 and TT sequence from strand 3 is transferred to strand 1. (c) Duplex 1'-2 now requires only gap filling to complete repair, while duplex 3'-4 can be repaired by excision repair (see Figure 7).

region of DNA containing the correct information. The two fundamental reactions involved are homologous pairing and strand exchange, both of which are performed by the *rec* A protein in the presence of ATP.[163.164] The new configuration can now be repaired by excision. The gapped DNA is also opposed by a strand containing complete information and can be filled in by repair replication. In bacteria, this repair pathway is controlled by the *rec* A gene product, mutations in which render the cells sensitive to UV.

Recently, a new mechanism, controlled by the *rec* B gene product has been proposed.[194] This mechanism involves double-strand exchanges between two DNA molecules and was termed sister duplex recombination to distinguish it from gap-filling recombinational repair.

In mammalian cells, the information with regard to postreplication repair is still sketchy. As in bacteria, DNA synthesized in mammalian cells after UV irradiation is shorter in size,[159] but whether it contains gaps and are these gaps opposite dimers has not been settled.[160] Also unsettled is how the gaps, if they exist, are filled. Initially it was thought that this is accomplished by *de novo* DNA synthesis.[159] More recently it was demonstrated that 1 to 3% of the dimers in human lymphocytes can be detected in the newly synthesized daughter strands at 34 to 45 hr after UV irradiation,[161] indicating the occurrence of recombination. Unlike bacteria, very little, if any, DNA can be detected by density-shift experiments to exchange between parent and daughter strands in mammalian cells.[162] Therefore the exchanges must involve relatively short segments of DNA. The lack of mammalian cells mutants analogous to bacterial *rec⁻* mutants has also hindered clarification of postreplication repair in mammals. An exception may be a class of XP patients, the XP variants, who show all clinical signs of XP but have normal capacity for excision repair (see Chapter 2, Volume II). There is also a lack of inhibitors specific for enzymes involved in postreplication repair, although caffeine is sometimes considered such an inhibitor.[159] In conclusion, this repair path appears to be of minor importance in ameliorating the cytocidal action of UV light in mammalian cells. However, since *de novo* filling of gaps is expected to be error prone, postreplication repair probably contributes to UV-induced mutagenesis.

D. SOS Repair and Other Inducible Repair Functions

Damage in DNA is normally produced at a very low rate. It would seem advantageous, therefore, for the cell to maintain a low level of repair enzymes constitutively, which can be induced by UV exposure and increased to a higher level. In bacterial cells, the existence of inducible repair paths has been well documented and is covered under the general term SOS repair.[165] This repair is induced by UV light and other DNA-damaging agents, prevented by the administration of protein-synthesis inhibitors after UV, and is error prone (i.e., mutagenic). The system regulating the SOS response in *E. coli* involves the action of two proteins: the *lex A* protein, which represses a set of unlinked genes (among them excision-repair and postreplication-repair genes), and the *rec A* protein. When the DNA is damaged, an inducing signal is produced which reversibly activates a specific protease activity of the *rec A* protein, and this protease cleaves and inactivates the *lex A* repressor. In consequence, the products of the SOS target genes are expressed at much higher levels. When DNA damage is repaired, the level of the signal molecule drops, the protease activity of the *rec A* protein disappears, and *lex A* protein accumulates and repress the SOS genes once again. At low levels of DNA damage, a subinduced state exists in which repressor level is reduced by a low level of cleavage.[166] A mutagenic activity, error-prone repair pathway, controlled by the *umuC* gene product, is also induced as a part of the SOS system.[167] This function is responsible for Weigle reactivation and mutagenesis (see Section III) but its biochemical mechanism has not been established. One possibility is that under SOS-induced conditions, fidelity requirements for DNA polymerase are relaxed and incorrect nucleotides can be incorporated opposite damaged sites in DNA.[168]

Interestingly, with increasing wavelength ($\lambda > 290$ nm), damage induced by solar UV radiations becomes increasingly less susceptible to SOS-induced repair systems.[169] Damage produced by 313 nm no longer induces, and is not being repaired by, the SOS system. Instead a new repair system is induced in *E. coli* by UVA.[170] Its nature is still unknown, but its fluence response is within the range of physiological exposure to UVA, suggesting that this type of repair may be an adaptation to environmental conditions.

Is DNA repair inducible in mammalian cells? A major experimental approach has been the use of viral probes. The results indicate that prior UV exposure of human[72] and monkey cells[171] induces enhanced survival and mutagenesis of UV-irradiated infecting viruses. This strongly suggests the presence of an inducible, error-prone DNA repair system. Although this repair system has not been firmly identified, dose-fractionation studies suggest enhancement of postreplication repair in Chinese hamster cells by a conditioning UV exposure.[172] Painter[173] has questioned the interpretation of such experiments but later studies seem to support it.[174] Of particular interest are the observations that UV light induces the synthesis of plasminogen activator in human cells.[175] Lower fluence (1 J/m²) is required for induction in XP fibroblasts compared to XP heterozygotes (20 J/m²). These results suggest that plasminogen activator induction in human cells is caused by unrepaired DNA damage and represents a mammalian SOS-like function. More recently it was shown that exposure of human fibroblasts to low doses of UV induces synthesis of a protein involved in a metabolic pathway that transiently enhances the capacity of cells to repair potentially lethal damage resulting from a subsequent dose of UV.[201]

VI. CELLULAR RECOVERY FROM UV DAMAGE

A. Repair of Sublethal Damage

Sublethal damage (SLD) is a type of damage which must be accumulated for a lethal effect to occur. Its presence in UV-irradiated mammalian cells in culture is evident from the shoulder which is often part of the survival curve (Figure 5). Such damage is subject to repair which is studied by splitting a UV fluence with a time interval between the two exposures, or by exposing the cells at a low fluence rate.[177] The operation of repair under these conditions results in enhanced survival. During a split-dose experiment, the repair of SLD is inferred from the reappearance of the shoulder on the survival curve. Continuous exposure at a low fluence rate results in a survival curve that is less steep than that obtained after acute exposure. In bacteria, enhanced survival due to fluence fractionation is partly due to excision repair, since the effect is reduced in *uvr⁻* strains.[178] However, the principal factor apparently is that the number of lesions present at any time remains low, allowing for a more efficient repair. In principle, SOS repair could be induced under these conditions; however, its possible contribution has not been determined.

In mammalian cells, repair of UV-induced SLD was first observed in a Chinese hamster cell-line whose survival curve possessed a pronounced shoulder.[179] Another Chinese hamster cell-line with a small shoulder did not display SLD repair. In order to repair SLD, rodent cells have to pass through S phase after the first exposure to UV.[179-181] This suggests the involvement of postreplication repair in the recovery from SLD, but a definite proof is lacking. Similar results were obtained with human cells.[182] There are no experiments in which mammalian cells were exposed to UV at a low fluence rate during a prolonged period. Also, information with regard to SLD repair following exposure to UVA and UVB is not available. Such information is relevant to the response of human skin to sunlight exposure.

B. Repair of Potentially Lethal Damage

When cells are held under nongrowth conditions following exposure to UV light and before plating to allow colony formation, their survival usually increases. This phenomenon is termed liquid holding recovery (LHR) in bacteria and repair of potentially lethal damage (PLD) in mammalian cells. LHR occurs only in *uvr⁺* bacterial strains,[178,183] suggesting that removal of Pyr <> Pyr by excision repair is responsible for LHR. A complicating factor in bacteria is the temporary inhibition of respiration 1 hr after UV irradiation, controlled by UV damage in DNA.[184] Heat treatment of UV-irradiated *E. coli* prevents the turn-off of respiration and is accompanied by an early increase in viability (thermal reactivation).[185] This implies that continuous energy flow is necessary for LHR, a conclusion which is supported by studies in yeast cells.[186]

Repair of PLD in mammalian cells, observed by delayed plating, occurs only in plateau phase. In mouse fibroblasts, it was suggested that PLD repair is associated with excision repair of UV damage in DNA.[187] The elimination of PLD repair in UV-irradiated human[114] and monkey cells[188] by hydroxyurea and aphidicolin, respectively, strongly supports this view. The strongest evidence that PLD repair in human cells depends on excision of Pyr <> Pyr comes from the work of Maher et al.[189] They showed that skin fibroblasts from normal individuals eliminate potentially cytotoxic (and mutagenic) lesions induced by UVC if held ∿20 hr in plateau phase. In contrast, fibroblasts from XP patients with no excision-repair activity, showed no increase in survival even when held for 7 days in confluence after UV irradiation. However, PLD repair may depend on factors in addition to excision. Thus, fibroblasts from a patient with Gardner's syndrome exhibit no PLD repair[190] although their excision-repair capacity is indistinguishable from that of normal cells.[191]

Repair of PLD in log-phase cells can be demonstrated by postirradiation treatments that enhance UV-induced cell killing. Such treatments presumably cause expression of PLD by inhibiting its repair. Caffeine is the most potent drug in this respect. However, it affects only rodent cells,[192] while human cells appear to be refractory to its action.[193] This difference may be explained by assuming that caffeine inhibits postreplication repair but not excision. The latter is more important for survival in human cells than in rodent cells. However, caffeine has many pleiotropic effects in mammalian cells and exactly how it potentiates UV-induced cytotoxicity is still not clear.

VII. CONCLUDING REMARKS

From the foregoing it is evident that lesions in DNA are the main cause of the biological damage inflicted on cells exposed to UV from germicidal lamp, sunlamp, or sunlight. The DNA photoproduct of major biological importance is Pyr <> Pyr, although other photoproducts contribute more or less, depending on the wavelength. Photodamage in DNA is repaired enzymatically by various mechanisms which are subject to regulation. The level of repair enzymes varies with the species, the age or developmental stage of the organism, the tissue, and even the growth state of cells in culture. It is thus dangerous to rely on measurements of repair in cultured cells without actually testing repair in the intact organism.

DNA damage that fails to be corrected may not lead to cell death at low levels and may not be detectable on a cellular or organismal level. It may be in a noncoding DNA segment; ambiguity in the genetic code may allow insertion of the correct amino acid into the resulting protein; and even if the coding change results in the insertion of a new amino acid, it may be a conservative substitution allowing adequate enzyme function. In spite of all this, it is also clear that UV does induce cancers in animals and humans. This and other effects of light in man will be discussed in detail in the other chapters of this volume, using the information in the previous and present chapters as a basis.

REFERENCES

1. Beukers, R. and Berends, W., Isolation and identification of the irradiation product of thymine, *Biochim. Biophys. Acta*, 41, 550, 1960.
2. Weinblum, D. and Johns, H. E., Isolation and properties of isomeric thymine dimers, *Biochim. Biophys. Acta,* 114, 450, 1966.
3. Ben-Hur, E., Elad, D., and Ben-Ishai, R., The photosensitized dimerization of thymidine in solution, *Biochim. Biophys. Acta,* 149, 355, 1967.
4. Patrick, M. H. and Rahn, R. O., Photochemistry of DNA and polynucleotides: photoproducts, in *Photochemistry and Photobiology of Nucleic Acids,* Vol. 2, Wang, S. Y., Ed., Academic Press, New York, 1976, chap. 2.
5. Ben-Hur, E. and Ben-Ishai, R., *Trans-syn* thymine dimers in ultraviolet-irradiated denatured DNA: identification and photoreactivability, *Biochim. Biophys. Acta,* 166, 9, 1968.
6. Riklis, E., Studies on the mechanism of repair of ultraviolet-irradiated viral and bacterial DNA *in vivo* and *in vitro, Can. J. Biochem.,* 43, 1207, 1965.
7. Patrick, M. H. and Gray, D. M., Independence of photoproduct formation on DNA conformation, *Photochem. Photobiol.,* 24, 507, 1976.
8. Unrau, P., Wheatcroft, R., Cox, B., and Olive, T., The formation of pyrimidine dimers in the DNA of fungi and bacteria, *Biochim. Biophys. Acta,* 312, 626, 1973.
9. Hayes, F. N., Williams, D. L., Ratliff, R. L., Varghese, A. J., and Rupert, C. S., Effect of a single thymine photodimer on the oligodeoxythymidilate-polydeoxyadenilate interaction, *J. Am. Chem. Soc.,* 93, 4940, 1971.
10. Shafranovskaya, N. N., Trifonov, E. N., Lazurkin, Y. S., and Frank-Kamenetskii, M. D., Clustering of thymine dimers in ultraviolet irradiated DNA and the long-range transfer of electronic excitation along the molecule, *Nature (London) New Biol.,* 241, 58, 1973.
11. Ciarrocchi, G. and Pedrini, A. M., Determination of pyrimidine dimer unwinding angle by measurement of DNA electrophoretic mobility, *J. Mol. Biol.,* 155, 177, 1982.
12. Cozzarelli, N. R., DNA gyrase and the supercoiling of DNA, *Science,* 207, 953, 1980.
13. Benham, C. J., Theoretical analysis of competitive conformational transitions in torsionally stressed DNA, *J. Mol. Biol.,* 150, 43, 1981.
14. Brunk, C. F., Distribution of dimers in ultraviolet-irradiated DNA, *Nature (London) New Biol.,* 241, 74, 1973.

15. Rahn, R. O. and Stafford, R. S., Measurements of defects in ultraviolet-irradiated DNA by the kinetic formaldehyde method, *Nature (London)*, 248, 52, 1974.
16. Yonker, L. S. and Blok, J., Evidence against clustering of thymine dimers in ultraviolet-irradiated DNA, *Nature (London)*, 255, 245, 1975.
17. Wilkins, R. J., The non-random distribution of pyrimidine dimers in ultraviolet-irradiated DNA, *Int. J. Radiat. Biol.*, 35, 381, 1979.
18. Donnelan, J. E. and Setlow, R. B., Thymine photoproducts but not thymine dimers found in UV-irradiated bacterial spores, *Science*, 149, 308, 1965.
19. Smith, K. C. and Yoshikawa, H., Variation in the photochemical reactivity of thymine in the DNA of *B. subtilis* spores, vegetative cells and spores germinated in chloramphenicol, *Photochem. Photobiol.*, 5, 777, 1966.
20. Varghese, A. J., 5-Thyminyl-5,6-dihydrothymine from UV-irradiated DNA, *Biochem. Biophys. Res. Commun.*, 38, 484, 1970.
21. Lindsay, J. A. and Murrell, W. G., A comparison of UV induced DNA photoproducts from isolated and non-isolated developing bacterial forespores, *Biochem. Biophys. Res. Commun.*, 113, 618, 1983.
22. Varghese, A. J. and Wang, S. Y., UV-irradiation of DNA produces a third thymine-derived product, *Science*, 156, 955, 1967.
23. Varghese, A. J. and Wang, S. Y., Thymine-thymine adduct as a photoproduct of thymine, *Science*, 160, 186, 1968.
24. Patrick, M. H., Studies on thymine-derived UV photoproducts in DNA-I. Formation and biological role of pyrimidine adducts in DNA, *Photochem. Photobiol.*, 25, 357, 1977.
25. Vanderhoek, J. Y. and Cerutti, P. A., The stability of deoxycytidine photohydrates in the mononucleotide, oligodeoxynucleotides and DNA, *Biochem. Biophys. Res. Commun.*, 52, 1156, 1973.
26. Remsen, J. F., Mattern, M., Miller, N., and Cerutti, P. A., Photohydration of uridine in the ribonucleic acid of coliphage R17. Lethality of uridine photohydrates and nonlethality of cyclobutane-type photodimers, *Biochemistry*, 10, 524, 1971.
27. Yamane, T., Wyluda, B. J., and Shulman, R. G., Dihydrothymine from UV-irradiated DNA, *Proc. Natl. Acad. Sci. U.S.A.*, 58, 439, 1967.
28. Hariharan, P. V. and Cerutti, P. A., Formation of products of the 5,6-dihydroxydihydrothymine type by ultraviolet light in HeLa cells, *Biochemistry*, 16, 2791, 1977.
29. Porschke, D., A specific photoreaction in polydeoxyadenylic acid, *Proc. Natl. Acad. Sci. U.S.A.*, 70, 2683, 1973.
30. Ben-Ishai, R., Green, M., Graff, E., Elad, D., Steinmaus, H., and Salomon, J., Photoalkylation of purines in DNA, *Photochem. Photobiol.*, 17, 155, 1973.
31. Bose, S. N., Davies, R. J. H., Sethi, S. K., and McCloskey, J. A., Formation of an adenine-thymine photoadduct in the deoxynucleoside monophosphate d(TpA) and in DNA, *Science*, 220, 723, 1983.
32. Tyrrell, R. M., Ley, R. D., and Webb, R. B., Induction of single-strand breaks (alkali-labile bonds) in bacterial and phage DNA by near-UV (365 nm) radiation, *Photochem. Photobiol.*, 20, 395, 1974.
33. Bujard, H., Electron microscopy of single-stranded DNA, *J. Mol. Biol.*, 49, 125, 1970.
34. Rahn, R. O. and Patrick, M. H., Photochemistry of DNA, secondary structure, photosensitization, base substitution, and exogenous molecules, in *Photochemistry and Photobiology of Nucleic Acids*, Vol. 2, Wang, S. Y., Ed., Academic Press, New York, 1976, chap. 3.
35. Alexander, P. and Moroson, H., Cross-linking of deoxyribonucleic acid to protein following ultraviolet irradiation of different cells, *Nature (London)*, 194, 882, 1962.
36. Varghese, A. J., Properties of photoaddition products of thymine and cysteine, *Biochemistry*, 12, 2725, 1973.
37. Todd, P. and Han, A., UV-induced DNA to protein cross-linking in mammalian cells, in *Aging, Carcinogenesis, and Radiation Biology*, Smith, K. C., Ed., Plenum Press, New York, 1976, 83.
38. Smith, K. C., The radiation-induced addition of proteins and other molecules to nucleic acids, in *Photochemistry and Photobiology of Nucleic Acids*, Vol. 2, Wang, S. Y., Ed., Academic Press, New York, 1976, chap. 5.
39. Jagger, J., Ultraviolet inactivation of biological systems, in *Photochemistry and Photobiology of Nucleic Acids*, Vol. 2, Wang, S. Y., Ed., Academic Press, New York, 1976, chap. 4.
40. Setlow, J. K., Effects of UV on DNA: correlations among biological changes, physical changes and repair mechanisms, *Photochem. Photobiol.*, 3, 405, 1964.
41. Beattie, K. L. and Setlow, J. K., Killing of *Haemophilus influenzae* by integrated ultraviolet-induced lesions from transforming deoxyribonucleic acid, *J. Bacteriol.*, 100, 1284, 1969.
42. Hutchinson, F. and Kohnlein, W., The photochemistry of 5-bromouracil and 5-iodouracil in DNA, in *Progress in Molecular and Subcellular Biology*, Vol. 7, Hahn, F. E., Kersten, H., Kersten, W., and Szybalski, W., Eds., Springer-Verlag, Berlin, 1980, 1.
43. Foote, C. S., Photosensitized oxidation and singlet oxygen: consequences in biological systems, in *Free Radicals in Biology*, Vol. 2, Pryor, W. A., Ed., Academic Press, New York, 1976, 85.

44. Allison, A. E., Magnus, I. A., and Young, M. R., Role of lysosomes and of cell membranes in photosensitization, *Nature (London),* 209, 874, 1966.

45. Spikes, J. D. and Livingston, R., The molecular biology of photodynamic action: sensitized photoautoxidations in biological systems, *Adv. Radiat. Biol.,* 3, 29, 1969.

46. Ben-Hur, E. and Song, P. S., The photochemistry and photobiology of furocoumarins (psoralens), *Adv. Radiat. Biol.,* 11, 131, 1984.

47. Ben-Ishai, R., Ben-Hur, E., and Horenfeld, Y., Photosensitized dimerization of thymine and cytosine in DNA, *Isr. J. Chem.,* 6, 769, 1968.

48. Tyrrell, R. M., Induction of pyrimidine dimers in bacterial DNA by 365 nm radiation, *Photochem. Photobiol.,* 17, 69, 1973.

49. Niggli, H. J. and Cerutti, P. A., Temperature dependence of induction of cyclobutane-type pyrimidine photodimers in human fibroblasts by 313 nm light, *Photochem. Photobiol.,* 37, 467, 1983.

50. Webb, R. B., Lethal and mutagenic effects of near-ultraviolet radiation, in *Photochemical and Photobiological Reviews,* Vol. 2, Smith, K. C., Ed., Plenum Press, New York, 1977, 169.

51. Sutherland, J. and Griffin, K., Monomerization of pyrimidine dimers in DNA by tryptophan-containing peptides: wavelength dependence, *Radiat. Res.,* 83, 529, 1980.

52. Gantt, R., Jones, G. M., Stephens, E. N., Baeck, A. E., and Sanford, K. K., Visible light-induced DNA crosslinks in cultured mouse and human cells, *Biochim. Biophys. Acta,* 565, 231, 1979.

53. Rothman, R. H. and Setlow, R. B., An action spectrum for cell killing and pyrimidine dimer formation in Chinese hamster V-79 cells, *Photochem. Photobiol.,* 29, 57, 1979.

54. Moss, S. H. and Smith, K. C., Membrane damage can be a significant factor in the inactivation of *Escherichia coli* by near-ultraviolet radiation, *Photochem. Photobiol.,* 33, 203, 1981.

55. Ito, A. and Ito, T., Possible involvement of membrane damage in the inactivation by broad-band near-UV radiation in *Saccharomyces cerevisiae* cells, *Photochem. Photobiol.,* 37, 395, 1983.

56. Cleaver, J. E., Excision repair: our current knowledge based on human (xeroderma pigmentosum) and cattle cells, in *Molecular and Cellular Repair Processes,* Beers, R. F., Herriott, R. M., and Tilghman, R. C., Eds., Johns Hopkins University Press, Baltimore, 1972, 195.

57. Ben-Hur, E. and Elkind, M. M., DNA damage and its repair in hyperthermic mammalian cells: relation to enhanced cell killing, in *Radiation Research — Biomedical, Chemical and Physical Perspectives,* Nygaard, O. F., Adler, H. I., and Sinclair, W. K., Eds., Academic Press, New York, 1975, 703.

58. Stroud, A. N., Rounds, D. E., Creter, S., and El Kadi, S. S., Reproductive integrity of cells after ultraviolet laser irradiation, *Int. J. Radiat. Biol.,* 19, 157, 1971.

59. Rosenstein, B. S. and Ducore, J. M., Induction of DNA strand breaks in normal human fibroblasts exposed to monochromatic ultraviolet and visible wavelengths in the 240—546 nm range, *Photochem. Photobiol.,* 38, 51, 1983.

60. Scaife, J. F. and Brohee, H., Pyknotic interphase death of cultured human kidney cells after high doses of ultraviolet radiation, *Int. J. Radiat. Biol.,* 13, 531, 1968.

61. Han, A. and Sinclair, W. K., Sensitivity of synchronized Chinese hamster cells to ultraviolet light, *Biophys. J.,* 9, 1171, 1969.

62. Downes, C. S., Collins, A. R. S., and Johnson, R. T., DNA damage in synchronized HeLa cells irradiated with ultraviolet, *Biophys. J.,* 25, 129, 1979.

63. Han, A. M., Korbelick, M., and Ban, J., DNA-to-protein crosslinking in synchronous HeLa cells exposed to ultraviolet light, *Int. J. Radiat. Biol.,* 27, 63, 1975.

64. Singh, B. and Gupta, R. S., Mutagenic response to ultraviolet light and x-rays at five independent genetic loci in Chinese hamster ovary cells, *Environ. Mutagenesis,* 4, 543, 1982.

65. Kondo, S. and Jagger, J., Action spectra for photoreactivation of mutation to prototrophy in *Escherichia coli* phr⁺ and phr⁻, *Photochem. Photobiol.,* 5, 189, 1966.

66. Witkin, E. M., Ultraviolet light mutagenesis and inducible DNA repair in *Escherichia coli, Bacteriol. Rev.,* 40, 869, 1976.

67. Fix, D. and Bockrath, R., Targeted mutation at cytosine-containing pyrimidine dimers: studies of *Escherichia coli* B/r with acetophenone and 313-nm light, *Proc. Natl. Acad. Sci. U.S.A.,* 80, 4446, 1983.

68. Brash, D. E. and Haseltine, W. A., UV-induced mutation hotspots occur at DNA damage hotspots, *Nature (London),* 198, 189, 1982.

69. Todd, P. A. and Glickman, B. W., Mutational specificity of UV light in *Escherichia coli:* indication for a role of DNA secondary structure, *Proc. Natl. Acad. Sci. U.S.A.,* 79, 4123, 1982.

70. Weigle, J., Induction of mutations in a bacterial virus, *Proc. Natl. Acad. Sci. U.S.A.,* 39, 628, 1953.

71. Lawrence, C. W., Are pyrimidine dimers non-instructive lesions?, *Mol. Gen. Genet.,* 192, 511, 1981.

72. Lytle, C. D. and Knott, D. C., Enhanced mutagenesis parallels enhanced reactivation of herpes virus in a human cell line, *EMBO J.,* 1, 701, 1982.

73. Stone-Wolff, D. S. and Rossman, T. G., Effects of inhibitors of de novo protein synthesis on UV-mutagenesis in Chinese hamster cells. Evidence against mutagenesis via inducible, error-prone DNA repair, *Mutat. Res.*, 82, 147, 1981.

74. Peterson, A. R., Landolph, J. R., Peterson, H., and Heidelberger, C., Mutagenesis of Chinese hamster cells is facilitated by thymidine and deoxycytidine, *Nature (London)*, 276, 508, 1978.

75. Kunkel, T. A., Silber, J. R., and Loeb, L. A., The mutagenic effect of deoxynucleotide substrate imbalances during DNA synthesis with mammalian DNA polymerases, *Mutat. Res.*, 94, 413, 1982.

76. Thompson, L. H., Brookman, K. W., Dillehay, L. E., Mooney, C. L., and Carrano, A. V., Hypersensitivity to mutation and sister-chromatid-exchange induction in CHO cell mutants defective in incising DNA containing UV lesions, *Somat. Cell Genet.*, 8, 759, 1982.

77. Grosovsky, A. J. and Little, J. B., Mutagenesis and lethality following S phase irradiation of xeroderma pigmentosum and normal human diploid fibroblasts with ultraviolet light, *Carcinogenesis*, 4, 1389, 1983.

78. Zelle, B., Reynolds, R. J., Kottenhagen, M. J., Schuite, A., and Lohman, P. H. M., The influence of the wavelength of ultraviolet radiation on survival, mutation induction and DNA repair in irradiated Chinese hamster cells, *Mutat. Res.*, 72, 491, 1980.

79. Jacobson, E. D., Krell, K., and Dempsey, M. H., The wavelength dependence of ultraviolet light-induced cell killing and mutagenesis in L5178Y mouse lymphoma cells, *Photochem. Photobiol.*, 33, 257, 1981.

80. Chan, G. L. and Little, J. B., Induction of oncogenic transformation *in vitro* by ultraviolet light, *Nature (London)*, 264, 442, 1976.

81. Doniger, J., Jacobson, E. D., Krell, K., and DiPaolo, J. A., Ultraviolet light action spectra for neoplastic transformation and lethality of Syrian hamster embryo cells correlate with spectrum for pyrimidine dimer formation in cellular DNA, *Proc. Natl. Acad. Sci. U.S.A.*, 78, 2378, 1981.

82. Chan, G. L. and Little, J. B., Effects of fluence fractionation on UV-induced malignant transformation and cell killing in non-cycling plateau phase mouse cells, *Photochem. Photobiol.*, 36, 409, 1982.

84. Hall, J. D., Transformation of ultraviolet-irradiated human fibroblasts by simian virus 40 is enhanced by cellular DNA repair functions, *Biochim. Biophys. Acta*, 652, 314, 1981.

85. Chu, E. H. Y., Effect of ultraviolet radiation on mammalian cells. I. Induction of chromosome aberrations, *Mutat. Res.*, 2, 75, 1965.

86. Bender, M. A., Griggs, H. G., and Walker, P. L., Mechanisms of chromosomal aberration production. I. Aberration induction by ultraviolet light, *Mutat. Res.*, 20, 387, 1973.

87. Reynolds, R. J., Natarajan, A. T., and Lohman, P. H. M., *Micrococcus luteus* UV-endonuclease-sensitive sites and sister-chromatid exchanges in Chinese hamster ovary cells, *Mutat. Res.*, 64, 353, 1979.

88. Natarajan, A. T., Van Zeeland, A. A., Verdegaal-Immerzeel, E. A. M., and Filon, A. R., Studies on the influence of photoreactivation on the frequencies of UV-induced chromosomal aberrations, sister-chromatid exchanges and pyrimidine dimers in chicken embryonic fibroblasts, *Mutat. Res.*, 69, 307, 1979.

89. Sasaki, M. S., DNA repair capacity and susceptibility to chromosome breakage in xeroderma pigmentosum cells, *Mutat. Res.*, 20, 291, 1973.

90. Timson, J., Caffeine, *Mutat. Res.*, 47, 1, 1977.

91. Cremer, C., Gremer, T., and Simickova, M., Induction of chromosome shattering and micronuclei by ultraviolet light and caffeine. I. Temporal relationship and antagonistic effects of the four deoxyribonucleotides, *Environ. Mutagenesis*, 2, 338, 1980.

92. Kellow, G. N. and Graves, J. A. M., Evidence for an indirect effect of radiation on mammalian chromosomes. II. UV-induced isochromosome formation in cell hybrids, *Cancer Genet. Cytogenet.*, 8, 297, 1983.

93. Graves, J. A. M. and Kellow, G. N., Evidence for an indirect effect of radiation on mammalian chromosomes. III. UV- and x-ray-induced sister-chromatid exchanges in heterokaryons, *Cancer Genet. Cytogenet.*, 8, 307, 1983.

94. Allison, A. C. and Paton, G. R., Chromosome damage in human diploid cells following activation of lysosomal enzymes, *Nature (London)*, 207, 1170, 1965.

95. Fisher, M. S., Kripke, M. S., and Chan, G. L., Antigenic similarity between cells transformed by ultraviolet radiation *in vitro* and *in vivo*, *Science*, 223, 593, 1984.

96. Masker, W. E. and Kuemmerle, N. B., In vitro replication of bacteriophage T7 DNA damaged by ultraviolet radiation, *Biochim. Biophys. Acta*, 609, 61, 1980.

97. Villani, G., Boiteaux, S., and Radman, M., Mechanism of ultraviolet-induced mutagenesis: extent and fidelity of *in vitro* DNA synthesis on irradiated templates, *Proc. Natl. Acad. Sci. U.S.A.*, 75, 3037, 1978.

98. Trgovcevic, Z., Petranovic, D., Petranovic, M., and Salajsmic, E., *rec A* gene product is responsible for inhibition of DNA synthesis after ultraviolet irradiation, *J. Bacteriol.*, 143, 1506, 1980.

100. **Kaufmann, W. K. and Cleaver, J. E.,** Mechanisms of inhibition of DNA replication by ultraviolet light in normal human and xeroderma pigmentosum fibroblasts, *J. Mol. Biol.,* 149, 171, 1981.
101. **Edenberg, J. H.,** Inhibition of DNA replication by ultraviolet light, *Biophys. J.,* 16, 849, 1976.
102. **Rosenstein, B. S. and Setlow, R. B.,** DNA repair after ultraviolet irradiation of ICR 2A frog cells. Pyrimidine dimers are long acting blocks to nascent DNA synthesis, *Biophys. J.,* 31, 195, 1980.
103. **Cleaver, J. E., Kaufmann, W. K., Kapp, L. N., and Park, S. D.,** Replicon size and excision repair as factors in the inhibition and recovery of DNA synthesis from ultraviolet damage, *Biochim. Biophys. Acta,* 739, 207, 1983.
104. **Michalke, H. and Bremer, H.,** RNA synthesis in *Escherichia coli* after irradiation with ultraviolet light, *J. Mol. Biol.,* 41, 1, 1969.
105. **Eliceiri, G. L.,** Sensitivity of low molecular weight RNA synthesis to UV radiation, *Nature (London),* 179, 80, 1979.
106. **Nocentini, S.,** Inhibition and recovery of ribosomal RNA synthesis in ultraviolet-irradiated mammalian cells, *Biochim. Biophys. Acta,* 454, 114, 1976.
107. **Ali, R. and Sauerbier, W.,** Effects of ultraviolet irradiation and postirradiation incubation on heterogeneous nuclear RNA size in murine cells, *Biophys. J.,* 22, 393, 1978.
108. **Mayne, L. V. and Lehmann, A. R.,** Failure of RNA synthesis to recover after UV irradiation: an early defect in cells from individuals with Cockayne's syndrome and xeroderma pigmentosum, *Cancer Res.,* 42, 1472, 1982.
109. **Kantor, G. J. and Hull, D. R.,** An effect of UV light on RNA and protein synthesis in nondividing human fibroblasts, *Biophys. J.,* 27, 359, 1979.
110. **Brunschede, H. and Bremer, H.,** Protein synthesis in *Escherichia coli* after irradiation with ultraviolet light, *J. Mol. Biol.,* 41, 25, 1969.
111. **Takeda, S., Naruse, S., and Yatani, R.,** Effects of UV microbeam irradiation of various sites in HeLa cells on the synthesis of RNA, DNA and protein, *Nature (London),* 213, 696, 1967.
112. **Fukuyama, K., Epstein, W. J., and Epstein, J. H.,** Effect of ultraviolet light on RNA and protein synthesis in differentiated epidermal cells, *Nature (London),* 216, 1031, 1967.
113. **Bushnell, D. E., Yager, J. D., Becker, J. E., and Potter, V. R.,** Inhibition of messenger RNA accumulation but not translation in ultraviolet irradiated hepatoma cells, *Biochem. Biophys. Res. Commun.,* 57, 949, 1974.
114. **Ben-Hur, E., Prager, A., and Buonaguro, F.,** Recovery from inhibition by UV-irradiation of ornithine decarboxylase induction in human cells: implication of excision repair, *Photochem. Photobiol.,* 35, 671, 1982.
115. **Kelner, A.,** Effect of visible light on the recovery of *Streptomyces griseus* conidia from ultraviolet irradiation injury, *Proc. Natl. Acad. Sci. U.S.A.,* 35, 73, 1949.
116. **Sutherland, B. M.,** Photoreactivation, *Bioscience,* 31, 439, 1981.
117. **Rupert, C. S.,** Photoenzymatic repair of ultraviolet damage in DNA. I. Kinetics of the reaction, *J. Gen. Physiol.,* 45, 703, 1962.
118. **Rupert, C. S.,** Photoenzymatic repair of ultraviolet damage in DNA. II. Formation of an enzyme-substrate complex, *J. Gen. Physiol.,* 45, 725, 1962.
119. **Setlow, J. K., Boling, M. E., and Bollum, F. J.,** The chemical nature of photoreactivable lesions in DNA, *Proc. Natl. Acad. Sci. U.S.A.,* 53, 1430, 1965.
120. **Cook, J. S.,** Direct demonstration of the monomerization of thymine-containing dimers in UV-irradiated DNA by yeast photoreactivating enzyme and light, *Photochem. Photobiol.,* 6, 97, 1967.
121. **Bronk, B. V. and Van de Merwe, W. P.,** The shape of the blacklight dose photoreactivation curve for chick embryo fibroblasts, *Mutat. Res.,* 112, 109, 1983.
122. **Sutherland, J. C. and Sutherland, B. M.,** Human photoreactivation enzyme: action spectrum and safelight conditions, *Biophys. J.,* 15, 435, 1975.
123. **Chiang, T. and Rupert, C. S.,** Action spectrum for photoreactivation of ultraviolet irradiated marsupial cells in tissue culture, *Photochem. Photobiol.,* 30, 525, 1979.
124. **Iwatsuki, N., Joe, C. O., and Werbin, H.,** Evidence that deoxyribonucleic acid photolyase from baker's yeast is a flavoprotein, *Biochemistry,* 19, 1172, 1980.
125. **Eker, A. P. M., Dekker, R. H., and Berends, W.,** Photoreactivating enzyme from *Streptomyces griseus.* I. On the nature of the chromophoric cofactor in *Streptomyces griseus* photoreactivating enzyme, *Photochem. Photobiol.,* 33, 65, 1981.
126. **Cook, J. S. and McGrath, J. R.,** Photoreactivating enzyme activity in metazoa, *Proc. Natl. Acad. Sci. U.S.A.,* 58, 1359, 1967.
127. **Ananthaswamy, H. N. and Fisher, M. S.,** Photoreactivation of ultraviolet radiation-induced pyrimidine dimers in neonatal BALBc mouse skin, *Cancer Res.,* 41, 1829, 1981.
128. **D'Ambrosio, S. M., Whetsone, J. W., Slazinski, L., and Lowney, E.,** Photorepair of pyrimidine dimers in human skin *in vivo, Photochem. Photobiol.,* 34, 461, 1981.
129. **Sutherland, B. M. and Oliver, R.,** Inheritance of photoreactivating enzyme deficiencies in human cells, *Photochem. Photobiol.,* 24, 449, 1976.

130. Setlow, R. B. and Carrier, W. L., The disappearance of thymine dimers from DNA: an error correcting mechanism, *Proc. Natl. Acad. Sci. U.S.A.,* 51, 226, 1964.
131. Boyce, R. P. and Howard-Flanders, P., Release of ultraviolet light induced thymine dimers from DNA of *Escherichia coli* K-12, *Proc. Natl. Acad. Sci. U.S.A.,* 51, 293, 1964.
132. Haseltine, W. A., Gordon, L. K., Lindan, C. P., Grafstrom, R. H., Shaper, J. L., and Grossman, L., Cleavage of pyrimidine dimers in specific DNA sequences by a pyrimidine dimer DNA-glycosylase of *M. luteus, Nature (London),* 285, 240, 1980.
133. Gordon, L. K. and Haseltine, W. A., Comparison of the cleavage of pyrimidine dimers by the bacteriophage T4 and *Micrococcus luteus* UV-specific endonucleases, *J. Biol. Chem.,* 255, 12047, 1980.
134. Sancar, A. and Rupp, W. D., A novel repair enzyme: UVRABC excision nuclease of *E. coli* cuts a DNA strand on both sides of the damaged region, *Cell,* 33, 249, 1983.
135. Grossman, L., Enzymes involved in the repair of damaged DNA, *Arch. Biochem. Biophys.,* 211, 511, 1981.
136. Friedberg, E. C., Rude, J. M., Cook, K. H., Ehmann, U. K., Mortelman, K., Cleaver, J. E., and Slor, H., in *DNA Repair Processes,* Nichols, W. W. and Murphey, D. G., Eds., Miami Symposia Specialists, Miami, 1977, 21.
137. Strauss, B., Rose, K., Alfimirano, M., Sklar, P., and Tatsumi, K., in *DNA Repair Mechanisms,* Hanawalt, P. C., Friedberg, E. C., and Fox, C. F., Eds., Academic Press, New York, 1978, 621.
138. Park, S. D., Choi, K. H., Hong, S. W., and Cleaver, J. E., Inhibition of excision-repair of ultraviolet damage in human cells by exposure to methyl methanesulfonate, *Mutat. Res.,* 82, 365, 1981.
139. Dresler, S. L. and Lieberman, M. W., Identification of DNA polymerases involved in excision repair in diploid human fibroblasts, *J. Biol. Chem.,* 258, 9990, 1983.
140. Youngs, D. A. and Smith, K. C., The involvement of polynucleotide ligase in the repair of UV-induced DNA damage in *Escherichia coli* K-12 cells, *Mol. Gen. Genet.,* 152, 37, 1978.
141. Soderhall, S. and Lindahl, T., Mammalian DNA ligases, *J. Biol. Chem.,* 250, 8438, 1975.
142. Cleaver, J. E., Defective repair replication of DNA in xeroderma pigmentosum, *Nature (London),* 218, 652, 1968.
143. Collins, A. R. S. and Johnson, R. T., The inhibition of DNA repair, *Adv. Radiat. Biol.,* 11, 71, 1984.
144. Ben-Hur, E. and Ben-Ishai, R., DNA repair in ultraviolet light irradiated HeLa cells and its reversible inhibition by hydroxyurea, *Photochem. Photobiol.,* 13, 337, 1971.
145. Ahmed, F. E. and Setlow, R. B., Saturation of DNA repair in mammalian cells, *Photochem. Photobiol.,* 29, 983, 1979.
146. Eggset, G., Volden, G., and Krokan, H., UV-induced DNA damage and its repair in human skin *in vivo* studied by sensitive immunohistochemical methods, *Carcinogenesis,* 4, 745, 1983.
147. Edenberg, H. and Hanawalt, P., Size of repair patches in the DNA of ultraviolet-irradiated HeLa cells, *Biochim. Biophys. Acta,* 272, 361, 1971.
148. Collier, I. E., Olson, W. H., and Regan, J. D., A mechanism for the control of patch size in mammalian cell DNA excision repair, *J. Theor. Biol.,* 102, 487, 1983.
149. Smith, C. A., Cooper, P. K., and Hanawalt, P. C., Measurement of repair replication by equilibrium sedimentation, in *DNA Repair: A Laboratory Manual of Research Procedures,* Vol. 1 (Part B), Friedberg, E. C. and Hanawalt, P. C., Eds., Marcel Dekker, New York, 1981, chap. 24.
150. Setlow, R. B. and Regan, J. D., Measurement of repair synthesis by photolysis of bromouracil, in *DNA Repair: A Laboratory Manual of Research Procedures,* Vol. 1 (Part B), Friedberg, E. C. and Hanawalt, P. C., Eds., Marcel Dekker, New York, 1981, chap. 25.
152. Mezzina, M. and Nocentini, S., DNA ligase activity in UV-irradiated monkey kidney cells, *Nucleic Acid Res.,* 5, 4317, 1978.
153. Ben-Hur, E., The involvement of poly (ADP-ribose) in the radiation response of mammalian cells, *Int. J. Radiat. Biol.,* 46, 659, 1984.
154. Smerdon, M. J. and Lieberman, M. W., Nucleosome rearrangement in human chromatin during UV-induced DNA repair synthesis, *Proc. Natl. Acad. Sci. U.S.A.,* 75, 4238, 1978.
155. Lambert, B., Ringborg, U., and Skoog, L., Age-related decrease of ultraviolet light-induced DNA repair synthesis in human peripheral leukocytes, *Cancer Res.,* 39, 2792, 1979.
156. Hart, R. W. and Setlow, R. B., Correlation between DNA excision-repair and life-span in a number of mammalian species, *Proc. Natl. Acad. Sci. U.S.A.,* 71, 2169, 1974.
157. Francis, A. A., Lee, W. H., and Regan, J. D., The relationship of DNA excision repair of ultraviolet-induced lesions to the maximum life span of mammals, *Mech. Ageing Dev.,* 16, 181, 1981.
158. Rupp, W. D. and Howard-Flanders, P., Discontinuities in the DNA synthesized in an excision-defective strain of *Escherichia coli* following ultraviolet irradiation, *J. Mol. Biol.,* 31, 291, 1968.
159. Lehman, A. R., Postreplication repair of DNA in mammalian cells, *Life Sci.,* 15, 2005, 1975.
160. Park, S. D. and Cleaver, J. E., Postreplication repair: questions of its definition and possible alteration in xeroderma pigmentosum cell strains, *Proc. Natl. Acad. Sci. U.S.A.,* 76, 3927, 1979.

161. Fornace, A. J., Recombination of parent and daughter strand DNA after UV-irradiation in mammalian cells, *Nature (London)*, 304, 552, 1983.
162. Fujiwara, Y. and Tatsumi, M., Low-level DNA exchanges in normal human and xeroderma pigmentosum cells after UV-irradiation, *Mutat. Res.*, 43, 279, 1977.
163. West, S. C., Cassuto, E., and Howard-Flanders, P., Mechanism of *E. coli* Rec A protein directed strand exchanges in post-replication repair of DNA, *Nature (London)*, 294, 659, 1981.
164. West, S. C., Cassuto, E., and Howard-Flanders, P., Postreplication repair in *E. coli* strand exchange reactions of gapped DNA by Rec A protein, *Mol. Gen. Genet.*, 187, 209, 1982.
165. Little, J. W. and Mount, D. W., The SOS regulatory system of *Escherichia coli*, *Cell*, 29, 11, 1982.
166. Little, J. W., The SOS regulatory system: control of its state by the level of Rec A protease, *J. Mol. Biol.*, 167, 791, 1983.
167. Bagg, A., Kenyon, D. J., and Walker, G. C., Inducibility of a gene product required for UV and chemical mutagenesis in *Escherichia coli*, *Proc. Natl. Acad. Sci. U.S.A.*, 78, 5749, 1981.
168. Schaaper, R. M. and Loeb, L. A., Depurination causes mutations in SOS-induced cells, *Proc. Natl. Acad. Sci. U.S.A.*, 78, 1772, 1981.
169. Menezes, S. and Tyrrell, R. M., Damage by solar radiation at defined wavelengths: involvement of inducible repair systems, *Photochem. Photobiol.*, 36, 313, 1982.
170. Peters, J. and Jagger, J., Inducible repair of near-UV radiation lethal damage in *E. coli*, *Nature (London)*, 289, 194, 1981.
171. Sarasin, A. and Benoit, A., Induction of an error-prone mode of DNA repair in UV-irradiated monkey kidney cells, *Mutat. Res.*, 70, 71, 1980.
172. D'Ambrosio, S. M. and Setlow, R. B., Enhancement of postreplication repair in Chinese hamster cells, *Proc. Natl. Acad. Sci. U.S.A.*, 73, 2396, 1976.
173. Painter, R. B., Does ultraviolet light enhance postreplication repair in mammalian cells?, *Nature (London)*, 275, 243, 1978.
174. Pirsel, M., Masek, F., and Sedliakova, M., Inducible nature of tolerance to lesions produced by ultraviolet light in DNA of Chinese hamster V79 cells, *Neoplasma*, 29, 685, 1982.
175. Miskin, R. and Ben-Ishai, R., Induction of plasminogen activator by UV light in normal and xeroderma pigmentosum fibroblasts, *Proc. Natl. Acad. Sci. U.S.A.*, 78, 6236, 1981.
176. Caradonna, S. J. and Cheng, Y. C., DNA glycosylases, *Mol. Cell. Biochem.*, 46, 49, 1982.
177. Elkind, M. M. and Whitmore, G. F., Recovery from radiation damage, in *The Radiobiology of Cultured Mammalian Cells*, Gordon & Breach, New York, 1967, chap. 6.
178. Harm, W., Effects of dose fractionation on ultraviolet survival of *Escherichia coli*, *Photochem. Photobiol.*, 7, 73, 1968.
179. Humphrey, R. M., Sedita, B. A., and Meyn, R. E., Recovery of Chinese hamster cells from ultraviolet irradiation damage, *Int. J. Radiat. Biol.*, 18, 61, 1970.
180. Domon, M. and Rauth, A. M., Cell cycle specific recovery from fractionated exposures of ultraviolet light, *Radiat. Res.*, 55, 81, 1973.
181. Todd, P., Fractionated ultraviolet light irradiation of cultured Chinese hamster cells, *Radiat. Res.*, 55, 93, 1973.
182. Todd, P., Dalen, H., and Schroy, C. B., Survival of synchronized cultured human liver cells following single and fractionated exposures to ultraviolet light, *Radiat. Res.*, 69, 573, 1977.
183. Tang, M. S. and Patrick, M. H., Repair of UV damage in *Escherichia coli* under non-growth conditions, *Photochem. Photobiol.*, 26, 247, 1977.
184. Swenson, P. A. and Schenley, R. L., Evidence for the control of respiration by DNA in ultraviolet-irradiated *Escherichia coli* B/r cells, *Mutat. Res.*, 9, 443, 1970.
185. Swenson, P. A., Boyle, J. M., and Schenley, R. L., Thermal reactivation of ultraviolet-irradiated *Escherichia coli*: relationship to respiration, *Photochem. Photobiol.*, 19, 1, 1974.
186. Jain, V. K., Gupta, I., and Lata, K., Energetics of cellular repair processes in a respiratory-deficient mutant of yeast, *Radiat. Res.*, 92, 436, 1982.
187. Chan, G. L. and Little, J. B., Response of plateau-phase mouse embryo fibroblasts to ultra-violet light, *Int. J. Radiat. Biol.*, 92, 436, 1982.
188. Nocentini, S., Effects of aphidicolin on the recovery of ribosomal RNA synthesis and on the repair of potentially lethal damage in UV irradiated simian and human cells, *Biochem. Biophys. Res. Commun.*, 109, 603, 1982.
189. Maher, V. M., Dorney, D. J., Mendrala, A. L., Konze-Thomas, B., and McCormick, J. J., DNA excision-repair processes in human cells can eliminate the cytotoxic and mutagenic consequences of ultraviolet irradiation, *Mutat. Res.*, 62, 311, 1979.
190. Little, J. B. and Nagasawa, H., Repair of potentially lethal damage in UV-irradiated Gardner's syndrome fibroblasts: effects on survival and sister chromatid exchanges, *Radiat. Res.*, 83, 474, 1980.
191. Henson, P., Fornace, A. J., and Little, J. B., Normal repair of ultraviolet-induced DNA damage in a hypersensitive strain of fibroblasts from a patient with Gardner's syndrome, *Mutat. Res.*, 112, 383, 1983.

192. Domon, M. and Rauth, A. M., Effects of caffeine on ultraviolet-irradiated mouse L cells, *Radiat. Res.,* 39, 207, 1969.
193. Wilkinson, R., Kiefer, J., and Nias, A. H. W., Effects of post-treatment with caffeine on the sensitivity to ultraviolet light irradiation of two lines of HeLa cells, *Mutat. Res.,* 10, 67, 1970.
194. Wang, T. C. V. and Smith, K. C., Mechanisms for *recF*-dependent and *recB*-dependent pathways of postreplication repair in UV-irradiated *Escherichia coli uvrB, J. Bacteriol.,* 156, 1093, 1983.
195. Lieberman, M. W., Beach, L. R., and Palmiter, R. D., Ultraviolet radiation-induced metallothionein-I gene activation is associated with extensive DNA demethylation, *Cell,* 35, 207, 1983.
196. Kastan, M. B., Gowans, B. J., and Lieberman, M. W., Methylation of deoxycytidine incorporated by excision-repair synthesis of DNA, *Cell,* 30, 509, 1982.
197. Peak, J. G., Peak, M. J., and MacCoss, M., DNA breakage caused by 334 nm ultraviolet light is enhanced by naturally occurring nucleic acids components and nucleotide coenzymes, *Photochem. Photobiol.,* 39, 713, 1984.
198. Peak, J. G. and Peak, M. J., Lethality in repair-proficient *Escherichia coli* after 365 nm ultraviolet light irradiation is dependent on fluence rate, *Photochem. Photobiol.,* 36, 103, 1982.
199. Bourre, F. and Sarasin, A., Targeted mutagenesis of SV40 DNA induced by UV light, *Nature (London),* 305, 68, 1983.
200. Plesko, M. M. and Richardson, A., Age-related changes in unscheduled DNA synthesis by rat hepatocytes, *Biochem. Biophys. Res. Commun.,* 118, 730, 1984.
201. Tyrrell, R. M., Exposure of nondividing populations of primary human fibroblasts to UV (254 nm) radiation induces a transient enhancement in capacity to repair potentially lethal cellular damage, *Proc. Natl. Acad. Sci. U.S.A.,* 81, 781, 1984.

Chapter 3

ACUTE CUTANEOUS EFFECTS OF LIGHT

Farrington Daniels, Jr.

TABLE OF CONTENTS

Since the basic work of Finsen, photobiology has developed into a major science . . . The central question and the most difficult problem of experimental phototherapy lies in the question of the "depth effect" of the light.[1]

I. INTRODUCTION

UV erythema, sunburn, has been studied for at least 90 years. Until the last 15 years the picture appeared simple, but the fact that the established data are not yet clearly linked in an overall reaction diagram indicates a previously unexpected complexity. An older overview would have said that UVB, that portion of sunlight which is cut out by window glass, was absorbed by a target, a chromophore. This photochemical event could lead to the release of a diffusible mediator which dilated the capillaries and the subpapillary venous plexus. The delay between exposure and erythema was explained by the diffusion time. Conversely, UVA could cause transient darkening of melanin without other biological effect, while UVC could produce a pale erythema with little subsequent pigmentation, and with a flatter dose-response curve than UVB.

The tremendous recent advances in medical photobiology brought the subject of acute cutaneous reactions to the fore.[2-8] In this review truncation and generalization have been resorted to because of the very large number of publications in this area. This leads the author to believe that the subject of acute effects of ultraviolet radiation (UVR) on skin can no longer be encompassed by a book chapter; the next review will probably require a monograph of its own.

Actually, a great deal was learned about effects of UVR between Finsen's cure of skin tuberculosis for which he received the Nobel Prize in 1903, and the advent of sulfonamides and antibiotics in the 1930s and 1940s. Phototherapy was the only available treatment for some forms of tuberculosis and streptococcal skin infections. It is still profitable to read Mayer,[9] Laurens,[10] and Blum.[11] Every student of medical photobiology should read Urbach's[12] translation of Hausser and Vahle's classic article.

A common denominator of many conditions treated with UVR was the diagnosis of "asthenia". Van der Leun[13] has suggested that many of the patients may have been deficient in vitamin D. Now that it is known that vitamin D is involved in neuromuscular junctions,[14] brain, skin, and many other sites outside the gut and bone,[15,16] the benefits of UVR in asthenia can be rationalized. Another major advance in understanding skin photobiology was the finding that the epidermal effects characterized by sunburn cells are separate from the dermal effects among which erythema is the most evident.[17-20]

II. KERATINOCYTES, THE SUNBURN CELL, AND SERIAL HISTOLOGY

Although reactions of the skin involve interactions between keratinocytes, melanocytes, Langerhans, and perhaps other dendritic cells, the author will use the changes in the keratinocytes to outline the events, since these are the most conspicuous following UVB and UVC. The keratinocyte begins as a stem cell among the basal cells and differentiates[21] through prickle cells, and granular cells, to form a "dead" plastic film that makes life out of the sea possible.[22] After exposure to UVR, the penetration of radioactive iodine into the skin shows a transient increase and then a 2 to 3 day period of reduced permeability.[23]

The sunburn cell is not unique to sunburn but it is a characteristic of it. It is a "dyskeratotic" or prematurely cornified cell appearing at 12 hr and reaching a peak 24 hr after UVB radiation. As shown in Figure 1 the sunburn cells are scattered through

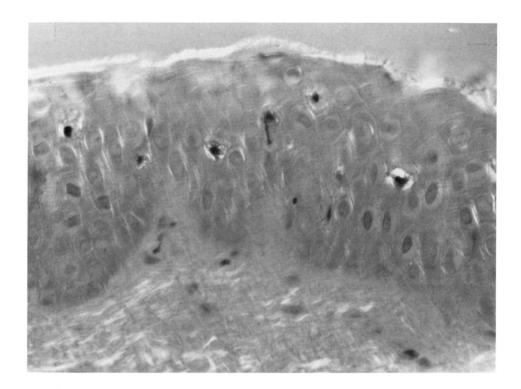

FIGURE 1. "Sunburn cells" at 24 hr after 2 minimal erythema doses (MED) of UVB radiation. Examined with crossed polarizers which bring out the keratin in the sunburn cells. However, note the general spacing and level which suggests Langerhans cells. In the dermis, polarization brings out collagen fibers. The keratinizing structures are vertical at the basal cell and became horizontal at the stratum corneum.

the epidermis, but most tend to be about two thirds of the way from the basal to granular layer. They tend to be spaced laterally at about equal distances, and presumably something was modified in some component of the cytoskeleton. In the sunburn cells are granules identified as melanin,[24] that show up with phase-contrast or high-magnification microscopy. That the sunburn cell is a keratinocyte is confirmed by the polarization shown in Figure 1, and by keratin, prekeratin, mucin (KPM) stain of Dane and Herman[25] as shown in color plates in other publications.[3,26]

Basal-cell accumulation of glycogen occurs 12 hr after administration of a UVB burn[27] and is characteristic of epidermal damage but not dermal damage.[28] By 48 hr, glycogen is more diffusely distributed in midepidermis.[3]

Basal-cell mitoses appear somewhere between 24 and 48 hr after UVR and reach a maximum at 72 hr. Mitoses reach a maximum at 48 hr after tape stripping, which may indicate an immediate chalone interruption by stripping and at the time of sunburn cell appearance.[6] There are no observations on how the melanocytes increase in number without recognized mitoses.

Vacuolization and shrinking of the cells around the sunburn cell spreads with the appearance of a transected sphere, until a band of globules covers the entire upper epidermis. The damaged upper epidermal cells shrink, and retain pyknotic nuclei, hence becoming parakeratotic. Underneath the shedding layer there is hyperplasia, acanthosis, cellular disorder, and heavy staining or fluorochroming for RNA. Beginning at about 72 hr, a new granular layer starts to form under the condensed upper "old" epidermis.

Figure 2 shows the histologic appearance 48 hr after UVB irradiation. This is a case

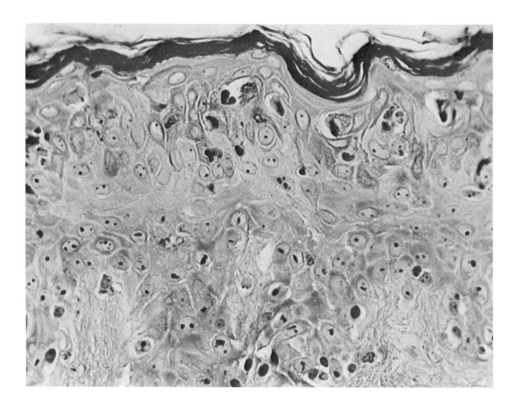

FIGURE 2.   Giemsa stain. Severe UVB burn at 48 hr. Rounded, presumably spherical collections of dead or dying keratinocytes, suggesting a distribution around Langerhans cells. Mitotic figures and small and multiple nucleoli at basal level. Melanocytes have deep-stained nuclei and pale cytoplasm.

of severe sunburn. Instead of isolated sunburn cells, there are now nests of necrotic cells giving the impression of a globular configuration. The epidermis is markedly thickened. Figure 3 shows a biopsy taken at the same time and in the same individual as in Figure 2. However, this is 8-methoxypsoralen photosensitization. The destruction is so different that the author has never accepted the idea of referring to PUVA as an exaggerated sunburn. Finally, Figure 4 shows the histology 72 hr after UVB exposure. The old upper third of the epidermis is being cast off and a new granular layer is forming under it. By 5 days, the main finding is epidermal thickening as the remainder of acanthosis. An increase in the number of melanocytes at the basal level is evident.

III. TARGETS IN CUTANEOUS PHOTOBIOLOGY

A. Nucleic Acids

DNA is probably the most studied of possible UVR targets in skin under the general heading of photobiology. Its damage and repair are discussed in Chapter 2.

In serial biopsy studies by Daniels et al.,[4,6,27] the important features related to DNA were blanching or swelling of upper-level prickle cell nuclei at 4 and 7 hr. The methods used included the Feulgen reaction. Beginning between 24 and 48 hr, there was an increase in basal-level mitoses, reaching a maximum at 72 hr. That DNA is damaged by UVR is further indicated by the fact that it becomes antigenic.[29,30] Volden et al.[31] showed that DNA was damaged by UVB at half of MED, and that the erythema was better correlated with DNA damage than with the dose of UVB. The information

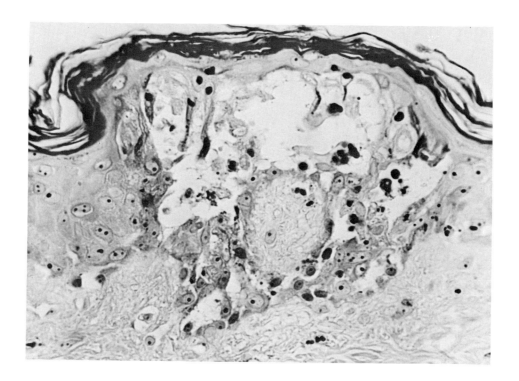

FIGURE 3. Same subject as Figure 2, 48 hr after UVA exposure with 8-methoxypsoralen as a photosensitizer.

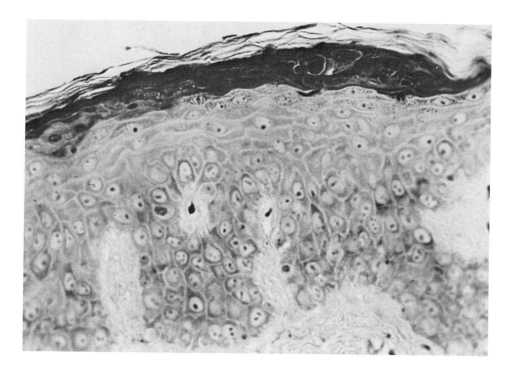

FIGURE 4. Histological appearance at 72 hr after UVB exposure.

stored in DNA is transcribed in the nucleolus to RNA. When the RNA synthesis is enhanced there is an increase in the size of the nucleolus. Nucleolar size increases in the basal layer as one of the earliest manifestations of the beginning of tissue repair. These changes due to UVB burn as seen with the electron microscope were described.[32] Baden and Pearlman[33] showed reduced incorporation of radiolabeled uridine into RNA following UVB irradiation. Epstein et al.[34,35] showed a decrease followed by an increase in RNA synthesis following UVR. Hanke[36] observed a decrease in RNA, as well as metachromasia. Daniels et al.[3,27] have shown that with the toluidine blue staining, the sunburn cells and desquamating upper epidermis remained orthochromatic, whereas the remainder of the epidermis became metachromatic, an indication of RNA accumulation. The metachromasia was confirmed by removal with ribonuclease. Changes were also seen with the methyl green pyronine stain for RNA. The most dramatic demonstration of RNA was with acridine orange fluorochroming which gives DNA a light-green fluorescence and RNA a bright-orange fluorescence.[37]

A refractory period of several days follows one episode of UV erythema. This has usually been explained by stratum corneum and epidermal thickening. It could as logically be loss of a target, such as the Langerhans cell. The appearance of RNA with hyperplasia is shown in Figure 4. At 72 hr after 2 MED of UVB irradiation, the beginning of a new granular layer is evident. We assume that there is nothing unique to the role of RNA and hyperplasia following UVR, and the description[38] of hyperplasia after two other forms of injury is applicable. An increased uptake of radiolabeled uridine and an increase in ribosomes was found. The author is therefore suggesting that the accumulation of RNA during epidermal hyperplasia serves as a UV filter that probably plays a role in the "tolerance" that develops at 72 hr and lasts for about 10 days before erythema can be reinduced with UVB.

B. Histidine, Urocanic Acid, and the Granular Layer

Histidine seems to have an important role as a chromophore in the skin reactions to UVR. Histidine enters the sunburn picture in at least two ways. Its decarboxylation product, histamine, is incorporated into the mast cells. It is of interest that histidine is incorporated in a differentiating part of the epidermis, the granular layer.[39,40] Second, the histidine-rich layer has opened a new vista in the functions of urocanic acid. Urocanic acid was first described as a possible sunscreen in sweat.[41] It was shown to increase in the skin after solar exposure,[42] but was then found to be an epidermal component eluted in the sweat.[43] Changes in isomerization of urocanic acid were found to be a means of dissipating the UV energy.[44,45] In the stationary state, about 60% of epidermal urocanic acid is in the *cis* form; sunlight shifts the balance to about 70% in the *trans* form. This transformation appears to take place in the lower parts of the stratum corneum. It has been also indicated that urocanic acid photoreceptors act on both antigen processing and in the circulation on suppressor T cells.[46,47] Thus, the inhibitory effects of UVR on immune responses are not entirely due to Langerhans cells.[48] The absorption maximum of urocanic acid is at 260 nm, so it is a better screen against DNA damage than erythema. Urocanic acid also reacts with excited singlet oxygen about twice as rapidly as histidine, suggesting that it might fulfill more functions than simply isomerization.

The granular layer has long been recognized as the level at which keratinocytes suddenly become part of the stratum corneum. In the histology of serial biopsies after UVB irradiation, the "keratohyalin" granules of the old granular layer either disappear or are swept up in the destruction of the upper level of the epidermis. After 72 hr there is a somewhat diffuse, two to three cells thick formation of a new granular layer. By 5 days, the new granular layer is conspicuous under the desquamating surface.

Daniels[49] has previously shown the usefulness of dark-field microscopy in demon-

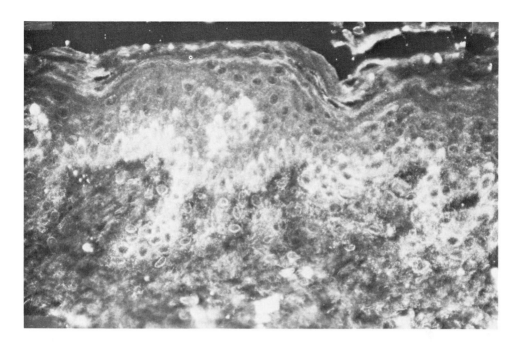

FIGURE 5.   A dark-field photomicrograph of a formalin-fixed section 24 hr after UVB exposure.

strating melanin granules without the need for silver staining. Figure 5 is a dark-field examination of a formalin-fixed section of a 24-hr UVB burn. The melanin caps over the basal cell nuclei are prominent. Some of the sunburn cells are also brightly lit by the melanin granules. The granular layer is also outlined in bright light, presumably from particle scattering. The ramifications of this observation require further study.

An electron microscopy study on human skin exposed to 4-MED UVB at times up to 1 week, indicated no decrease in keratohyaline, an increased thickness of the granular layer, and the presence of dense round 50- to 200-nm bodies. The granular layer became normal in 1 week.[50]

It has long been assumed that the chalky white color of vitiligo was due not only to reflectance from dermis but also reflectance and scatter from the granular layer, as with Wickham's striae of lichen planus. After all, albinos do look pinker than vitiligo. In vitiligo, acquired tolerance to sunburn, lack of elastosis, and the low incidence of skin cancer, have long been puzzling. Van der Leun[51] studied UV erythema in vitiligo patients and found the depigmented areas were more sensitive to 254- and 365-nm radiation than the surrounding pigmented skin. He confirmed that the depigmented areas, were less sensitive to 300-nm radiation than the pigmented areas, thereby implicating a diffusing mediator in the 300-nm erythema. Sunburn cells in vitiligo hardly increased in number with 16 MED, which was attributed to a lack of melanin in keratinocyte phagolysosomes.[24] In preparing this review the author has reexamined some sunburn cells in vitiligo sections stained with the Dane (KPM) stain,[25] for keratin, prekeratin, and mucin. This stain is also useful for heavy brown-to-black staining of keratohyaline granules and bright-red staining of erythrocytes. Packing of red cells in small vessels in erythema is striking. In the pigmented part of human skin with 1, 4, and 8 MED of radiation from a bank of four 20-W fluorescent sunlamps, there is an increased number of sunburn cells with dose, and an even more impressive increase in the number of surrounding keratinocytes that show vacuolation and other damage. In the pigmented skin at 24 hr, the granular layer appears intact and one-cell chick. The vitiligo areas at 24 hr after 1, 4, and 8 MED UVB radiation are strikingly different, with fewer sunburn cells, with much less reaction around them, and little increase in their number with increasing dose. In the vitiliginous areas, the granular layer is intact and thicker with one to three cells. Is it possible that vitiligo is a disease of the granular layer rather than of melanocytes?

C. Membrane Constituents

Routine light microscopy with its treatment of tissue with organic solvents and paraffin for sectioning, has hidden the fact that cells and organelles are organized by lipid membranes. Electron microscopy not only increased magnification but the fixation techniques using osmium emphasized the membranes. Tickner[52] found that after UV radiation of skin there was no change in nucleic acid content, but a decrease in phospholipids with a concomitant increase in acid-soluble phosphate. Johnson[53] found a decrease in phospholipids in mouse skin after UVR. Norins[54] demonstrated free-radical formation in UV-irradiated skin. A paper presented at the 1st International Congress on Photobiology[55] described lipid peroxidation following UVR. Changes in membrane metabolism in cultured keratinocytes exposed to UVR are another indication of the importance of membranes.[56] There are many reviews on lipid membranes, including the one edited by Kummerow.[57] Even though the evidence was very strong that lipid membrane peroxidation was an important feature of UV damage,[58-62] there remained the question of the chromophore. Though the fatty acids contain double bonds they do not absorb in the UVB range.

Lysosomes were originally described as single-membrane bound organelles containing a number of acid hydrolases, and were originally considered to be intracellular "suicide packets".[63-65] Part of the rationale in studying lysosomes in sunburn cells was that it would appear they would have the ideal arrangement for the digestion of DNA, RNA, and proteins, in the general process of keratinocyte cornification.[66] Lysosome function has gone beyond the suicide packet, and the lysosomes are now believed to have roles in the uptake, storage, and discharge of materials from outside the cell; in effect serving as the gastrointestinal and urinary tracts of the cell.

It was established earlier[64] that lysosomes could be disrupted by UVR, and that the membranes were stabilized by adrenocortical steroids. It was also found that the lysosome membrane was stabilized by 7-dehydrocholesterol, and lysed by vitamins A and D. Lysosomal damage with the azo-coupling method for acid phosphatase was found first in mice, then in men.[67-69] By differential incubation, an initial increase in staining intensity was interpreted as sufficient membrane damage to increase substrate penetration. Later, diffusion, disorganization, and then fading were found.[8]

An interesting feature of the sunburn cell is that it frequently has more ingested melanin than the adjacent keratinocytes, tending to confirm that phagolysosomes are more vulnerable to UV damage than primary lysosomes, or that melanin-containing lysosomes have more acid phosphatase.[24]

Conversion of 7-dehydrocholesterol in the epidermis to previtamin D_3 is due to UVR exposure. The lysosomal membrane is stabilized by 7-dehydrocholesterol and not by vitamin D.[68,69] It is noteworthy[70] that the vitamin D metabolite produced by single hydroxylation in the liver is toxic and that it may influence the structure of lipid bilayer membranes. The circulating level of 25-hydroxy vitamin D is influenced by UV exposure of the skin. The final and most active metabolite (hormone), 1,25-dihydroxy vitamin D_3 is end-product regulated. Targets for this metabolite have been identified in epidermal keratinocytes,[71] and in line with the other information on the granular layer it is of interest that in vitamin D-deficient rats the basal cells are elongated and there is a marked reduction in the granular layer.[72]

Histamine[73] and kinins[74] had been ruled out as mediators of erythema but as each new group of mediators was identified, it was considered a factor in UV erythema. Thus, prostaglandins (PGs) were also implicated.[56,58-62] The recent medical literature is replete with reviews of the cyclooxygenase and lipoxygenase pathway of products derived from arachidonic acid (AA). Many of these have offered hope of explaining the UV erythema, but the time course and the persistence of the erythema long after the bolus of mediator would have passed have made them identified as involved; however, this does not explain the entire picture.

The role of leukotrienes as mediators, particularly of allergic reactions, has received its interest in turn. Soter et al.[75] have probably spared us a long period of speculation by injecting a series of leukotrienes into human skin and clearly producing effects that differ markedly from a UVB burn. Of interest were the different sensory effects in different subjects.

Tryptophan and its photoproducts have been recognized as key items in the effects of UVA on the lens,[76-78] and as the dominant chromophore present in cell membranes.[79] The finding that tryptophan is the chromophore in lipid membranes brings amino acids back into the picture after almost being eclipsed by DNA. Conversion of tryptophan to tryptamine by UVR was described.[80]

IV. DYNAMICS OF THE UV ERYTHEMAS AND TANNING

The MED or minimal perceptible erythema (MPE) is the minimum dose to produce an erythema. The minimum dose to produce melanization, or the minimum dose to produce vesiculation can also be used. While the use of a threshold of visual detection makes investigators feel uncomfortable because of its subjective nature, the MED has been and continues to be a useful clinical standard. Daniels et al. studied visual grading in evaluating sunburn and tanning in comparison to reflectance readings and found that in large samples the grading of +, ++, +++, and ++++ fell on a straight line on a log scale,[81] and when a field experiment added a +++++ category,[82] it fell on the same line. With television techniques, nothing could be seen below an MED.[83]

Hausser and Vahle[12] in a widely reproduced graph based on color standard grading of erythema, showed that the erythema increased almost vertically at 297 nm at a ++ erythema. With UVC the slope is much flatter and the maximum reached is ++, while the UVB goes to +++++ on their scale. The UVC erythema stays pink, whereas at longer wavelengths erythema go to deep red. Erythema is only one manifestation of injury and attention must be paid to edema, vesiculation, desquamation, and pigmentation. Buettner[84] suggested that the subvesicular dose was less variable than the minimal erythema. Adams et al.[85] compared the data of Hausser and Vahle[12] to the process of photography. They presented an interesting plot of the different degrees of erythema with energy of different wavelengths. By combining the erythema curve and the spectrum of sunlight reaching the earth they found a "peak effectiveness" at 306 nm.[86] If the square root of dye concentration in the standard is plotted against the log of the exposure, straight lines are obtained, and at 334 and 365 nm, the slope of erythema as a function of dose is so large that "taking it as infinite would not greatly change the calculated exposure."[85] Recording reflectance spectrophotometers have been used to measure skin reflectance at IR, visible, and UV wavelengths.[87-89] Melanin has a broad absorption band but no specific peaks. Aside from slight absorption from carotene at 482 nm, of interest are the absorption peaks of oxyhemoglobin at 542 and 576 nm. The reduced hemoglobin maximum at 556 nm is not usually separable from the two oxyhemoglobin bands. Usually a green filter (or an interference filter with peak transmission at 542 or 576 nm) is used to measure erythema, and the red filter (or a 610-nm peak transmission filter), to sample melanin. Reflectance spectra for Caucasian, black, sunburned, and suntanned skin are given elsewhere.[4]

Reflectance meters have been used extensively by anthropologists to measure skin color in different human populations,[90,91] and by skin photobiologists in following the effects of different wavelengths of UVR. Interference filters of 544 and 661 nm were used in a reflectance meter to follow the erythemas produced by cold quartz (254-nm) lamps, fluorescent sunlamps, three sources of predominantly UVB, and sunlight.[92] The 254-nm erythema appeared earliest and faded in 5 days for 1 MED and in 10 days with 4 MED. The other three sources had a much slower decrease from the peak erythema. Wan et al.[93] calculated the blood content of the skin based on reflectance spectroscopy measurements. In line with other observations that UVA erythema requires 1000 to 3000 times the dose of UVB, their data are presented as J/cm^2 for UVA, and mJ/cm^2 of UVB. It is, however, reiterated that there may be as much as 100 times the intensity of UVA in sunlight as compared to UVB.[94]

Reciprocity is the characteristic of photochemical reactions in which the multiplication of intensity and time is constant. Claesson[95] demonstrated that UVB effects on skin exhibit reciprocity over a 10 million-fold range. Two[96,97] independent studies have put the upper limit of reciprocity for human UVB erythema at about 8 hr.

The usual method for identifying a target in a photobiological system is by comparing an action spectrum with the absorption spectrum of potential molecular targets. An action spectrum is defined by determining the reciprocal of the dose of each wavelength required to produce a certain reaction, which in the case of sunburn has usually been erythema. The question of erythema action spectrum constitutes a major portion of reviews on the cutaneous effects of UVR.[4,51,98-100] However, with the finding that dermal and epidermal effects of UVR are largely separated, there is less reason to try to explain erythema by epidermal chromophores.

V. EPIDERMAL LANGERHANS CELLS (ELC) IN THE SKIN REACTION TO UVR

Figure 1 shows sunburn cells in a pattern resembling the distribution of ELC. In 1962, Daniels[6] suggested that ELC might be UV targets. In 1964, Daniels et al. found damage to the dendrites and body of the ELC in a 24-hr UVB burn using gold chloride and osmium zinc iodide techniques. Gilchrest[102,103] found that sunburn cells were keratinocytes in contact with UV-damaged ELC. The ELC disappeared at 24 hr, at which time only a minority of keratinocytes displayed marked vacuolization or dyskeratosis. The spreading of damage in a globular cluster of keratinocytes[104] around the initial sunburn cell is best explained by the linking of the keratinocytes in the "Langerhans cell-epidermal unit".[105,106] In the dose range 1 to 30 mJ/cm^2 for UVB and 1×40 to 2×100 J/cm^2 of UVA, ELC were the only epidermal cells to show damage.[107] In mice, 40 mJ/cm^2 of UVB or 300 J/cm^2 of UVA had no discernible effect on keratinocytes, but 40 to 60 mJ/cm^2 of UVB produced an almost complete elimination of ATPase-positive cells.[108] ATPase and Ia-reactive cells were markedly reduced by 100 J/cm^2 of UVA. It is not yet known why ELC damage in UVA does not lead to sunburn cells. Potter[109] has argued that the inverse relationship between epidermal hyperplasia and the presence of ELC suggest that the ELC might be the source of the G_1 chalone. In describing the histologic and histochemical changes following UVB Lobitz et al.[110] suggested that the keratinocyte chalone production was interrupted at the time the sunburn cells appeared, because the number of basal level mitoses was maximal at 72 hr, as compared to the 48 hr following tape stripping. This suggestion was supported by Iverson.[111]

ELC disappear for about 2 weeks after UVB irradiation, and return as the hyperplasia subsides. As indicated,[108] the upper dendrites of Langerhans cells are located in the granular layer, with an appearance suggesting termination at the nucleus of the granular-layer cells. In their own 15-μm sections with osmium zinc iodide Daniels et al. have observed by focusing up and down with phase contrast that the appearance of terminating at a granular-layer cell nucleus is often seen. After UVB irradiation, a new granular layer is formed, and with the return of ELC, the conspicuous link between basal cells and the granular layer is reestablished. In spite of the identification of the ELC as the front line of the immune system, this does not exclude other functions. With ATPase and osmium zinc iodide there is the appearance of wires or pipes in ELC, connecting the granular layer with the basal layer. Because it is known that a message is sent to regulate basal-cell mitoses, it is hard to ignore the appearance of these connections provided by the ELC.

VI. MELANOCYTES AND MELANIN SYSTEM IN THE ACUTE REACTIONS OF THE SKIN TO UVR

This subject could easily require an entire chapter, so only a few highlights will be given. For reviews see References 112 to 117.

Paling of melanocytes has been noted on histologic sections[102] but has not been studied as systematically as other cells. The 72-hr findings are visible in Figure 4.

Some subjects, when exposed to UVA or even visible light, develop darkening as a result of oxidation of preformed melanin.[118-121] More recent work emphasized the role of cytoskeletal elements. Since the immediate tanning peaks in 1 to 3 hr and fades variably, the cosmetic appeal of "tan without burn" has to be watched, particularly during the current craze for UVA boxes.

Rosdahl[113] has shown that local UVR causes a general increase in the number of skin melanocytes. Is this due to the "circulating solar factors" that appear in the epidemiology of malignant melanomas?

VII. EFFECTS OF UVA, UVB, AND UVC ON THE DERMIS

Erythema is produced by engorgement of small blood vessels, mostly in the subpapillary venous plexus. The term "small vessels" is used to avoid "capillaries", since capillary loops would not have a sufficient coverage to produce uniform erythema. Van der Luen[51,122] suggested that the greater warmth of a UVB erythema compared to a UVC erythema is probably due to arteriolar involvement. He has also presented evidence that UVC and UVA erythemas involve direct action on blood vessels, while that of UVB involves a diffusable mediator. Sams and Winkelman[123] have shown direct effects of UV on isolated blood vessels, and Epstein et al.[124] have shown that there must be direct vessel damage, because of unscheduled DNA synthesis following UVR.

Rosario et al.[104] studied the different erythemas with equally erythemogenic doses. In general, UVB and UVC produced more damage in the epidermis, whereas UVA produced more dermal effects. With UVA, papillary edema was evident at 72 hr and at 7 days. In UVB erythema, endothelial cell enlargement followed the UVB irradiation in a matter of minutes, which suggests direct action and not a diffusing mediator. There is also a discrepancy between the clinical and the histopathologic pictures. The clinical picture is of blood-filled vessels; the pathologic picture is of occlusion of blood-vessel lumen by endothelial cells protruding into it.[103] Merrill Chase[125] has told the author that in his studies of allergic contact dermatitis in guinea pigs he always clamped off perforating arteries and veins before fixing the tissue, so that he could see the erythema in the pathology. Daniels[126] saw vessels occluded by red cells in frostbite or the equivalent cryosurgery, where extravasation of the fluid following mast-cell rupture is believed to leave a thrombus of red cells. In the normal skin or in erythema one might expect the vessels to contain not only the red cells but plasma as well, and hence one would expect more evident blood vessels. A punch biopsy of a sunburned area is a bloody biopsy and Daniels suggests that the erythema has drained out of the biopsy specimen. If true, this has considerable general importance because the clinician sees erythema and the pathologist does not.

A suggestion[127] that histamine might be involved in the UVR reaction was settled by the finding that a histamine liberator did not prevent subsequent UV erythema.[128] Mast cells were found to be important in inflammation but not in sunburn cell production.[129]

Hawk and Parrish[130] found some polymorphonuclear (PMN) leukocytes in UVA erythema, which they considered might be due to a thermal effect. They also noted that neutrophils are not found in UVB burn in man but they are found in rodents. Potter[109] suggests that the shedding epidermis is not an invasive foreign body or an enclosed area of necrosis, and that epidermal cells release their own interleukins and other mediators without the intervention of the neutrophils. The author does not believe sunburn is a typical inflammation any more than he believes that it is an example of a first-degree thermal burn.

VIII. CONCLUDING REMARKS

There are some incompletely answered questions: (1) Why is there a wavelength-dependent time lag in the onset of erythema? (2) What is/are the mediator(s) of the erythema? A diffusable mediator is an easy explanation for the latent period between UV irradiation and the appearance of erythema. However, what is the reason for the persistence of the erythema, and particularly its prolongation in the skin cancer-prone subject? Whatever causes the erythema has to include the finding that the erythema does not blanch with injected epinephrine. Why does the slope of response to dose vary so consistently with wavelength? (3) What is the adaptive value of the basic skin melanization? There is a strong negative correlation between human skin color and latitude. Is this due to an almost-closed melanin shutter near the equator, and an almost-open melanin shutter toward the North Pole for the regulation of vitamin D synthesis? If not vitamin D, what?

A. Areas of Current Rapid Progress

The Langerhans cell has turned out to be even more interesting than when the reviewer suggested it as a UVR target in 1962. It organizes a unit of keratinocytes, and in serial biopsies it appears that this unit is damaged by UVB burn, as well as the ELC itself. ELC acts as the front line of immunological defense, and the fact remains that morphologically it should regulate epidermal thickness by communicating between the granular layer and the basal cells. That a cell can have more than one function is evident from the survival of cells in culture.

REFERENCES

1. Rothman, S., Untersuchungen über die Physiologie der Lichtwurkungen, *Z. Gesamte Exp. Med.*, 36, 398, 1923.
2. Daniels, F., Jr., Man and radiant energy: solar radiation, in *Handbook of Physiology, Section 4,* Dill, D. B., Ed., Williams & Wilkins, Baltimore, 1964, 969.
3. Daniels, F., Jr., Ultraviolet radiation and dermatology, in *Therpeutic Electricity and Ultraviolet Radiation,* Vol. 4, 2nd ed., Licht, S., Ed., Licht Publishing, New Haven, Conn., 1967, 370.
4. Johnson, B. E., Daniels, F., Jr., and Magnus, I. A., Responses of the human skin to ultraviolet light, in *Photophysiology,* Vol. 4, Giese, A. C., Ed., Academic Press, New York, 1968, 139.

5. Daniels, F., Jr., The physiological effects of sunlight, *J. Invest. Dermatol.,* 32, 147, 1959.

6. Daniels, F., Jr., Ultraviolet carcinogenesis in man, in The 1st Conference on Biology of Cutaneous Cancer, National Cancer Institute Monogr. No. 10, Urbach, F., Ed., NCI, Bethesda, Md., 1962, 407.

7. Daniels, F., Jr., Solar radiation, in *Environmental Physiology,* Slonim, B., Ed., C. V. Mosby, St. Louis, 1974, 276.

8. Daniels, F., Jr. and Johnson, B. E., Normal physiologic and pathologic effects of solar radiation on the skin, in *Sunlight and Man,* Fitzpatrick, T. B., Pathak, M. A., Harber, L. C., Seiji, M., and Kukita, A., Eds., University of Tokyo Press, Tokyo, 1974, 117.

9. Mayer, E., *Clinical Application of Sunlight and Artificial Radiation,* Williams & Wilkins, Baltimore, 1926.

10. Laurens, H., *The Physiological Effects of Radiant Energy,* Chemical Catalog, New York, 1933.

11. Blum, H. F., *Photodynamic Action and Disease Caused by Light,* (reprinted ed.), Hafner, New York, 1964.

12. Hausser, K. W. and Vahle, W., Sunburn and suntanning, *Wiss. Veroeff. Siemens Konzern,* 6, 101, 1927; translated by Urbach, F., in *The Biologic Effects of Ultraviolet Radiation,* Urbach, F., Ed., Pergamon Press, Oxford, 1969, 3.

13. Van der Leun, J. C., Personal communication.

14. Birge, S. and Haddad, J. G., 25-hydroxycholecalciferol stimulation on muscle metabolism, *J. Clin. Invest.,* 56, 1100, 1975.

15. Stumpf, W. E., Madhabananda, S., Reid, F. A., Tanaka, U., and DeLuca, H. F., Target cells for 1,25-dihydroxy vitamin D_3 in intestinal tract, stomach, kidney, skin, pituitary, and parathyroid, *Science,* 206, 1188, 1979.

16. Stumpf, W. E., Sar, M., Clarck, S. A., and DeLuca, H. F., Brain target sites for 1,25-dihydroxy vitamin D_3, *Science,* 215, 1403, 1982.

17. Snyder, D. S., Cutaneous effects of topical indomethacin, an inhibitor of prostaglandin synthesis on UV-damaged skin, *J. Invest. Dermatol.,* 64, 322, 1975.

18. Kaidbey, K. H. and Kurban, A. K., The influence of corticosteroids and topical indomethacin on sunburn erythema, *J. Invest. Dermatol.,* 66, 153, 1976.

19. Pearse, A. D., Wolska, H., and Marks, R., Do sunscreens prevent premalignant change in the epidermis?, *Br. J. Dermatol.,* 101(Suppl. 17), 1979.

20. Sambuco, C. P., Forbes, P. D., Davies, R. D., and Urbach, F., An animal model to determine sunscreen protectiveness against both vascular injury and epidermal cell damage, *J. Am. Acad. Dermatol.,* 10, 737, 1984.

21. Green, H., The keratinocyte as differentiated cell type, *Harvey Lect.,* 74, 101, 1979.

22. Kligman, A. M., Comments on the stratum corneum, in *The Biologic Effects of Ultraviolet Radiation,* Urbach, F., Ed., Pergamon Press, Oxford, 1969, 165.

23. Maizelis, M. Y., Effect of solar radiation upon skin permeability, *Vestn. Dermatol. Venerol.,* 3, 10, 1957.

24. Johnson, B. E., Mandell, G., and Daniels, F., Jr., Melanin and cellular reactions to ultraviolet radiation, *Nature (London) New Biol.,* 235, 147, 1972.

25. Dane, E. T. and Herman, D. L., Haematoxylin-phloxine-alcian blue-orange G differential staining of prekeratin, keratin and mucin, *Stain Technol.,* 38, 97, 1963.

26. Daniels, F., Jr., Van der Leun, J. C., and Johnson, B. E., Sunburn, *Sci. Am.,* 219, 38, 1968.

27. Daniels, F., Jr., Brophy, D., and Lobitz, W. C., Jr., Histochemical responses of human skin following ultraviolet irradiation, *J. Invest. Dermatol.,* 37, 351, 1961.

28. Lobitz, W. C., Jr., Brophy, D., Larner, A. E., and Daniels, F., Jr., Glycogen response in epidermal basal cells, *Arch. Dermatol.,* 86, 207, 1962.

29. Tan, E. M. and Stoughton, R. B., Ultraviolet light induced damage to deoxyribonucleic acid in human skin, *J. Invest. Dermatol.,* 52, 537, 1969.

30. LeFeber, W. P., Norris, D. A., Huff, J. C., Kub, M., Ryan, S. R., and Weston, W. L., Induction of nuclear antigen expression in human keratinocytes by ultraviolet light, *J. Invest. Dermatol.,* 80, 328, 1983.

31. Volden, G., Eggset, G., Krokan, H., and Kavli, G., UV-induced DNA damage and its repair in human skin *in vivo* correlated to erythema, tanning and light penetration, *J. Invest. Dermatol.,* 82, 550, 1984.

32. Nix, T. E., Jr., Nordquist, R. E., and Scott, J. R., An ultrastructural study of nucleolar enlargement following ultraviolet irradiation of human epidermis, *J. Invest. Dermatol.,* 45, 114, 1965.

33. Baden, H. F. and Pearlman, C., The effect of ultraviolet light on protein and nucleic acid synthesis in the epidermis, *J. Invest. Dermatol.,* 43, 7, 1964.

34. Fukuyama, K., Epstein, W. L., and Epstein, J. H., Effect of ultraviolet light on RNA and protein synthesis in differentiated epidermal cells, *Nature (London),* 216, 1031, 1967.

35. Epstein, J. H., Fukuyama, K., and Fye, K., Effects of ultraviolet radiation on the mitotic cycle and DNA, RNA, and protein synthesis in mammalian epidermis *in vivo, Photochem. Photobiol.*, 12, 57, 1970.

36. Hanke, W., Die Bedeutung von Latenzzeiten für U.V.-Strahlenbedingte Veranderungen am lebenden Gewebe, in *Progress in Photobiology, The Finsen Memorial Congress,* Christensen, B. and Buchmann, B., Eds., Elsevier, Amsterdam, 1961, 336.

37. Daniels, F., Jr., Johnson, B. E., Beaghen, S., and Binford, R. T., Histology and histochemistry of acute sunburn, Exhibit at American Academy of Dermatology, Bal Harbour, Fla., December 3 to 8, 1966.

38. Argyris, T. S., Ribosomal RNA synthesis through epidermal hyperplasia induced by abrasion or treatment with tetradecanoyl phorbol-13-acetate, *J. Invest. Dermatol.,* 76, 388, 1981.

39. Fukuyama, K., Nakamura, T., and Bernstein, I. A., Differentially localized incorporation of amino acids in relation to epidermal keratinization in the newborn rat, *Anat. Rec.,* 152, 525, 1965.

40. Voorhees, J. D., Chakrabarti, S. G., and Bernstein, I. A., The metabolism of "histidine-rich" protein in normal and psoriatic keratinization, *J. Invest. Dermatol.,* 51, 344, 1968.

41. Zenisek, A. and Kral, J. A., Sunscreening effect of urocanic acid, *Biochem. Biophys. Acta,* 18, 589, 1959.

42. Hais, I. M. and Strych, A., Increase in urocanic acid concentration in human epidermis following insolation, *Coll. Czech. Commun.,* 34, 649, 1969.

43. Brusilow, S. L. and Ikai, K., Urocanic acid in sweat: an artifact of elution from the epidermis, *Science,* 160, 1257, 1968.

44. Baden, H. P. and Pathak, M. A., The metabolism and function of urocanic acid in skin, *J. Invest. Dermatol.,* 48, 11, 1967.

45. Anglin, J. G. and Batten, W. H., Studies on *cis* urocanic acid, *J. Invest. Dermatol.,* 50, 463, 1968.

46. DeFabo, E., Noonan, F., Fisher, M., Burns, J., and Kacser, H., Further evidence that the photoreceptor mediated UV-induced systemic immune supprecion is urocanic acid, *J. Invest. Dermatol.,* 80, 319, 1983.

47. DeFabo, E., Noonan, F., Fisher, M., Burns, J., and Kacser, H., Mice deficient in skin urocanic acid are unable to be systemically immunosuppressed by UV radiation, *Photochem. Photobiol.,* 37, S36, 1983.

48. Shelley, W. B. and Juhlin, L., The Langerhans cell: its origin, nature, and function, *Acta Derm.,* Suppl. 79, 7, 1978.

49. Daniels, F., Jr., Optics of the skin as related to ultraviolet radiation, in *The Biologic Effects of Ultraviolet Radiation,* Urbach, F., Ed., Pergamon Press, Elmsford, N.Y., 1969, 151.

50. Nix, T. E., Jr., Nordquist, R. E., and Everett, M. A., Ultrastructural changes induced by ultraviolet light in human epidermis: granular and transitional cell layers, *J. Ultrastruct. Res.,* 12, 547, 1965.

51. Van der Luen, J. C., Ultraviolet Erythema: a Study of Diffusion Processes in Human Skin, Ph.D. thesis, University of Utrecht, Utrecht, the Netherlands, 1966.

52. Tickner, A., Changes in phospholipids of mouse skin after ultraviolet irradiation *in vitro, Biochem. J.,* 88, 80, 1963.

53. Johnson, B. E., A Study of the Physiological Effects of Ultraviolet Radiation on Mammalian Skin, Ph.D. thesis, University of London, 1965.

54. Norins, A. L., Free radical formation in the skin following exposure to ultraviolet light, *J. Invest. Dermatol.,* 39, 445, 1962.

55. Dubouloz, P. and Dumas, J., Sur la formation de peroxide lipideques dan la peau sous l'action des radiation, in *Proc. 1st Int. Photobiological Congr.,* Veenman and Zonen, Wageningen, the Netherlands, 1954, 247.

56. De Leo, V. A., Horlick, H., Hanson, D., Eisinger, M., and Harber, L. C., Ultraviolet radiation induces changes in membrane metabolism of human keratinocytes in culture, *J. Invest. Dermatol.,* 83, 323, 1984.

57. Kummerow, F. A., Benga, G., and Holmes, R. P., Biomembranes and cell function, *Ann. N.Y. Acad. Sci.,* 414, 1983.

58. Eaglstein, W. H. and Weinstein, G. D., Prostaglandin and DNA synthesis in human skin: possible relationship to ultraviolet light effects, *J. Invest. Dermatol.,* 64, 386, 1975.

59. Snyder, D. S., Cutaneous effects of topical indomethacin, an inhibitor of prostaglandin synthesis on UV damaged skin, *J. Invest. Dermatol.,* 64, 322, 1975.

60. Camp, R. D., Greaves, M. W., Hensby, C. N., Plummer, M. A., and Warin, A. P., Irradiation of human skin by short wavelength ultraviolet radiation (200—290 nm) (UVC): increased concentrations of arachidonic acid and prostaglandins E_2 and F_{2a}, *Br. J. Clin. Pharmacol.,* 6, 145, 1978.

61. Zibon, V. A., Casebolt, T. L., Marcelo, C. L., and Voorhees, J. J., Lipoxygenation of arachidonic acid by subcellular preparation from murine keratinocytes, *J. Invest. Dermatol.,* 83, 248, 1984.

62. Hawk, J. L. M., Black, A. K., Jaenicke, K. F., Barr, R. M., Soter, N., Mallett, A. I., Gilchrest, B. A., Hensby, C. N., Parrish, J. A., and Greaves, M., Increased concentrations of arachidonic acid, prostaglandin E_2, D_2, and 6-oxo-F_1 and histamine in human skin following UVA irradiation, *J. Invest. Dermatol.*, 80, 496, 1983.

63. DeDuve, C. and Wattiaux, R., Functions of lysosomes, *Annu. Rev. Physiol.*, 28, 435, 1966.

64. Weissmann, G. and Dingle, J. T., Release of lysosomal protease by UV irradiation and inhibition by hydrocortisone, *Exp. Cell Res.*, 25, 207, 1961.

65. Weissmann, G. and Fell, H. B., The effect of hydrocortisone on the response of fetal rat skin in culture to ultraviolet irradiation, *J. Exp. Med.*, 365, 1968.

66. Frienkel, R. K. and Traczyk, T. N., Acid hydrolases of the epidermis: subcellular localization and relationship to cornification, *J. Invest. Dermatol.*, 80, 441, 1983.

67. Johnson, E. B., Ultraviolet radiation and lysosomes in skin, *Nature (London)*, 219, 1258, 1968.

68. Johnson, E. B. and Daniels, F., Jr., Lysosomes and reactions of skin to ultraviolet radiation, *J. Invest. Dermatol.*, 53, 85, 1969.

69. Johnson, E. B., Lysosomal damage by UV-irradiation of the skin, in 6th Int. Congr. Photobiology, Schenk, G. O., Ed., Bochum, West Germany, 1972.

70. Kummerow, F. A., Modification of cell membrane composition by dietary lipids and its implications for atherosclerosis, *Ann. N.Y. Acad. Sci.*, 414, 29, 1983.

71. Feldman, D., Chen, T., and Hirst, M., Demonstration of 1,25 dihydroxy vitamin D receptors in human skin biopsies, *J. Clin. Endocrinol.*, 51, 1463, 1980.

72. Pavlovitch, J. H. and Delescluse, C., Vitamin D and the metabolism of epidermis, *Int. J. Dermatol.*, 22, 98, 1983.

73. Weber, G., Excited states in proteins, in *Light and Life*, McElroy, W. D. and Glass, B., Eds., Johns Hopkins University Press, Baltimore, 1961, 82.

74. Yeargers, E., Ultraviolet light effects on proteins, in *The Biologic Effects of Ultraviolet Radiation*, Urbach, F., Ed., Pergamon Press, Oxford, 1969, 37.

75. Soter, N. A., Lewis, R. A., Corey, E. J., and Austen, K. F., Local effects of synthetic leukotrienes (LTC_4, LTD_4, LTE_4, LTB_4) in human skin, *J. Invest. Dermatol.*, 80, 115, 1983.

76. Walrant, P., Santis, R., and Grossweiner, L. I., Photosensitizing properties of N_1-formylkynurenine, *Photochem. Photobiol.*, 22, 63, 1975.

77. Zigman, S., Schultz, J., Yolo, T., and Griess, G., Possible roles of near UV light in the cataractous process, *Exp. Eye Res.*, 15, 201, 1973.

78. Zigman, S., The role of sunlight in human cataract formation, *Surv. Ophthalmol.*, 27, 317, 1983.

79. Kochevar, I. E. and Yoon, M., Photosensitization of methyl linoleate oxidation by tryptophan in peptides, *Photochem. Photobiol.*, 37, 279, 1983.

80. Wiskemann, A., Die heutigen Kenntnisse über die Mechanismen der UV-Wirkung auf die menschliche haut, *Strahlentherapie*, 122, 463, 1963.

81. Daniels, F., Jr. and Van der Luen, J. C., Problems in quantifying skin reactions, *Arch. Dermatol.*, 97, 553, 1968.

82. Daniels, F., Jr. and Imbrie, J. D., Comparison between visual grading and reflectance measurements of erythema produced by sunlight, *J. Invest. Dermatol.*, 30, 295, 1958.

83. Van der Luen, J. C., Presentation at the 6th Int. Congr. Photobiology, Bochum, West Germany, 1972.

84. Buettner, K. J. K., The effects of natural sunlight on human skin, in *The Biologic Effects of Ultraviolet Radiation*, Urbach, F., Ed., Pergamon Press, Oxford, 1969, 237.

85. Adams, E. Q., Barnes, B. T., and Forsythe, W. E., Erythema due to ultraviolet radiation, *J. Opt. Soc. Am.*, 21, 207, 1931.

86. Schulze, R. and Grafe, K., Consideration of sky ultraviolet radiation in the measurement of solar ultraviolet radiation, in *The Biologic Effects of Ultraviolet Radiation*, Urbach, F., Ed., Pergamon Press, Oxford, 1969.

87. Edwards, E. A. and Duntley, S. Q., An analysis of skin pigment changes after exposure to sunlight, *Science*, 90, 235, 1939.

88. Jansen, M. T., A reflection spectrophotometric study of ultraviolet erythema and pigmentation, *J. Clin. Invest.*, 32, 1053, 1953.

89. Jacquez, J. A., Kuppenheim, H. F., Dimitroff, J. M., McKeehan, W., and Huss, J., Spectral reflectance of human skin in the region 235—700 nm, *J. Appl. Physiol.*, 8, 212, 1955.

90. Lasker, G. W., Photoelectric measurement of skin color in a Mexican Mestizo population, *Am. J. Phys. Anthropol.*, 12, 115, 1954.

91. Weiner, J. S., Harisson, G. A., Singer, R., Harris, R., and Jopp, W., Skin color in southern Africa, *Hum. Biol.*, 36, 294, 1964.

92. Breit, R. and Kligman, A. M., Measurement of erythemal and pigmentary responses to ultraviolet radiation of different spectral properties, in *The Biologic Effects of Ultraviolet Radiation*, Urbach, F., Ed., Pergamon Press, Oxford, 1969, 267.

93. Wan, S., Jaenicke, K. F., and Parrish, J. A., Comparison of the erythemogenic effectiveness of ultraviolet-B (290—320 nm) and ultraviolet-A (320—400 nm) radiation by skin reflectance, *Photochem. Photobiol.,* 37, 547, 1983.

94. Parrish, J. A., Anderson, R. R., Urbach, F., and Pitts, D., *UVA: Biological Effects of Ultraviolet Radiation with Emphasis on Human Responses to Longwave Ultraviolet,* Plenum Press, New York, 1978, 7—14 and 65—73.

95. Claesson, S., Juhlin, L., and Wettermark, G., The reciprocity law of UV-irradiation effects, *Acta Derm.,* 38, 123, 1958.

96. Berger, D., Personal communication, 1979.

97. Colsky, L. D., Halprin, K. M., Taylor, J. R., Comerford, M., and Kramer, J. R., UVB is additive when repeated within an 8-hour interval, *J. Am. Acad. Dermatol.,* 8, 760, 1983.

98. Everett, W. A., Sayer, R. M., and Olson, R. L., Physiologic response of human skin to UV light, in *The Biologic Effects of Ultraviolet Radiation,* Urbach, F., Ed., Pergamon Press, Oxford, 1969, 181.

99. Van der Leun, A. C., On the action spectrum of ultraviolet erythema, in *Research Progress in Organic, Biological and Medicinal Chemistry,* North-Holland, Amsterdam, 1972, 711.

100. Parrish, J. A., Ying, C. Y., Pathak, M. A., and Fitzpatrick, T. B., Erythemogenic properties of long-wave ultraviolet light, in *Sunlight and Man,* Pathak, M. A., Harber, L. C., Seiji, M., Kukita, A., and Fitzpatrick, T. B., Eds., University of Tokyo Press, Tokyo, 1974, 131.

101. Johnson, B. E., Reactions of normal skin to solar radiation, in *The Physiology and Pathophysiology of the Skin,* Vol. 8, Jarrett, A., Ed., 1984, 2413.

102. Gilchrest, B. A., Soter, N. A., Stoff, J. S., and Mihm, M. C., Human sunburn reaction: histologic and biochemical studies, *J. Am. Acad. Dermatol.,* 5, 411, 1981.

103. Gilchrest, B. A., Murphy, G. F., and Soter, N. A., Effect of chronological aging and ultraviolet irradiation on Langerhans cells in human epidermis, *J. Invest. Dermatol.,* 79, 85, 1982.

104. Rosario, R., Mark, G. J., Parrish, J. A., and Mihm, M. C., Histologic changes produced in skin by equally erythemogenic doses of UVA, UVB, UVC, and UVA with psoralens, *Br. J. Dermatol.,* 101, 299, 1979.

105. Wolff, K. and Winklemann, R. F., Ultrastructural localization of nucleoside triphosphatase in Langerhans cells, *J. Invest. Dermatol.,* 48, 50, 1967.

106. Potten, C. S. and Allen, T. D., A model implicating the Langerhans cell in keratinocyte proliferation control, *Differentiation,* 5, 43, 1976.

107. Aberer, W., Schuler, G., Stingl, G., and Wolff, K., Ultraviolet light depletes surface markers of Langerhans cells, *J. Invest. Dermatol.,* 76, 202, 1981.

108. Stingl, G., New aspects of Langerhans cell function, *Int. J. Dermatol.,* 19, 289, 1980.

109. Potter, G., Langerhans Cell: Studies in Epidermal Cell Culture and Clinical Applications, Ph.D. thesis, Cornell University, Ithaca, N.Y., 1981.

110. Lobitz, W. C., Jr., Brophy, D., Larner, A. E., and Daniels, F., Jr., Glycogen response in human epidermal basal cell, *Arch. Dermatol.,* 86, 207, 1962.

111. Iverson, O., Discussion, in 1st Int. Conf. Biology of Cutaneous Cancer, National Cancer Institute Monograph No. 10, Urbach, F., Ed., NCI, Bethesda, Md., 1963, 418.

112. Riley, V., Ed., *Pigmentation: Its Genesis and Biologic Control,* Appleton-Century-Crofts, New York, 1972.

113. Kawamura, T., Ed., *Biology of Normal and Abnormal Melanocytes,* University of Tokyo Press, Tokyo, 1974.

114. Jimbow, K., Pathak, M. A., Szabo, G., and Fitzpatrick, T. B., Ultrastructural changes in human melanocytes after ultraviolet radiation, in *Sunlight and Man,* Pathak, M. A., Harber, L. C., Seiji, M., Kukita, A., and Fitzpatrick, T. B., Eds., University of Tokyo Press, Tokyo, 1974.

115. Riley, V., Ed., *Pigment Cell,* Vol. 3, S. Karger, Basel, 1975.

116. Carter, D. M., The Yale conference on pigment cell biology, *Yale J. Biol. Med.,* 46, 331, 1973.

117. Fitzpatrick, T. B., Szabo, G., Seiji, M., and Quevedo, W. C., Jr., Biology of the melanin pigmentary system, in *Dermatology in General Medicine,* 2nd ed., Fitzpatrick, T. B., Eisen, A. Z., Wolff, K., Freedberg, I. M., and Austen, K. F., Eds., McGraw-Hill, New York, 1979.

118. Miescher, G. and Minder, H., Untersuchungen über die durch langwelliges Ultraviolett hervorgerufene Pigmentdunkelun, *Strahlentherapie,* 66, 6, 1939.

119. Wiskemann, A. and Winser, H., Die Beziehung der direkten Pigmentiertung zur Konstitution, *Strahlentherapie,* 99, 594, 1956.

120. Lorincz, A. L., Pigmentation, in *Physiology and Biochemistry of the Skin,* Rothman, S., Ed., University of Chicago Press, Chicago, 1954, 515.

121. Rosdahl, I. K., Local and systemic effects on the epidermal melanocyte population in UV-irradiated mouse skin, *J. Invest. Dermatol.,* 73, 306, 1979.

122. Van der Luen, A. C., On the action spectrum of ultraviolet erythema, in *Research Progress in Organic, Biological, and Medicinal Chemistry,* North-Holland, Amsterdam, 1972, 711.

123. Sams, W. J. and Winkelmann, R. K., The effect of ultraviolet light on isolated cutaneous blood vessels, *J. Invest. Dermatol.*, 53, 79, 1969.
124. Epstein, W. L., Fukuyama, K., and Epstein, J. H., Early effects of ultraviolet light on DNA synthesis in human skin *in vivo, Arch. Dermatol.*, 100, 84, 1969.
125. Chase, M., Personal communication.
126. Daniels, F., Jr., Some of the cryobiology behind cryosurgery, *Cutis,* 16, 421, 1975.
127. Lewis, T., *The Blood Vessels of the Human Skin and their Responses,* Shaw & Sons, London, 1927.
128. Partington, M. W., The vascular response of the skin to ultraviolet light, *Clin. Sci.*, 13, 425, 1954.
129. Ikai, T., Danno, K., Horop, T., and Narumya, S., Effect of ultraviolet radiation on mast cell deficient mice, *J. Invest. Dermatol.*, 82, 391, 1984.
130. Hawk, J. L. M. and Parrish, J. A., Responses of normal skin to ultraviolet radiation, in *The Science of Photomedicine,* Regan, J. D. and Parrish, J. A., Eds., Plenum Press, New York, 1982, 219.

Chapter 4

THE HOMOLOGY OF UV-MEDIATED CUTANEOUS CARCINOGENIC AND AGING PROCESSES

Homer S. Black

TABLE OF CONTENTS

I. INTRODUCTION

Skin cancer represents a group of diseases that occur with common frequency in white-skinned populations. Indeed, the yearly reported incidence of new skin cancer cases among white Americans nearly equals the combined annual incidence of all other malignancies![1] For the purpose of this discussion, skin cancer is herein limited to non-melanoma, epithelial cancers — both basal and squamous cell carcinomas.

Although treatment of skin cancer results in a high cure rate (well over 90%), this disease, for those individuals so prediposed, demonstrates a great propensity for repeated occurrence.[2] Because skin cancer does not normally appear until the fourth or fifth decade of life, it is often found in conjunction with other conditions generally associated with aging skin. These manifestations of cutaneous aging also represent physiologic states which markedly diminish the quality of life among age groups comprising an ever-increasing percentage of our population. The U.S. Bureau of Labor Statistics reports that skin disorders account for upwards of 40% of all reported occupational diseases. The level of skin disorders in the elderly is even greater — reaching 65% of persons over age 65.[3] Collectively then, the conditions associated with skin aging and cancer represent problems of significant personal, societal, and economic impact.

That a relationship exists between cancer and aging is not a new concept.[4] Epidemiologic studies have demonstrated that the incidence of cancer increases with age in both human and animal populations. The probability that a human will develop cancer in the succeeding 5-year period is 50 times greater at age 65 than at 25.[5] Recent studies have shown that given the same amount of sun exposure, individuals over 60 years of age are at a significantly greater risk of developing skin cancer than those under 60.[6]

Experimental evidence suggests that tumor response reflects two distinguishable aspects of aging.[7] First, passage of time required by repeated exposure to the carcinogen that results in accumulated damage and second, the "physiological age" of the target tissue which correlates with passage of time. It is the latter of which little is known. Whether the influence of physiological age on carcinogenesis results from morphologic and/or pathologic changes occurring in the target tissue, biochemical properties of the respective tissue, or physiological properties of the organism (systemic factors) is unknown. It has been suggested that if cancer developed in old age because of the breakdown of systemic control, the induction of cancer by carcinogenic agents should become progressively easier with advancing age.[8] Under a wide range of experimental protocols, the reverse has been most often observed with UV carcinogenesis, i.e., older animals appear *less* susceptible to formation of UV-induced tumors.[7,9-11] Moreover, an increased cancer incidence with age may actually result as a consequence of prolonged local exposure to the carcinogenic agent. The conclusion drawn from one study in which benzo(a)pyrene was used to induce skin cancer is that aging per se is irrelevant — the observed increase in cancer incidence with time being a direct result of the duration of local exposure.[5] Thus the crucial question remains unanswered. How are the manifestations of actinically aged skin related to the observed increased incidence of UV-induced skin cancers? Are they independent, interdependent, or dependent phenomena? This chapter reviews the pertinent theories of aging as they relate to carcinogenesis with the emphasis placed on experimental aspects. It is hoped that information provided here will serve as a guide in establishing the rationale and as a catalyst for future research when addressing the question of a relationship between actinic aging and carcinogenesis of the skin.

II. GENERAL THEORIES

Many theories of aging and carcinogenesis evoke remarkably similar mechanisms. Generally these are based upon:

1. Some malfunction of genetic material, i.e., either inability to preserve informational DNA in its original, functional form or to transcribe or translate the genetic information into functional cellular activities.
2. The formation and/or accumulation of harmful products.
3. Programmed aging in which some type of biological clock, presumably contained in the genetic material, tracks elapsed time and which initiates and programs the aging sequence at the appropriate time. Of course, this mechanism must be relatively impervious to environmental factors (inmutable) and must dictate the life span of each respective species or tissue with utmost accuracy. An analogous circumstance for carcinogenesis might involve some type of endogenous chronic insult (wear and tear) that results in gradual loss of metabolic control until expression of neoplasia ultimately occurs.

A. The Aging Process

Strehler[12] has conveniently defined aging as a set of deteriorative processes characterized by the following common properties:

1. General deleterious processes occur in all species and are thus *universal* in nature.
2. These processes are *intrinsic* — a part of the genetic makeup of the respective species. The life span of each species is fixed and only through environmental modification can such parameters as mean life expectancy be influenced.
3. Aging is a *progressive* process, i.e., it occurs gradually with time.
4. Aging processes are *deleterious*. They diminish the functional capacity of the system to withstand challenges from the environment or within the system.

B. The Carcinogenic Process

On the other hand, carcinogenesis is a process represented by a series of events, usually initiated by *extrinsic* factors, in which functional deletion of metabolic control sites occur resulting in abnormal *new* tissue growth. Becker[13] has characterized the carcinogenic process as involving five distinct phases:

1. A *toxic* phase in which extrinsic factors initiate the process. This phase is most often characterized by inhibition of normal functions, i.e., decreased nucleic acid synthesis, etc.
2. An *escape* phase in which persistent cell division occurs, allowing selected cells to be identified by morphological and functional characteristics differing from normal cells.
3. A period in which rapid *growth* of the "escaped" cells occurs. It is possible that the stages of carcinogenesis to this point are reversible.
4. The subsequent stage of *autonomy* is characterized by retention of phenotypic diversity and abnormal structure and an enhanced capacity for cell division, presumably having escaped normal regulatory controls.
5. The final stage is that of frank malignancy, characterized by ability to invade surrounding tissues and irreversibility of its growth pattern.

There are obvious differences in the general processes of aging and carcinogenesis. Cancer is not universal, although we have alluded to the increased incidence of cancer associated with passage of chronological time. It may be, with respect to oncogenes, that the propensity to cancer expression with age is intrinsic. However, for most forms of cancer the preponderance of evidence is that expression occurs in response to environmental insult. This is particularly apparent for ultraviolet radiation (UVR). Certainly it appears that for both processes the only intervention possible is through environmental modification; here again, advances in our paradigm of scientific wisdom, particularly in the area of genetic engineering, may alter our thinking on this matter in the future. Cancer and the aging processes certainly diminish the functional capacity of the system, but is the growth pattern exhibited by a neoplasm representative of this general property? Etymologically, the contrary is indicated. Thus, comparisons of general characteristics of these two processes provide only interesting parallels, and it would appear that relationships of aging to carcinogenesis must be sought at the cellular and molecular levels.

III. BIOCHEMICAL ASPECTS

A. Aging

The error-accumulation hypothesis of aging generally holds that cellular reproduction is not perfect and that defective cell components are occasionally generated. If these errors are not repaired, this misinformation can be passed to subsequent generations, resulting in eventual impairment of cell function. If, for example, an accumulation of mutations occurred within the DNA of a cell, functionally impaired enzymes might result (Orgel hypothesis)[14] — perhaps DNA repair or replication enzymes — which could eventually bring cell division to a halt.

As noted, the most relevant and serious manifestations of aging would appear to be those of intrinsic origin and which affect the genetic composition of the cell, i.e., its DNA. Unfortunately, these forms of damage are the least understood, as compared to model DNA damaging agents such as UV.[15] Irrespective that the specific mechanics of DNA damage induced by intrinsic and extrinsic insult may differ, similar categories of extrinsic stimuli would be expected to produce similar damage and/or evoke similar repair steps, some of which would be expected to mimic effects of intrinsic factors. For example, it is well established that UV insult causes unscheduled DNA synthesis (UDS), a type of synthesis indicative of excision repair. Thus, Hart and Setlow[16] examined the relationship between life span and ability to repair DNA. Using cells derived from superficial dermis of several animal species of varying life spans, these investigators demonstrated that both the rate and extent of UDS, following UV insult, increased with life span of the respective species. The measured parameters were assumed to reflect the numbers of repaired regions per unit length of DNA. Thus, a mouse, with low excision-repair capacity, would accumulate more damage per unit length of its DNA than would man. Such damage could result in more rapid deterioration of the fidelity of transcription and translation processes which, in turn, could lead to a shortened life span.

A considerable literature in cellular senescence has accrued since the observation that human and animal cells demonstrate a determinant number of population doublings when grown in culture.[17,18] Such cells are predestined to undergo irreversible functional decrements that mimic age changes in the whole organism. This maximum potential for cell doubling is diminished in cells derived from older donors and appears to be inversely proportional to their age.[19-21] In addition, the limitation on doubling potential of cultured normal cells is expressed in vivo when serial transplants are made. There is some evidence, by at least one established in vitro criterion, that UV plays a role in accelerating skin aging. It has been shown that prior chronic sun exposure decreases the life span of cultured human skin fibroblasts and keratinocytes.[22,23]

Although a number of cellular functional activities have been reported to occur in aging cells that could account for loss of doubling potential, a diminished nucleic acid synthetic and repair capacity has been suggested as playing a major role. In general, the proportion of cells able to synthesize DNA declines with age and the ability of cells to repair the DNA they synthesize decreases.[24-26] Further, cells derived from patients suffering from progeria, a genetically transmitted disease in which aging manifestations are accelerated, have been reported to exhibit a reduced life span and a marked lack of repair after gamma radiation.[27] However, the relationship of UDS to aging is in no way certain. Goldstein[28] reported very little change in UDS between early- and late-passage cells. Hart and Setlow,[29] while finding that aged cells in culture synthesize less DNA, concluded that failure of repair is not a causal event in failure of late-passage cells to divide. Likewise, Regan and Setlow[30] found no reduced ability for DNA repair in progeroid cells and suggested that results obtained in previous reports could have resulted from trypsin sensitivity imposed by the culture methods. Thus, the evidence for deficient DNA repair levels in aging cell populations remains incomplete.

B. Carcinogenesis

Perhaps the most encouraging efforts to discern mechanisms of UV carcinogenesis have stemmed from studies of humans afflicted with *Xeroderma pigmentosum* (XP). This disease is genetically transmitted and attributable to an autosomal recessive gene. Persons suffering from the syndrome are extremely susceptible to effects of UV and as a consequence of exposure, develop multiple skin cancers.[31] The biochemical defect in XP that leads to skin cancer is thought to be due to a mutation resulting in dysfunction of endonuclease, the enzyme that initiates the repair process by making a single-strand break in DNA next to the aberrant pyrimidine dimer. Just as progeria cells exhibit different repair rates in response to gamma and UV radiation, XP cells have a normal repair in X-ray-induced DNA strand breaks but a much slower capacity to remove UV-induced dimers.[33-37] In both homozygous XP fibroblasts and in vivo, there occurs no increase in repair synthesis upon UV exposure as does occur in normal fibroblasts or subjects.[38] The yield of pyrimidine dimers in XP cells is a linear function of UV dose when measured immediately postirradiation — the same as occurs in normal cells. However, 24 hr after irradiation, the percent of dimers in normal cells has fallen, whereas virtually no change occurs in XP cells.[39] These data indicate deficient repair systems as a probable cause of skin cancer. Nevertheless, the relationship of DNA repair defects to oncologic clinical manifestations of XP is obscured by the finding of a group of patients, designated "XP variants", who presented the clinical manifestations of the disease but whose cells lacked the repair defects as conventionally defined.[31,40] In this respect, newer techniques have indicated that a number of the XP variant cell lines are, indeed, less efficient than normal cells in their DNA repair processes. These data point to the complexity of repair processes but do not indicate which processes are deficient. At this time, the evidence linking deficient DNA repair capacity in both aging and carcinogenesis remains equivocal and says nothing about the fidelity of repair mechanisms in these processes.

DNA repair is but one of many functional parameters that have been examined as a potential determinant in the aging and carcinogenic processes. Accumulation of altered proteins (Orgel hypothesis), RNA metabolism, and error catastrophe are but a few others that have received attention with respect to aging. No clear-cut impairment of function, due to some type of accumulated damage, has yet been demonstrated.[41] Indeed, as Cutler[42] points out, "on analyzing deeper into the cellular and biochemical properties of the animal, the obvious macroscopic manifestations of age begin to diminish to the point that most cellular and biochemical properties appear unchanged". It is suggested that aging may be the result of cells simply drifting away from their proper state of differentiation — a process referred to as "dysdifferentiation". This process would be akin to the thermodynamic behavior of systems undergoing decay from a higher-ordered state. In this respect aging and cancer would be more related than previously noted in that both would represent aberrant states which result from escape of control.

Foremost among potential processes that might act to dysdifferentiate cells would be various by-products of normal cellular metabolism. These toxic by-products, as exemplified by the formation of peroxides, would have the ability to act as epigenetic-like inducers of dysdifferentiation at concentrations far below the levels required to produce obvious cell damage. This brings us to the potential role of free radicals in the processes of aging and carcinogenesis.

IV. FREE-RADICAL THEORY OF AGING AND CARCINOGENESIS

Harman [43,44] advanced the thesis that mutation, cancer, and aging are attributable to the side effects of endogenously formed free radicals. Free radicals are highly reactive chemical species that are unique in that they possess an unpaired electron. As a result of this property, free radicals are extremely reactive with neighboring molecules and consequently have only a transient life span. Because of the ubiquitous nature of free-radical reactions that occur in living organisms (free radicals are thought to arise endogenously by reduction of oxygen in respiring tissues to the reactive radical anion), defense mechanisms which limit the damage from these reactions have evolved. Some representative defense mechanisms include antioxidants, e.g., endogenous vitamin E and carotene; certain enzymes, e.g., selenium and heme-containing peroxidases and superoxide dismutase; and the previously discussed DNA repair mechanisms.

Whereas the reactivity of free radicals may proceed via several routes, of particular interest in regard to aging and cancer are those reactions that result in lipid peroxidation.[45] Lipid peroxides result from the chain-propagated free-radical attack upon polyunsaturated fatty acids and are themselves highly toxic.[46] Further, they are subjected to a number of metabolic fates, one being degradation to the three-carbon dialdehyde or malonaldehyde. Whereas malonaldehyde has been shown to be mutagenic,[47,48] it may also react with amines to form fluorescent conjugated Schiff bases that possess spectral properties nearly identical to that of the age pigment, lipofuscin.[49] The accumulation of lipofuscin is the most prominent age-associated alteration thus far observed in a variety of postmitotic cell types and in many phylogenetically divergent organisms.[50]

If free-radical reactions are involved in the degradative (dysdifferention) responses manifested in aging and cancer, then compounds that possess a capacity for scavenging free radicals, inhibiting their formation, or terminating chain reactions initiated by them, should produce a salutary effect upon both processes. Compounds capable of inhibiting free-radical reactions are broadly defined as antioxidants. Thus, Harman[44] has proposed three intervention strategies to reduce the potential damage of free-radical reactions:

1. Lower caloric intake, thereby lowering the level of free-radical reactions arising during the course of normal metabolism.
2. Reduce levels of dietary constituents that tend to increase the level of free-radical reactions, i.e., polyunsaturated lipids.
3. Addition of dietary free-radical reaction inhibitors (antioxidants).

Some evidence supports Harman's thesis. Berg and Simms[51] have shown that caloric restriction in rats significantly extends their mean life span. One explanation for such an effect is based upon the expected reduction in free-radical-mediated damage throughout the cells, but particularly to the mitochondria where about 90% of the oxygen consumed by an animal is utilized. Mitochondria possess their own complement of DNA and protein-synthesizing machinery and, to a degree, are self-replicating. If free radicals are generated at a rate dependent upon the rate of oxygen consumption, as it is generally assumed, then excessive caloric intake could accelerate those normally gradual deleterious effects that impair the mitochondrial, and ultimately the cells', proliferative capacity. Harman[52] has also reported that by increasing the amount and/ or degree of unsaturation of dietary fat, the mean life span of CH3 mice is significantly decreased. By adding certain antioxidants, such as 2-mercaptoethylamine or butylated hydroxytoluene (BHT), an increase in mean life expectancy is observed.[53]

It has been suggested that free radicals play a major role in mediating UV-induced epidermal cell damage.[54,55] Indeed, formation of free radicals has been shown to occur in UV-radiated skin.[56] As a result, several investigations have been undertaken to examine the effects of antiradicals upon UV-mediated biological responses. Lo and Black,[57] while examining the potential role of cholesterol photooxidation products in UV carcinogenesis, found that formation of these oxidation products was greatly diminished by systemic administration of a mixture of antioxidants. An inverse relationship was found to exist between levels of oxidation product formed and tissue antioxidant levels. The antioxidant mixture consisted of ascorbic acid, dl-α-tocopherol acetate, reduced glutathione, and BHT. When the mixture was tested in the hairless mouse/UV-carcinogenesis model, it was found to inhibit both tumor latency and severity.[58,59] Subsequently, DeRios et al.[60] demonstrated that the same antioxidant mixture protected against UV-induced erythema, providing a systemic sun protection factor (SPF) of 2. Of the mixture, only BHT afforded protection when administered individually, the degree of protection being equivalent to that provided by the complete mixture. It was assumed that BHT was the active principal in the mixture and subsequently it was shown to inhibit UV carcinogenesis.[61]

Other scavengers of active oxygen species have also been examined in the UV-carcinogenesis model. β-Carotene, a carotenoid pigment of plant origin, accumulates at very low levels in human skin and affords some protection against the harmful effects of UV when subjects are made carotenemic by administration of large amounts of this agent. Mathews-Roth et al.[62] have reported that carotene provides a limited, but statistically significant, increase in the UV-induced erythema threshold. Epstein[63] demonstrated the photoprotective effects of β-carotene against UV-induced carcinogenesis in hairless mice, both in regard to delayed appearance and reduced tumor growth rates. Mathews-Roth[64] expanded these studies and examined two other carotenoid pigments for photoprotective properties. Canthaxanthin, like β-carotene, is a free-radical inhibitor and singlet oxygen quencher, but cannot be metabolized to vitamin A as can β-carotene. Phytoene can also inhibit free-radical formation and absorb UV radiation. β-Carotene, canthaxanthin, and phytoene, irrespective of vitamin A activity, provided significant protection against UV-induced tumor formation. Although the exact mechanism of carotenoid pigments in inhibiting UV carcinogenesis is uncertain at present, the involvement of these pigments in some sort of reactive oxygen species-mediated responses appears certain.[65]

Pauling et al.[66] corroborated the earlier observations concerning the inhibitory effect of antioxidants on UV carcinogenesis. However, Forbes,[67] using a semipurified diet containing an identical antioxidant mixture, observed no effect upon carcinogenic sensitivity. The fact that dietary factors could modify the photoprotective effect of antioxidants had been noted previously.[68] Indeed, the free-radical theory would predict that dietary factors that enhance free-radical reactions would increase the antioxidant requirements. Thus, a closer examination of dietary influence upon antioxidant-modified UV carcinogenesis was indicated.

Several studies have now confirmed the early observation that dietary lipid plays an important role in predisposition to UV carcinogenesis.[69] The degree of dietary lipid saturation has been shown to have a significant effect upon UV-induced tumor expression. Unsaturated lipid, just as in some types of chemical carcinogenesis, exacerbates UV-tumor formation.[70] Two independent studies have demonstrated that for the respective ranges examined, dietary-lipid level has a direct effect upon carcinogenic response to UV in regard to both tumor latency and multiplicity.[71,72] Mathews-Roth and Krinsky[72] reported that as dietary fat was increased, the ability of β-carotene to protect animals against UV-induced skin tumors declined. Black et al.[71] found that antioxidants produced an inhibitory effect almost equal to the degree of carcinogenic enhancement evoked by increasing dietary lipid levels.

The influence of dietary-lipid level and antioxidants upon lipid peroxidation has also been examined.[73] Levels of thiobarbituric acid (TBA) reacting materials in epidermal homogenates increased almost proportionately to the level of dietary lipid. TBA values for antioxidant-supplemented animals remained relatively constant and consistently low, regardless of lipid level. The relationship of dietary-lipid level, UV carcinogenesis, epidermal lipid-peroxidative capacity, and antioxidant effects upon these processes are summarized in Figure 1. These data indirectly implicate peroxidative reactions in UV carcinogenesis and demonstrate that antioxidants can inhibit such events. Interestingly, Meffert et al.[74] had demonstrated that levels of similar lipid-peroxidation products increased in human skin (1) after UV radiation, (2) in chronically sun-exposed areas, as well as (3) with advancing age. One potential manifestation of lipid peroxidation would be labilization of cell membranes. This effect, particularly with respect to lysosomal membranes, has been observed in both acute and chronically irradiated skin.[75,76]

Evidence for the involvement of free radicals or their reactions in UV carcinogenesis is summarized in Table 1.

V. IMMUNOLOGIC ASPECTS OF AGING AND CARCINOGENESIS

Aging is characterized by a declining capability of organisms to adapt to environmental stress, exemplified by an inability to maintain homeostasis.[79] This loss of physiologic control is manifested in age-associated increases in susceptibility to infectious diseases and frequency of cancer, both occurring when immunologic responsiveness is declining.[80,81] With respect to UV carcinogenesis, immunologic involvement is now well documented, although evidence of the specific immunologic factors that participate in carcinogenesis is unclear.

Whereas Baumann and Rusch[69] first noted that UV-induced tumors were readily rejected upon transplantation, it was some 35 years later until the potential significance of this observation became apparent. Kripke[82] first demonstrated that rejection of UV-induced tumors was due to an immunologic response. Because of the unusually high degree of antigenicity of UV-induced tumors, the question arose as to how these tumors could survive immunologic rejection in the autochthonous host. The involvement of UV radiation became apparent when it was shown that (1) treatment of mice with UV radiation interfered with the rejection of UV-induced tumors at distant transplant sites,[83] (2) transplantation of UV-induced tumors into UV-radiated hosts resulted in tumor growth rather than rejection, and (3) injection of tumor cells resulted in pulmonary metastases in UV-radiated hosts but not in nonirradiated hosts.[84]

Studies of the nature of this immunologic involvement indicated that UV-mediated rejection incompetence was caused by an alteration in the recipients' lymphoid cells. It was determined that T lymphocytes from UV-radiated animals suppressed tumor rejection by normal lymphocytes.[85,86] T cells are lymphoid cells that serve as part of a regulatory system that normally controls immunologic responses. These UV-induced sup-

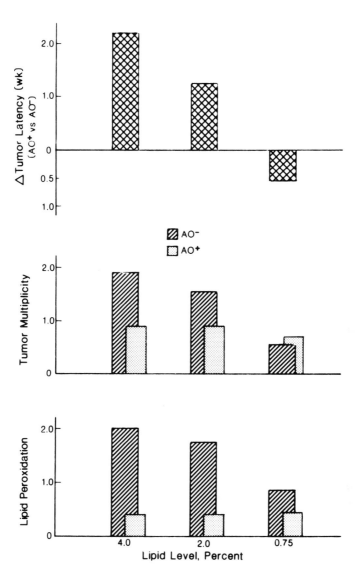

FIGURE 1. Relation of antioxidant supplementation and dietary lipid level to tumor latency, multiplicity, and epidermal lipid peroxidation in the hairless mouse/UV carcinogenesis model. The deviation bar graph (top) represents the effects of antioxidants on tumor latency at varying dietary-lipid levels. At the highest dietary-lipid level (4%) antioxidants increase tumor latency by 2 weeks. This increase is approximately equal to the decrease of tumor latency affected by increasing the dietary-lipid level from 0.75 to 4.0%. The effect of antioxidants decrease with decreasing lipid levels. The center bar graph reflects the effects of antioxidants on tumor multiplicity (mean number of tumors per animal) for the respective lipid levels. The lower bar graph depicts the effects of antioxidants and varying lipid level on epidermal lipid peroxidation (expressed as nanomole TBA reacting materials per milligram epidermal protein per hour). Antioxidants negate the dietary lipid-related elevation of both tumor multiplicity and lipid peroxidation.[71,73]

pressor cells inhibit the immune response to UV-induced tumors in what appears to be a specific manner, i.e., the suppressor cells do not evoke an immune response to chemically induced tumors or tissue allografts.[85,87]

Recently de Gruijl and van der Leun[88] demonstrated that UV carcinogenesis is accelerated in animals that have been previously irradiated at a site removed from that of tumor induction. Further, the presence or absence of UV-induced suppressor cells dictates whether visible tumors develop in UV-irradiated skin.[89] These data, along with

Table 1
EVIDENCE FOR INVOLVEMENT OF FREE-RADICAL MEDIATED REACTIONS IN UV CARCINOGENESIS

1.   Free radicals are formed in skin upon response to UV radiation.[56]
2.   UV-induced oxidation of skin sterols results in formation of cholesterol epoxide[77] — a putative carcinogen, the formation of which is a sensitive indicator of lipid peroxidation.[78]
3.   Dietarily administered antioxidants inhibit the formation of cholesterol epoxide — its formation being inversely related to the skin antioxidant content.[57]
4.   UV radiation promotes the formation of stable lipid-peroxidation products in skin.[74]
5.   Antioxidants inhibit epidermal malonaldehyde formation — an empirical test for lipid peroxidation.[73]
6.   Biological effects of potential free-radical-mediated reactions, i.e., membrane labilization, have been shown to occur in acute and chronically irradiated skin.[75,76]
7.   Intake of free-radical stimulators, i.e., polyunsaturated fats, exacerbates UV carcinogenesis.[71,72]
8.   Antioxidants inhibit UV carcinogenesis at a level roughly equivalent to the degree of exacerbation induced by unsaturated lipid.[71]

those in which immunosuppressive agents have been shown to enhance UV carcinogenesis,[90,91] provide convincing evidence of an immunologic component to photocarcinogenesis and a link between UV radiation and the immune system.

Just as T-cell function has been implicated in the process of UV carcinogenesis, it is T-cell populations which primarily reflect age-associated immunologic change. Based upon the process of involution and atrophy through which the thymus begins to undergo shortly after puberty, proponents of the "biological clock" theory of aging suggest that the T-dependent lymphoid system is genetically programmed to decline in effectiveness.[79] In theory, the thymus would be under control of a genetically programmed clock mechanism set to self-destruct after having undergone a fixed number of cell divisions.

Regardless of the intrinsic nature of potential control mechanisms of immunocompetence, it has been shown that extrinsic factors, among them diet, can counteract age-related immunologic insufficiency. Just as reduced caloric intake has been demonstrated to inhibit carcinogenesis, Good et al.[92] observed that not only was life span increased in certain strains of animals receiving restricted dietary calories but that immunologic decline was forestalled. Dietary fat also played a significant role in ameliorating age-related autoimmune processes. It has been suggested that dietary restriction causes a delay in maturation of the immune system, with a subsequent increase in time span of immunocompetence.[93]

There is some evidence that endogenous free-radical reactions have an adverse effect on the immune system. Age-associated increases in random free-radical reactions are reflected in elevated serum oxidase activities and declining concentrations of mercaptans,[94,95] both conditions occurring concomitantly with increasing age and declining immunocompetence. Although there is no evidence that antioxidants slow the decline of age-related immune responses, these agents are capable of enhancing both humoral and cell-mediated immunologic parameters. Harman et al.[96] found that several free-radical inhibitors were as effective in eliciting a humoral response from spleen cells as levamisole, a known immune-system stimulant.

As yet, there have been no investigations into the possible role antioxidants might play in potentiating UV carcinogenesis by modulation of immune responses. However, considering the influence of UV upon immune response, its relation to UV carcinogenesis, and the photoprotective effects of antioxidants, it would be surprising if these agents did not diminish at least some of the known deleterious effects UV has upon skin-associated lymphoid tissues.[97,98]

VI. CONCLUSIONS

The involvement of UV radiation in either carcinogenic or aging processes of skin has been documented in numerous reviews.[99-103] Those cited are intended to be representative rather than exhaustive. Here, an attempt has been made to explore the mechanistic relationship between UV-influenced carcinogenesis and aging through general theories upon which both aging and carcinogenesis may converge. The areas of potential congruence through which homologies of these two processes have been sought include: (1) perturbations in the maintenance of genetic integrity, (2) formation and/ or accumulation of harmful materials, and (3) an intrinsically timed, but extrinsically influenced, biological clock that shuts down control of essential life processes.

Before recapping the evidence regarding each of these theories, a general comment regarding the nature of UV aging/carcinogenesis relationships should be noted. Epidemiologic evidence indicates that given equal actinic exposure, older individuals are more likely to develop skin cancer than are younger ones.[6] Indeed, data of this nature form the basis for seeking potential relationships between aging and cancer. Experimentally, however, it has been demonstrated that older animals are less susceptible to UV-induced tumor formation.[7,9,10] This paradox is further confounded by the observation that skin from old animals, when grafted to young recipients, is more susceptible to UV carcinogenesis but that more tumors develop in skin grafted to young recipients than in old, regardless of the age of the skin donor.[10] These observations led to the supposition that predisposition to UV carcinogenesis was not attributable to inherent properties of the skin per se, but was dependent upon physiological factors in the host that change as a function of age. If this were so, conventional wisdom might predict that older animals would be more susceptible to carcinogenesis when immunocompetence or other physiological controls were in decline — a circuitous argument that appears in conflict with the experimental data.

In addition, it must be stressed that most recognized aging effects attributable to UV are manifested in the dermis.[104-106] It seems reasonable that relationships between aging and carcinogenesis should be sought in the tissue where carcinogenesis occurs. If direct relationships exist at the mechanistic level, carcinogenesis might be considered as an acute manifestation of the underlying bases of aging. Certainly much more is known of the photocarcinogenic process in the epidermis than is known of aging. Aside from the general observation of age-associated epidermal atrophy, no biochemical indices are known which represent epidermal aging. Whereas the epidermis would be the logical tissue in which to pursue aging/carcinogenic relationships, this is not to say that the dermis does not influence those processes as they may be expressed in the epidermis. Indeed, some view the actinic changes that occur in the dermis to be of paramount importance to epidermal carcinogenesis.[107] Nor would one imagine that changes that occur in the epidermis be without effect upon the dermis.

With respect to mechanisms, considerable evidence points to a decline in DNA repair capacity as a factor in both aging and carcinogenesis. Impaired ability to repair DNA has been demonstrated in cells from both progeria and XP patients, disease states representing accelerated aging and extreme susceptibility to UV-induced skin cancer, respectively. Corroboration of these results has not always been forthcoming.[30,40] Evidence that UV plays a role in aging comes from cell-culture studies in which the number of population doublings decline in cells derived from chronically exposed sites. However, cells derived from these sites demonstrate an increased plating efficiency.[23] Further, while decreased DNA excision repair has been related to increased age, fibroblasts derived from chronically sun-exposed areas demonstrate a higher capacity for macromolecular synthesis and DNA repair.[108,109] Thus, the role of DNA repair in UV-mediated aging remains clouded and information concerning the fidelity of actinically impaired repair mechanisms is lacking.

Evidence for the formation and accumulation of toxic by-products and their involvement in aging and carcinogenesis is based largely upon the free-radical theory. By-products of free-radical reactions, such as malonaldehyde, are themselves mutagenic and affect DNA repair.[110] Whereas a considerable body of evidence, albeit indirect, points to involvement of free radicals in UV carcinogenesis, evidence for their involvement in aging is less convincing. Some have suggested a "wear and tear" mechanism for aging which would be reflected in a diminished capacity to safely cope with ever-present endogenously formed free radicals.[111] The result would be gradual accumulation of damage — an effect not incompatible with the error-accumulation or biological-clock theories. However, in at least one study, free-radical inhibitors were less effective in preventing UV carcinogenesis in older animals than in young ones — a time when wear and tear would be greatest, when the host would be least capable of coping with continuous insult, and when one would predict antiradicals would be most effective.[11] On the other hand, the wear and tear version of the free-radical theory would predict that older animals would be most susceptible to carcinogenesis, again, a prediction not borne out by the experimental evidence.

The immunologic influence upon carcinogenesis and aging perhaps provides the best associations in support of the biological-clock theory. The decline in immunocompetence with age, and consequent increase in cancer incidence, coincides with lymphoid cell decline. The latter is apparently intrinsically controlled, although it is obvious that extrinsic factors, while not altering the final outcome, can modify the response within time limits. Photoimmunology represents one of the most promising areas for future investigation into relationships of actinically mediated aging and carcinogenesis. However, the conflict between epidemiological and experimental evidence, with regard to age-associated carcinogenic susceptibility, should again be emphasized. This is a question that must be resolved! In addition, one should be mindful that much of our knowledge concerning general cellular and molecular parameters attributable to either aging or carcinogenic processes has been gleaned from studies of cell-culture systems, where systemic immunologic effect is absent.

The difficulty in seeking an unified theory with respect to the mechanistic relation of actinic aging and carcinogenesis will have become obvious. In areas where insight has been gained into specific influences of UV on carcinogenesis, knowledge is lacking for aging processes, and vice versa.

Further, Kligman[112] has cautioned about using cutaneous changes to support theoretical generalizations about the aging process, as it is unlikely that a single mechanism could account for the numerous and varied alterations that have been observed. If this be the case, the odds that a single theory could explain actinic-mediated mechanisms for both processes are even more remote. The French essayist Michel Montaigne's argument that the study of life is no more than one of decay may be more prophetic than realized. These two processes for which a relationship has been sought seem to be linked only by the general expression of dysfunction, dysfunction manifested by loss of physiologic control, i.e., decay (a change from a state of perfection). However, even in this general relationship it should be obvious that there are a number of mechanistic parallels between both processes that provide a starting point for more intense investigation.

ACKNOWLEDGMENT

The author is grateful to Mrs. Wanda Lenger for assistance in preparing the manuscript.

REFERENCES

1. Scott, J., Fears, T., Lisiecki, E., and Radosevich, S., Incidence of nonmelanoma skin cancer in the United States, 1977—78, Preliminary Report, Publ. No. (NIH) 80-2154, National Cancer Institute, U.S. Department of Health, Education and Welfare, Bethesda, Md., 1980.
2. Bergstresser, P. R. and Halprin, K. M., Multiple sequential skin cancers. The risk of skin cancer in patients with previous skin cancer, *Arch. Dermatol.,* 111, 995, 1975.
3. Johnson, M. L. T. and Robert, J., Relevance of Dermatological Disease Among Persons 1—74 years of age. Advance data from vital and health statistics of the National Center for Health Statistics, No. 4, U.S. Department of Health, Education and Welfare, Bethesda, Md., 1977.
4. Pitot, H. C., Carcinogenesis and aging — two related phenomena?, *Am. J. Pathol.,* 87, 440, 1977.
5. Peto, R., Roe, F. J. C., Lee, P. N., Levy, L., and Clack, J., Cancer and aging in mice and men, *Br. J. Cancer,* 32, 411, 1975.
6. Vitaliano, P. P. and Urbach, F., The relative importance of risk factors in nonmelanoma skin carcinoma, *Arch. Dermatol.,* 116, 454, 1980.
7. Forbes, P. D., Davies, R. E., and Urbach, F., Aging, environmental influences, and photocarcinogenesis, *J. Invest. Dermatol.,* 73, 131, 1979.
8. Doll, R., Incidence of cancer in humans, in *Origins of Human Cancer,* Hiatt, H. H., Watson, J. D., and Winsten, J. A., Eds., Cold Spring Harbor Laboratory, Cold Spring Harbor, N.Y., 1977, 1.
9. Blum, H. F., Grady, H. G., and Kirby-Smith, J. S., Relationships between dosage and rate of tumor induction by ultraviolet radiation, *J. Natl. Cancer Inst.,* 3, 91, 1942.
10. Ebbesen, P. and Kripke, M. L., Influences of age and anatomical site on ultraviolet carcinogenesis in BALB/c mice, *J. Natl. Cancer Inst.,* 68, 691, 1982.
11. Black, H. S., McCann, V., and Thornby, J. I., Influence of animal age upon antioxidant-modified UV carcinogenesis, *Photobiochem. Photobiophys.,* 4, 107, 1982.
12. Strehler, B. L., Aging theories and immunological senescence: perspects and prospects, in *Handbook of Immunology in Aging,* Kay, M. M. B. and Makinodan, T., Eds., CRC Press, Boca Raton, Fla., 1981, 3.
13. Becker, F. F., Evolution, chemical carcinogenesis, and mortality: the cycle of life, in *Carcinogens: Identification and Mechanisms of Action,* Griffin, A. C. and Shaw, C. R., Eds., Raven Press, New York, 1979, 5.
14. Orgel, L. E., The maintenance of the accuracy of protein synthesis and its relevance to ageing, *Proc. Natl. Acad. Sci. U.S.A.,* 49, 517, 1963.
15. Hart, R. W., D'Ambrosio, S. M., and Ng, K. J., Longevity, stability and DNA repair, *Mech. Ageing Dev.,* 9, 203, 1979.
16. Hart, R. W. and Setlow, R. B., Correlation between deoxyribonucleic acid excision-repair and lifespan in a number of mammalian species, *Proc. Natl. Acad. Sci. U.S.A.,* 71, 2169, 1974.
17. Hayflick, L. and Moorhead, P. S., The serial cultivation of human diploid cell strains, *Exp. Cell Res.,* 25, 585, 1961.
18. Hayflick, L., The limited *in vitro* lifetime of human diploid cell strains, *Exp. Cell Res.,* 37, 614, 1965.
19. Hayflick, L., The cell biology of aging, *J. Invest. Dermatol.,* 73, 8, 1979.
20. Martin, G. M., Sprague, C. A., and Epstein, C. J., Replicative life-span of cultivated human cells. Effects of donor's age and genotype, *Lab. Invest.,* 23, 86, 1970.
21. Schneider, E. L. and Mitsui, Y., The relationship between in vitro cellular aging and in vivo human age, *Proc. Natl. Acad. Sci. U.S.A.,* 73, 3584, 1976.
22. Gilchrest, B. A., Relationship between actinic damage and chronologic aging in keratinocyte cultures of human skin, *J. Invest. Dermatol.,* 72, 219, 1979.
23. Gilchrest, B. A., Prior chronic sun exposure decreases the lifespan of human skin fibroblasts *in vitro,* *J. Gerontol.,* 35, 537, 1980.
24. Cristofalo, V. T. and Sharf, B. B., Cellular senescence and DNA synthesis: thymidine incorporation as a measure of population age in human diploid cells, *Exp. Cell Res.* 76, 419, 1973.
25. Little, J. B., Relationships between DNA repair capacity and cellular aging, *Gerontology,* 22, 28, 1976.
26. Chan, A. C. and Walker, I. C., Loss of DNA repair capacity during successive subcultures of primary rat fibroblasts, *J. Cell Biol.,* 74, 365, 1977.
27. Epstein, J., Williams, J. R., and Little, J. B., Rate of DNA repair in progeric and normal human fibroblasts, *Biochem. Biophys. Res. Commun.,* 59, 850, 1974.
28. Goldstein, S., The role of DNA repair in aging of cultured fibroblasts from Xeroderma Pigmentosum and normals, *Proc. Soc. Exp. Biol. Med.,* 137, 730, 1971.
29. Hart, R. W. and Setlow, R. B., DNA repair in late-passage human cells, *Mech. Ageing Dev.,* 5, 67, 1976.
30. Regan, J. D. and Setlow, R. B., DNA repair in human progeroid cells, *Biochem. Biophys. Res. Commun.,* 59, 858, 1974.

31. Robbins, J. H., Kraemer, K. H., Lutzner, M. A., Festoff, B. W., and Coon, H. G., An inherited disease with sun sensitivity, multiple cutaneous neoplasms, and abnormal DNA repair, *Ann. Intern. Med.*, 80, 221, 1974.

32. Grossman, L., Braun, A., Feldberg, R., and Mahler, I., Enzymatic repair of DNA, *Annu. Rev. Biochem.*, 44, 19, 1975.

33. Epstein, J. H., Fukuyama, K., and Epstein, W. L., UVL induced stimulation of DNA synthesis in hairless mouse epidermis, *J. Invest. Dermatol.*, 51, 445, 1968.

34. Setlow, R. B., Regan, J. D., German, J., and Carrier, W. L., Evidence that Xeroderma Pigmentosum cells do not perform the first step in the repair of ultraviolet damage to their DNA, *Proc. Natl. Acad. Sci. U.S.A.*, 64, 1035, 1969.

35. Cleaver, J. E., Xeroderma Pigmentosum: a human disease in which an initial stage of DNA repair is defective, *Proc. Natl. Acad. Sci. U.S.A.*, 63, 428, 1969.

36. Cleaver, J. E., DNA repair and radiation sensitivity in human (Xeroderma Pigmentosum) cells, *Int. J. Radiat. Biol.*, 18, 557, 1970.

37. Kleijer, W. J., Lohman, P. H. M., Mulder, M. P., and Bootsma, D., Repair of X-ray damage in DNA of cultivated cells from patients having Xeroderma Pigmentosum, *Mutat. Res.*, 9, 517, 1970.

38. Epstein, W. L., Fukuyama, K., and Epstein, J. H., Ultraviolet light, DNA repair and skin carcinogenesis in man, *Fed. Proc.*, 30, 1766, 1971.

39. Cleaver, J. E., DNA damage and repair in light-sensitive human skin disease, *J. Invest. Dermatol.*, 54, 181, 1970.

40. Cleaver, J. E., Xeroderma Pigmentosum: variants with normal DNA repair and normal sensitivity to ultraviolet light, *J. Invest. Dermatol.*, 58, 124, 1972.

41. Kohn, R. R., Evidence against cellular aging theories, in *Testing the Theories of Aging*, Adelman, R. C. and Roth, G. S., Eds., CRC Press, Boca Raton, Fla., 1982, 221.

42. Cutler, R. G., Evolutionary biology of aging and longevity in mammalian species, in *Aging and Cell Function*, Johnson, J. E., Ed., Plenum Press, New York, 1984, 1.

43. Harman, D., Role of free radicals in mutation, cancer, aging and the maintenance of life, *Radiat. Res.*, 16, 753, 1962.

44. Harman, D., The free radical theory of aging, in *Free Radicals in Biology V*, Pryor, W. A., Ed., Academic Press, New York, 1982, 255.

45. Black, H. S., Chemoprevention of cutaneous carcinogenesis, *Cancer Bull.*, 35, 252, 1983.

46. Horgan, V. J., Philpot, J. St. L., Porter, B. W., and Roodyn, D. B., Toxicity of autoxidized squalene and linoleic acid and of simpler peroxides, in relation to toxicity of radiation, *Biochem. J.*, 67, 551, 1957.

47. Shamberger, R. J., Andereone, T. L., and Willis, C. E., Antioxidants and cancer. IV. Initiating activity of malonaldehyde as a carcinogen, *J. Natl. Cancer Inst.*, 53, 1771, 1974.

48. Shamberger, R. J., Corlett, C. L., Beaman, K. D., and Kasten, B. L., Antioxidants reduce the mutagenic effect of malonaldehyde and β-propiolactone. IX. Antioxidants and cancer, *Mutat. Res.*, 66, 349, 1979.

49. Chio, K. S. and Tappel, A. L., Synthesis and characterization of the fluorescent products derived from malonaldehyde and amino acids, *Biochemistry*, 7, 2821, 1969.

50. Donato, H., Jr., Lipid peroxidation, cross-linking reactions, and aging, in *Age Pigments*, Sohal, R. S., Ed., Elsevier/North-Holland, Amsterdam, 1981, 63.

51. Berg, B. N. and Simms, H. S., Nutrition and longevity in the rat. II. Longevity and onset of disease with different levels of food intake, *J. Nutr.*, 71, 255, 1960.

52. Harman, D., The free radical theory of aging: effect of the amount and degree of unsaturation of dietary fat on mortality rate, *J. Gerontol.*, 26, 451, 1971.

53. Harman, D., Free radical theory of aging: effect of free radical reaction inhibitors on the mortality rate of male LAF_1 mice, *J. Gerontol.*, 23, 476, 1968.

54. Daniels, F., Jr., The physiological effects of sunlight, *J. Invest. Dermatol.*, 32, 147, 1959.

55. Daniels, F., Jr. and Johnson, B. E., Normal, physiologic and pathologic effects of solar radiation on the skin, in *Sunlight and Man*, Fitzpatrick, T. B., Ed., University of Tokyo Press, Tokyo, 1974, 117.

56. Pathak, M. A. and Stratton, K., Free radicals in human skin before and after exposure to light, *Arch. Biochem. Biophys.*, 123, 468, 1968.

57. Lo, W. B. and Black, H. S., Inhibition of carcinogen formation in skin irradiated with UV, *Nature (London)*, 246, 489, 1973.

58. Black, H. S., Effects of dietary antioxidants on actinic tumor induction, *Res. Commun. Chem. Pathol. Pharmacol.*, 7, 783, 1974.

59. Black, H. S. and Chan, J. T., Suppression of ultraviolet light-induced tumor formation by dietary antioxidants, *J. Invest. Dermatol.*, 65, 412, 1975.

60. DeRios, G., Chan, J. T., Black, H. S. et al., Systemic protection by antioxidants against UVL-induced erythema, *J. Invest. Dermatol.*, 70, 123, 1978.

61. Black, H. S., Chan, J. T., and Brown, G. E., Effects of dietary constituents on ultraviolet light-mediated carcinogenesis, *Cancer Res.*, 38, 1384, 1978.

62. Mathews-Roth, M. M., Pathak, M. A., Fitzpatrick, T. B. et al., Beta-carotene therapy for Erythropoietic Protoporphyria and other photosensitivity diseases, *Arch. Dermatol.*, 113, 1229, 1977.

63. Epstein, J. H., Effects of Beta-carotene on UV induced cancer formation in the hairless mouse skin, *Photochem. Photobiol.*, 25, 211, 1977.

64. Mathews-Roth, M. M., Antitumor activity of β-carotene, canthaxanthin and phytoene, *Oncology*, 39, 33, 1982.

65. Krinsky, N. I. and Deneke, S. M., Interaction of oxygen and oxyradicals with carotenoids, *J. Natl. Cancer Inst.*, 69, 205, 1982.

66. Pauling, L., Willoughby, R., Reynolds, R., et al., Incidence of squamous cell carcinoma in hairless mice irradiated with ultraviolet light in relation to intake of ascorbic acid (vitamin C) and dl-*α*-tocopheryl acetate (vitamin E), in *Vitamin C:* new clinical applications in Immunology, lipid metabolism and cancer, Hanck, A., Ed., *Int. J. Vitam. Nutr. Res.*, 23(Suppl.), 53, 1982.

67. Forbes, P. D., Photocarcinogenesis: an overview, *J. Invest. Dermatol.*, 77, 139, 1981.

68. Black, H. S., Henderson, S. V., Kleinhans, C. M. et al., The effect of dietary cholesterol on ultraviolet-light carcinogenesis, *Cancer Res.*, 39, 5022, 1979.

69. Baumann, C. A. and Rusch, H. P., Effect of diet on tumors induced by ultraviolet light, *Am. J. Cancer*, 35, 213, 1939.

70. Black, H. S., Lenger, W., Phelps, A. W. et al., Influence of dietary lipid upon ultraviolet-light carcinogenesis, *Nutr. Cancer*, 5, 59, 1983.

71. Black, H. S., Lenger, W., MacCallum, M. et al., The influence of dietary lipid level on photocarcinogenesis, *Photochem. Photobiol.*, Suppl. 37, 539, 1983.

72. Mathews-Roth, M. M. and Krinsky, N. I., Effect of dietary fat level on UV-B induced skin tumors, and anti-tumor action of β-carotene, *Photochem. Photobiol.*, 40, 671, 1984.

73. Black, H. S. and Lenger, W., Inhibition of epidermal lipid peroxidation by dietarily administered antioxidants, *Proc. Am. Assoc. Cancer Res.*, 25, 132, 1984.

74. Meffert, H., Diezel, W., and Sonnichsen, N., Stable lipid peroxidation products in human skin: detection, ultraviolet light-induced increase, pathogenic importance, *Experientia*, 32, 1397, 1976.

75. Johnson, B. E. and Daniels, F., Jr., Lysosomes and the reactions of skin to ultraviolet radiation, *J. Invest. Dermatol.*, 53, 85, 1969.

76. Grossie, V. B., Jr. and Black, H. S., The effect of ultraviolet light (UVL) on the lysosomes of hairless mouse epidermis, *Experientia*, 33, 425, 1977.

77. Black, H. S. and Lo, W. B., Formation of a carcinogen in UV-irradiated human skin, *Nature (London)*, 234, 306, 1971.

78. Sevanian, A., Mead, J. F., and Stein, R. A., Epoxides as products of lipid autoxidation in rat lungs, *Lipids*, 14, 623, 1979.

79. Kay, M. M. B., The thymus: clock for immunologic aging?, *J. Invest. Dermatol.*, 73, 29, 1979.

80. Gross, L., Immunologic defect in aged populations and its relation to cancer, *Cancer*, 18, 201, 1965.

81. Gardner, I. D. and Remington, J. S., Age-related decline in the resistance of mice to infection with intracellular pathogens, *Infect. Immunol.*, 16, 593, 1977.

82. Kripke, M. L., Antigenicity of murine skin tumors induced by ultraviolet light, *J. Natl. Cancer Inst.*, 53, 1333, 1974.

83. Kripke, M. L. and Fisher, M. S., Immunologic parameters of ultraviolet carcinogenesis, *J. Natl. Cancer Inst.*, 57, 211, 1976.

84. Kripke, M. L. and Fidler, I. J., Enhanced experimental metastasis of ultraviolet light-induced fibrosarcomas in ultraviolet light-irradiated syngeneic mice, *Cancer Res.*, 40, 625, 1980.

85. Fisher, M. S. and Kripke, M. L., Further studies on the tumor-specific suppressor cells induced by ultraviolet radiation, *J. Immunol.*, 121, 1139, 1978.

86. Spellman, C. W. and Daynes, R. A., Properties of ultraviolet light-induced suppressor cells by ultraviolet radiation, *Cell Immunol.*, 31, 182, 1977.

87. Fisher, M. S. and Kripke, M. L., Systemic alteration induced in mice by ultraviolet light irradiation and its relationship to ultraviolet carcinogenesis, *Proc. Natl. Acad. Sci. U.S.A.*, 74, 1688, 1977.

88. de Gruijl, F. R. and van der Leun, J. C., Systemic influence of pre-irradiation of a limited skin area on UV-carcinogenesis, *Photochem. Photobiol.*, 35, 379, 1982.

89. Fisher, M. S. and Kripke, M. L., Suppressor T lymphocytes control the development of primary skin cancers in UV-irradiated mice, *Science*, 216, 1133, 1982.

90. Nathanson, R. B., Forbes, P. D., and Urbach, F., Modification of photocarcinogenesis by two immunosuppressive agents, *Cancer Lett.*, 1, 243, 1976.

91. Daynes, R. A., Harris, C. C., Connor, R. J., et al., Skin cancer development in mice exposed chronically to immunosuppressive agents, *J. Natl. Cancer Inst.*, 62, 1075, 1979.

92. Good, R. A., Fernandes, G., and West, A., Nutrition, immunologic aging, and disease, in *Aging and Immunity,* Singhal, S. K., Sinclair, N. R., and Stiller, C. R., Eds., Elsevier/North-Holland, New York, 1979, 141.

93. Watson, R. R. and Safranski, D. V., Dietary restrictions and immune responses in the aged, in *Handbook of Immunology in Aging,* Kay, M. M. B. and Makinodan, T., Eds., CRC Press, Boca Raton, Fla., 1981, 125.

94. Harman, D., The free radical theory of aging: effect of age on serum copper levels, *J. Gerontol.,* 20, 151, 1965.

95. Leto, S., Yiengst, M. J., and Barrows, C. H., Jr., The effect of age and protein deprivation on the sulfhydryl content of serum albumin, *J. Gerontol.,* 25, 4, 1970.

96. Harman, D., Heidrick, M. L., and Eddy, D. E., Free radical theory of aging: effect of free-radical reaction inhibitors on the immune response, *J. Am. Geriatr. Soc.,* 25, 400, 1977.

97. Streilein, J. W. and Tigelarr, R. E., SALT: skin associated lymphoid tissues, in *Photoimmunology,* Parrish, J. A., Kripke, M. L., and Morison, W. L., Eds., Plenum Press, New York, 1983, 95.

98. Bergstresser, P. R., Elmets, C. A., and Streilein, J. W., Local effects of ultraviolet radiation on immune function in mice, in *The Effect of Ultraviolet Radiation on the Immune System,* Parrish, J. A., Ed., Johnson & Johnson, Raritan, N.J., 1983, 73.

99. Emmett, E. A., Ultraviolet radiation as a cause of skin tumors, *CRC Crit. Rev. Toxicol.,* 2, 211, 1973.

100. Black, H. S. and Chan, J. T., Experimental ultraviolet light-carcinogenesis, *Photochem. Photobiol.,* 26, 183, 1977.

101. Montagna, W., Kligman, A. M., Wuepper, K. D., and Bentley, J. P., Eds., Special issue on aging, Proceedings of the 28th symposium on the biology of skin, *J. Invest. Dermatol.,* 73, 1, 1979.

102. Epstein, J. H., Photocarcinogenesis, skin cancer, and aging, *J. Am. Acad. Dermatol.,* 9, 487, 1983.

103. Gilchrest, B. A., *Skin and Aging Processes,* CRC Press, Boca Raton, Fla., 1984, 136.

104. Montagna, W., Morphology of aging skin: the cutaneous appendage, in *Advances in Biology of Skin,* Montagna, W., Ed., Pergamon Press, Oxford, 1965, 1.

105. Montagna, W. and Carlisle, K., Structural changes in aging human skin, *J. Invest. Dermatol.,* 73, 47, 1979.

106. Lavker, R. M., Structural alterations in exposed and unexposed aged skin, *J. Invest. Dermatol.,* 73, 59, 1979.

107. Mackie, B. S. and McGovern, V. J., The mechanism of solar carcinogenesis, *Arch. Dermatol.,* 78, 218, 1958.

108. Schneider, E. L., Aging and cultured human skin fibroblasts, *J. Invest. Dermatol.,* 73, 15, 1979.

109. Sbano, E., DNA repair after UV irradiation in skin fibroblasts from patients with actinic keratoses, *Arch. Dermatol. Res.,* 262, 55, 1978.

110. Munkres, K. D., Biochemical genetics of aging of *Neurospora crassa* and *Podospora anserina,* in *Age Pigments,* Sohal, R. S., Ed., Elsevier/North-Holland, New York, 1981, 83.

111. Pryor, W. A., The formation of free radicals and the consequences of their reactions *in vivo, Photochem. Photobiol.,* 28, 787, 1978.

112. Kligman, A. M., Perspectives and problems in cutaneous gerontology, *J. Invest. Dermatol.,* 73, 39, 1979.

Chapter 5

EFFECTS OF SUNLIGHT ON THE EYE

Sidney Lerman

TABLE OF CONTENTS

I. INTRODUCTION

The sun is the natural source for most of the electromagnetic radiation in our atmosphere. Depending on geographic location, we are constantly exposed to the nonionizing portion of the electromagnetic spectrum (mainly in the UV, visible, and IR regions) at much higher intensities compared with background ionizing radiation. Fortunately, the ozone, oxygen, water, and carbon dioxide molecules in our atmosphere filter out a significant portion of the more lethal wavelengths of such solar radiation (i.e., the shortwave UV (10 to 280 nm) rays).

It is estimated that approximately 8% (11 mW/cm²) of solar radiation above the atmosphere is in the 280- to 400-nm UV region. At sea level, this is decreased to 2 to 5 mW/cm², depending on geographic location and season.[1] Aside from solar radiation, man-made UV radiation also plays a role in ocular phototoxicity — a relatively small one in the phakic individual and a more significant one in the aphakic or pseudophakic eye. The spectral output of our most common fluorescent lamps is relatively low at these wavelengths and should not pose a problem except in patients who are being treated with photosensitizing drugs and in aphakes and pseudophakes. However, exposure to photo floodlamps or the black-light lamps frequently used in various laboratories might present a potential hazard since their output can approach approximately 5 to 10% of the average levels of solar radiation in our atmosphere.[1] Furthermore, a much more significant hazard exists in industries which utilize UV radiation in certain polymerization reactions. Recent studies have also demonstrated that UV and short wavelength visible radiation exposure from indirect ophthalmoscopy and the operating microscope can also induce photochemical damage in the retina.[2-6]

The eye is the only organ or tissue in the body (aside from the skin) that is particularly sensitive to the nonionizing wavelengths of optical radiation (280 to 1400 nm) normally present in our environment. In addition to IR and visible radiation, we are constantly exposed to UV radiation (solar and man-made) throughout life.

Since the normal cornea, aqueous, ocular lens, and vitreous are almost completely transparent to all but the shorter wavelengths of visible light (although the aging lens does absorb increasing amounts of shortwave visible radiation[1,7]), one would not anticipate photic damage to these tissues from visible radiation. Only the retina is susceptible to photodamage from visible radiation. Furthermore, in order for nonionizing radiation to exert an effect, it must be absorbed. While the retina contains chromophores whose function it is to absorb visible radiation (the photoreceptor rods and cones and the macular pigment), the other ocular tissues anterior to the retina have very few chromophores which can absorb such wavelengths. Nature has provided us with transparent ocular media which are avascular and contain very few visible wavelength-absorbing chromophores, in order to effectively transmit (as well as refract) the specific wavelengths required to initiate the visual process by photochemical reactions. However, these tissues do have the ability to absorb varying amounts of UV radiation (particularly the ocular lens). The shorter the wavelengths of radiation absorbed, the greater the potential for photic damage since there is an inverse relationship between wavelength and the photon energy associated with it (Figure 1). Thus, UV radiation is the nonionizing portion of the electromagnetic spectrum which could cause the most ocular damage, provided that it is absorbed. As we shall see, this applies to all the ocular tissues including the retina in the very young eye (where the lens has not as yet become an effective UV filter), but in particular, the ocular lens sustains the greatest amount of photochemical change during a lifetime of exposure to ambient UV radiation.

IR radiation (750 nm to 1400 nm) has a much lower photon energy than visible or

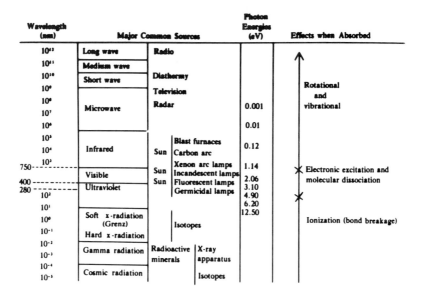

FIGURE 1.   The electromagnetic spectrum. (From Lerman, S., *Radiant Energy and the Eye*, Macmillan, New York, 1980. With permission.)

UV radiation (Figure 1) and exerts its action by increasing the motion of molecules, i.e., a heating effect. Under normal circumstances, ambient IR radiation is by itself incapable of exerting damage to ocular tissues. Although it is absorbed by water (hence by most biologic tissues), the amount of IR radiation we are normally exposed to is insufficient to cause any significant heating. Obviously, very high exposure levels (e.g., CO_2 laser or Nd:YAG laser) can exert significant damage due to acoustic gradients as well as intense heating.[8,9] Blast furnaces can also cause IR cataracts (Glass Blower's Cataract). However, normal daily life does not expose us to such levels of radiation, and the only effects of IR radiation at ambient levels are those associated with small temperature elevations (1 to 3°C) in the absorbing tissues (mainly the lens and retina) which could exert an effect by enhancing UV-induced photochemical changes.

UV-induced changes in human and animal ocular tissues can be attributed to two mechanisms: a direct or intrinsic process in which the radiation is absorbed by specific naturally occurring chromophores within these tissues (e.g., the nucleic acids or aromatic amino acid residues), and an indirect or photosensitized process in which the radiation is initially absorbed by photosensitizing drugs or other extrinsic compounds.

II. DIRECT RADIATION EFFECTS ON OCULAR TISSUES

Radiation must be absorbed in order to cause a change in the molecule since absorbed energy is required to promote a chemical change. Molecules in excited electronic states have different chemical and physical properties than their counterparts in the ground state (prior to absorption of energy). Thus, cells that do not contain chemical compounds absorbing at certain wavelengths will tend to transmit these wavelengths. For example, the nucleic acids and many proteins in a cell are essentially transparent to and transmit visible light but absorb certain wavelengths in the UV region (between 250 and 295 nm) and can be damaged by this form of radiation. The absorption of visible radiation gives the molecule its specific color (and characteristic absorption spectrum). Thus, rhodopsin (the visual pigment in the rod receptor cell of the retina) has a red color since it absorbs maximally in the blue-green portion of the visible spectrum and transmits or reflects all red light (above 600 nm). Hemoglobin has absorption peaks in the UV and visible region (275, 400, and 540 to 576 nm) which endows it with its characteristic color. These macromolecules can be damaged by visible radiation at their specific absorption wavelengths as well as by UV radiation. The recent therapeutic application involving phototherapy for certain types of malignancy makes use of these principles. Hematoporphyrin derivatives (HPD) are infused into a tumor and their absorption characteristics (in the red portion of the visible spectrum) enable one to destroy the malignancy with red light.[10] Attempts are currently under way to treat intraocular tumors in this manner.[11]

Since the effect of nonionizing radiation on a cell depends on the specific chemical composition within the cell, that is, on the presence of absorbing molecules (chromophores), a knowledge of the chemical composition as well as the morphology of the eye can be helpful in predicting the potential for photochemical damage occurring in specific ocular tissues during a lifetime of exposure to ambient optical radiation.

A. Cornea

The cornea and lens have similar optical functions. They must be transparent to visible light and capable of refracting the central core of incoming light so that it focuses properly on the appropriate region of the retina (macula) for normal visual acuity. The cornea is the major optical system in the eye, and its optical properties are determined by its refractive index, transparency to visible light (and UV radiation above 295 nm), and by its radius of curvature. The radius of curvature is determined by the growth and development of the normal cornea, the refractive index is determined by its chemical composition, and the transparency of the cornea is determined by its avascularity as well as its morphology and chemical composition. Although it is a relatively thin membrane, ranging from 0.5 to 0.57 mm in the center to about 0.66 to 0.67 mm at the periphery,[1] the cornea has a considerable amount of inherent tensile strength. This strength is due to the presence and arrangement of the collagen fibrils making up the lamellae within the corneal stroma. The collagen fibrils within the stromal lamellae run parallel to one another. Adjacent lamellae consist of fibrils lying parallel to but at right angles to one another, thereby forming a lattice network that is not interwoven. The fibrils and the lamellae are held together by a cement substance composed of a complex of mucopolysaccharides and proteins. Aside from endowing it with tensile strength, the geometric arrangement of the collagen fibrils (in an unwoven lattice pattern) plays a significant role in corneal transparency. The perfect lattice periodicity of these fibrils would result in zero intensity of scattered light in all directions, hence, transparency to visible light.[12] Benedek,[13,14] however, has noted that perfect lattice periodicity is not present in the cornea, but it is still transparent to visible light since the density of light-scattering particles is the same throughout this tissue. Thus, the total intensity of scattered light will be zero; i.e., the medium (cornea) is perfectly transparent if the density of scattered particles is uniform throughout. Corneal transparency is extremely sensitive to its state of hydration (about 75% of the cornea is composed of water). Even a small increase in the water content of the cornea will result in some loss of transparency. The metabolic activity of the cornea maintains the tissue in its proper state of deturgescence. The epithelium and endothelium play a major role in the metabolic maintenance of corneal transparency exerting their influence by an active as well as a passive process.[1] The relative importance of these two layers in the cornea is often reflected in clinical practice. It is well known that trauma to the endothelial surface during surgery will result in more severe and prolonged corneal edema than will damage to the epithelial surface.

It should also be noted that both optical systems of the eye are completely avascular. The peripheral cornea (limbal portion) receives its major nourishment from the perilimbal vessels present in the episclera and conjunctiva while the lens is a completely avascular tissue and cannot receive any nourishment directly from the bloodstream. The aqueous humor provides a significant amount of nourishment to the cornea, particularly to the inner layers, and completely nourishes the lens. The tear film is a third source of nourishment for the cornea. The corneal epithelium can obtain oxygen from the atmosphere, while the endothelium obtains its oxygen supply from the underlying aqueous humor. In contrast, the ocular lens can obtain oxygen only from the relatively low concentration present in the aqueous humor.[1] Thus, the metabolic activity in the corneal epithelium and particularly its reparative processes are much more active than those in the lens epithelial cells and this can play a significant role in determining the degree of UV radiation damage to these tissues.

Aside from its morphology which permit transparency of visible light, the chemical composition of the cornea provides further clues as to which wavelengths of radiation will be absorbed or transmitted. The cornea is made up of water (75%), protein (approximately 20%), polysaccharides (approximately 4% of the dry weight, or 1% of the wet weight), lipids, and nucleic acids. Aside from the small amount of the cytochromes that constitute the respiratory enzymes (responsible for oxidative phosphorylation), over 99% of the chemical composition of the cornea is composed of molecules that contain chromophores absorbing only in the UV region between 200 and 295 nm. The water and carbohydrate (polysaccharide) molecules will absorb UV radiation below 230 to 235 nm, the nucleic acids will absorb at approximately 250 to 260 nm, and the protein portion of the cornea will absorb in the 235- to 250-nm (for aliphatic amino acids) and in the 270- to 295-nm region (mainly due to the aromatic amino acids, phenylalanine, tyrosine, and tryptophan). The sugars comprising the corneal polysaccharides only absorb UV radiation below 250 nm. The ground substance of the corneal stroma is made up of a complex of mucopolysaccharides and protein. The protein portion of the ground substance of the cornea is responsible for absorption of UV radiation in the 275- to 295-nm region. The major portion of the corneal protein is composed of collagen (which comprises about two thirds of the total). Collagen has a relatively low absorbtion at 280 nm due its low content of the three aromatic amino acid residues mainly responsible for the 280-nm absorption spectra of most proteins.

The foregoing discussion on the morphology and composition of the cornea has demonstrated that this tissue should be transparent to and transmit all visible light (400 to 750 nm) and most of the UV radiation longer than 295 nm. This is borne out by data from several laboratories.[1] There is a sudden and marked decrease in the absorption spectra of human corneal tissue at approximately 295 nm. A corresponding increase in corneal transmission occurs above 295 nm, with this tissue transmitting over 90% of light above 400 nm in the young individual. The percent transmission of visible light decreases with age, as does the transmission of UV radiation between 300 and 400 nm (Figure 2). The latter decrease can be accounted for by the generation of a small amount of fluorescent chromophores as the cornea ages.[15,16] These photochemically derived pigments play an insignificant role in the cornea but assume much greater importance in the ocular lens.[1,15,16] It is true that other light-absorbing chromophores, such as the cytochromes, are present in both cornea (epithelium and endothelium) and lens (epithelium), but they represent a very minute proportion compared with the aforementioned chromophores and can be disregarded with respect to their potential effect on the UV and visible absorption and transmission characteristics of these two tissues.

From the foregoing discussion one can predict a UV action spectrum for corneal damage having at least two peaks — one at approximately 260 nm and the second at 280 to 295 nm. Such an action spectrum has been reported by various investiga-

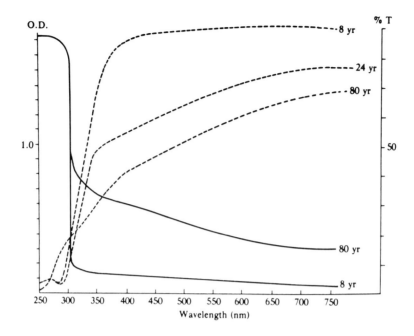

FIGURE 2.   Absorption (solid line) and transmission (dotted line) of the human cornea. (From Lerman, S., *Radiant Energy and the Eye,* Macmillan, New York, 1980. With permission.)

tors.[17-19] These investigators noted that the maximum efficiency for experimental photokeratitis and photokeratoconjunctivitis peaks sharply at 288 to 290 nm, with a smaller peak at 254 nm. This effect can be ascribed to absorption by the nucleotides (at 254 nm) and by tyrosine and tryptophan in the corneal epithelium. Studies on free-radical generation in human corneas exposed to 290 nm radiation show an interesting correlation with the UV action spectrum for photokeratitis reported by Sherashov[19] as shown in Figure 3. Clinically, corneal photodamage from UV radiation has long been appreciated, a typical example being snow blindness experienced by polar explorers. This type of photokeratitis is due to the relatively high levels of UV radiation which can be reflected by snow compared with less than 5% from earth or grass. Aside from the well-known polar and industrial photokeratitis, UV radiation has also been implicated in a variety of conjunctiveal and corneal lesions. These include pinngueculae and pterygiums, exposure keratosis (which involves epithelial changes related to actinic radiation and is analogous to actinic keratosis of the skin), nodular band-shaped keratopathy, experimentally induced tumors in animals, and the relatively rare dysplasia and intra-epithelial carcinoma. Certain corneal diseases can also be triggered by exposure to UV radiation; for example, herpes simplex keratitis and recurrent erosions of the cornea.

Since the cornea filters out UV radiation shorter than 295 nm, we are left with the question regarding the effect of longer wavelength UV radiation (300 to 400 nm) on the eye. The cornea transmits almost all of this radiation into the interior of the globe and the same can be said for the aqueous humor. The ocular lens absorbs a significantly increasing amount of this radiation, as well as visible light, as it ages.

B. Lens

A knowledge of the morphology and composition of the lens will not only explain its transparency to visible light but will also indicate why this organ is susceptible to UV-induced photochemical changes as it ages.

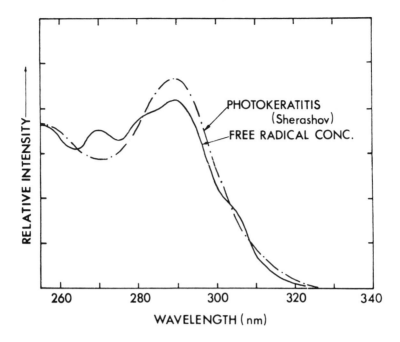

FIGURE 3.   Action spectrum for photokeratitis[19] and free radical generation in normal cornea exposed to monochromatic UV radiation.

The human crystalline lens, derived from the surface ectoderm at about the 4.5-mm stage of embryonic life, is a unique, biconvex, transparent, and avascular organ that represents a pure cell line and preserves the complete population of cells from fetal life until death. The mature strap-like lens-fiber cells lose their nuclei but remain viable with only scanty organelles. The lens fibers grow from all around the equatorial region and meet at radiating lines or sutures. During the first 8 weeks of life, the lens is a sphere. Since further growth of the lens depends on the continuous division of cells located in the germinative zone, there will be a gradual increase in the equatorial diameter of the lens in comparison with its axial diameter, and the organ will take on the more characteristic oval shape seen in the adult.

The adult human lens is a precisely formed structure containing about 65% water and 35% organic matter, the latter being chiefly structural proteins. Since the structural proteins (alpha, beta, and gamma crystallins and the insoluble protein fraction) constitute most of the dry weight of the lens, they must play a major role in the transmission as well as in the absorption and refraction of light through this organ. The degree of hydration and perhaps the action of the mucopolysaccharides as cement substances between the lens fibers may also play a role in lenticular transparency. In the infant, this organ does not contain any chromophores capable of absorbing a significant amount of visible radiation (400 to 750 nm), and the potential for absorbing UV radiation longer than 295 nm resides mainly in the tryptophan residues present in the lens proteins (and the relatively small amount of free tryptophan within the lens amino-acid pool). Aside from the minute amount of cytochromes in the lens epithelial cells, there are no other chromophores in the young lens capable of absorbing radiation wavelengths longer than 320 nm. The metabolic activity of the lens is mainly directed toward maintaining normal hydration (60 to 65%) and protein synthesis. The constituent lens proteins are densely packed and arranged in a high degree of spatial order within the intact fiber. There is little change in the density of scattering particles as one moves from point to point within the lens. According to Benedek[13,14] the changes in the index of refraction within specific anatomic zones of the lens still permit transparency. That is, "the scattered waves add up to give zero intensity in all directions except for those directions predicted for the bending of the primary beam by the laws of refraction in geometrical optics".[14] Refraction itself, therefore, is a consequence of scattering, and the refracted beam is the result of constructive interference of the scattered light. As Benedek[13] has pointed out "when lens proteins are extracted and mixed with water the constituent proteins are now dispersed throughout the solution. The proteins are no longer tightly packed and the density of proteins fluctuates markedly about its average value, hence, the solution can appear milky or turbid." In a simplified analogy, the accumulation of water within the lens results in a decreased transparency. Localized alterations in the density of packing of lens proteins, because of aggregation and/or configurational changes developing in various portions of the lens, will lead to changes in transparency; i.e., the development of opacities which could be due to localized changes in the refractive index.

Aging of the lens is reflected by pronounced changes at the molecular level, particularly with respect to the structural lens proteins, which constitute most of its dry weight. It seems that postsynthetic modifications mainly are involved, although errors at the translational level cannot be excluded. A variety of chemically or physically defined processes have been observed in lens proteins with aging. At birth, >95% of the human structural lens proteins are water soluble. One well-defined aging parameter is the progressive age-related increase in the amount of insoluble protein (to 40% or more of the total crystallin content), with a concomitant decrease in the total soluble protein (TSP) fraction.[1] The generation of a high molecular weight (HMW) fraction has been implicated in the increase in light scattering which develops as the lens ages.[20] There is also a marked change in the relative concentration of at least one of the soluble crystallin fractions. At birth, the gamma crystallins constitute over 50% of the TSP and then decrease progressively with age to about 10% in the old human lens (60+ age group) and in the 2-year-old rat lens.[1] The aggregation/insolubilization processes occurring with age appear to be associated with the formation of disulfide bridges and other covalent cross links. The latter may (at least in part) be due to chronic cumulative exposure to ambient UV radiation (over a 30 to 50 year span) resulting in the photochemical generation of a series of progressively longer wavelength UV and visible radiation-absorbing chromophores in the lens.[1,15,16,21] Thus, as the lens ages it displays an increasing absorbance in the 300- to 400-nm UV region, and in the visible region, which is associated with increased pigmentation of the lens core (nucleus). This is associated with increased lenticular fluorescence.

1. Intrinsic Fluorescence of the Lens

Before discussing the visible fluorescence of the lens, it is important to note that most proteins are endowed with an intrinsic UV-excited fluorescence because they contain aromatic amino acids (phenylalanine, tyrosine, and tryptophan). Of these three aromatic amino acids, phenylalanine has the lowest fluorescence quantum yield (approximately 1/10 to 1/20 of the latter two). Protein fluorescence spectra are thus generally considered only with respect to tyrosine and tryptophan. The presence of even one tryptophan residue in a protein (for example, horse serum albumin which has 17 tyrosines and 1 tryptophan) will result in an intrinsic fluorescence essentially that of tryptophan alone. Thus in most proteins containing at least one tryptophan residue, tyrosine appears to have a very low quantum efficiency so that the emission from this residue is markedly overshadowed by tryptophan fluorescence. However, tryptophan fluorescence in proteins appears to have quantum yields which in some cases are equivalent to the free amino acids.[22] It is also known that the tryptophan fluorescence maximum in proteins varies from 330 to 352 nm depending on the location of this amino acid within the protein, whereas free tryptophan has a characteristic fluorescence emission maximum at approximately 350 nm. It should be noted that tryptophan residues in native proteins are not necessarily present in identical locations nor are they equally influenced by their environment.[23,24]

The microenvironment of every residue is characterized by a particular set of physiochemical conditions such as polarizability, microviscosity, availability of charged groups, and possible specific interactions, that can influence chromophore fluorescence. Thus, protein (tryptophan) fluorescence is conditioned by the sum of fluorescent contributions of individual tryptophan residues which can vary over a relatively wide range. Studies using spectral band width, spectral maximum position, fluorescence quenching by external ionic quenchers, fluorescence lifetime, quantum yield, and changes upon denaturation of a variety of proteins indicate that fluorescence properties of various tryptophan residues in proteins can be delineated into three discrete spectral classes.[23,24] The Type I tryptophan residues are buried in nonpolar regions of the protein, and the Type II and III tryptophan residues are located on the protein surface, Type III being fully exposed to water and Type II being in limited contact with water. The following discussion will describe how these ideas can be applied to tryptophan fluorescence in lens proteins.

Lens proteins, in general, have a considerably higher content of tyrosine than tryptophan residues, but the presence of the latter results in an intrinsic protein fluorescence in the lens due to tryptophan alone.[21] The data show that the tryptophan fluorescence maximum in whole lenses is at 332 ± 2 nm with a band width of 47 nm. These results indicate that the majority of tryptophan residues in mammalian lenses belong to Type I of the Burstein classification,[23] i.e., they are buried in nonpolar regions of the proteins.

Fluorescence-lifetime measurements on intact lenses support the conclusions that lens protein tryptophan residues belong to Type I. Analysis of the decay data produces a fluorescence lifetime of 2.3 nsec, compared to a value of 2.8 nsec which is obtained for free tryptophan in aqueous solution. The value for tryptophan in the lens is consistent with these residues being located primarily in hydrophobic environments. Recent studies on bovine and human lens protein provide further substantiation that the tryptophan residues in the gamma crystallins are all buried or in crevice positions.[25-27] In the alpha and beta crystallins, most of the tryptophan residues are likewise buried, although one of the beta fractions may contain several surface tryptophans.

2. Extrinsic Fluorescence of the Lens

The visible fluorescence of the ocular lens was first noted well over 100 years ago,[28] but it was not until the last decade that this phenomenon was associated with increased yellow coloration of the lens nucleus by the increased visible and near-UV absorption. François et al.[29] noted the presence of a fluorescent peptide in primate lenses which could be activated by UV light. Specific fluorescent proteins in the human and other mammalian lenses have been demonstrated by a variety of investigators.[15,16,30-42] In addition to the fluorescence due to tryptophan, these proteins contain one or more fluorescent chromophores (fluorogens) with activation wavelengths of approximately 340 to 360 nm and 420 to 435 nm and emission maximums at 420 to 440 nm and 500 to 520 nm.[21] This type of fluorescence has been shown to be present in the soluble, HMW and insoluble fractions of the human lens (mainly in the latter) and to increase with age, particularly in the insoluble-protein fraction. These fluorogens are tightly bound to peptides derived from the insoluble lens protein.

In vitro UV-induced changes in human lenses include increased visible fluorescence intensities at 440 and 520 nm and increased pigmentation.[1,15,16] Similar fluorescence enhancement can be observed in UV-irradiated animal lenses both in vitro and in

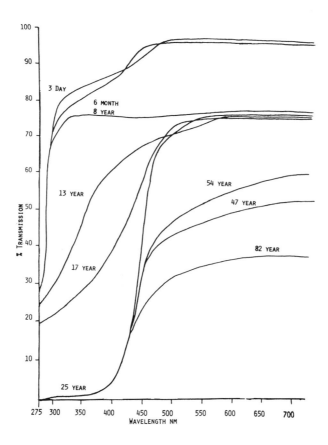

FIGURE 4.   Transmission changes in the aging ocular lens.

vivo.[1,15,43] These studies indicate that the photochemical changes are similar to the increasing fluorescence seen in normal human lenses as they age.[1,15,16,21] The cumulative effects of chronic exposure to ambient UV radiation include the generation of a series of fluorescent chromophores (absorbing at increasingly longer wavelengths), a deepening yellow color of the lens nucleus, and a progressive increase in the level of insoluble lens proteins. The latter phenomenon may be related to the cross linking of previously soluble polypeptides by some of the fluorescent pigments as well as by disulfide bond formation.

Since the human ocular lens is constantly exposed to ambient UV radiation (300 to 400 nm) throughout life, the consequence of cumulative photochemical damage is an increasing absorption of UV radiation and some visible light due to the presence of photochemically generated fluorescent chromophores which increase in concentration and in number as the lens ages. UV and visible-light transmission studies on normal human lenses ranging in age from 3 days to 82 years have shown that over 75% of the UV radiation (300 to 400 nm) is transmitted by lenses under 10 years of age, while the corresponding UV transmission in lenses above 25 years of age drops markedly (Figure 4). These data are consistent with the relative lack of UV-absorbing chromophores in the young lens and an increase in their concentration as the lens ages.[1] Accompanying the measured increase in these chromophores and decrease in light transmission, there is a concomitant increase in the yellow color of the lens nucleus as it ages. These pigments are mainly confined to the nucleus and may play a role in the development of nuclear sclerosis. However, nuclear sclerosis can also develop without significant discoloration. The discoloration is mainly confined to the lens nucleus since the cortex has much higher levels of glutathione and other compounds capable of aborting most of the photochemical reactions.[1,15,16] In about 10% of our population, this process progresses at a more rapid pace, resulting in the development of the brown (nuclear) cataract which is an extreme example of these age-related photochemical changes. This type of discoloration, in moderation, is actually beneficial since it enables the lens to become a very effective filter for UV and short-wavelength visible radiation (by the second to third decade) thus protecting the retina from cumulative photochemical damage which could occur during our lifetime. Recent studies have shown that such radiation can cause irreversible retinal photodamage in the aphakic Rhesus monkey and even in man.[2,6,44-47] It is interesting that nature has provided us with the ability to develop a lenticular UV filter to protect the retina from continuous radiation exposure which could be harmful, particularly in the older individual where the retinal metabolism and repair processes are no longer as effective as in the young. We are now beginning to see confirmation of the hypothesis that long-wavelength UV radiation may play a role in certain retinal diseases (e.g., cystoid macular edema) which tend to occur in older patients following removal of their cataractous lenses and even in degenerative processes (macular degeneration and retinitis pigmentosa).

Although only a small amount of UV radiation from the sun enters the eye under normal circumstances, the cumulative effect of many years exposure is significant, particularly when one considers man's ever-increasing life span. Epidemiologic surveys provide some support for the thesis that sunlight plays a role in lenticular aging and in the generation of senile cataracts.[48-51] For example, cataracts and the rate of cataract extraction are much higher in India, Pakistan, and certain areas of Africa than in the temperate zones. An epidemiologic investigation into the relationship between sunlight and cataract in the U.S. reported that " . . . cataract to control ratios for persons aged 65 years or older were significantly larger in locations with large amounts of sunlight . . . "[48]

Two recent epidemiologic studies involving Australian aborigines exposed to relatively intense solar radiation are of interest. Detailed personal histories were obtained on 350 individuals, and the possible role of a variety of environmental factors in cataractogenesis were investigated. Of the 350 individuals studied by Taylor,[49] all of whom were over 30 years of age, 116 had lens opacities as determined by slit-lamp examination. These findings indicate a relationship between cataracts, increased hours of sunlight, and higher annual UV radiation levels. Aside from age, no other factors studied appeared to be associated with cataractogenesis. Hollows and Moran's study,[50] involving a much greater geographical area and over 50% of the total aborigine population, found a statistically significant correlation between environmental UV irradiation and the prevalence of cataract. Cataracts occurred much more frequently in the younger age group (40 to 59 years) in zones with high UV radiation than in zones with low UV radiation. Brilliant et al.[51] studied the relationship between the prevalence of cataracts, altitude, and hours of sunlight exposure in Nepal. Exposure to an average of 12 hr of sunlight resulted in 3.8 times the number of cataracts compared with individuals exposed to 7 hr or less of sunlight. These epidemiologic studies support the hypothesis that senile cataracts are associated with higher exposure to sunlight. Obviously other factors play a role in cataractogenesis, including heredity, nutrition, metabolism, etc.

Aside from the effects of chronic exposure to ambient UV radiation, exposure to higher radiation levels can produce cortical opacities in human, rat, and rabbit lenses in vitro and in vivo.[52-54] Thus, more intense UV radiation (300 nm and longer) can induce lens changes involving the cortex, while chronic exposure affects mainly the lens nucleus. These effects appear to be dose and time related.[55] There is also the possibility that more intense UV radiation may affect the protein/water order within the lens, resulting in the formation of "water lakes" associated with protein aggregates. This would give rise to localized areas of marked changes in refractive index in the injured site resulting in light scattering and opacification. Studies on rabbit lenses exposed to 337-nm laser irradiation demonstrate marked changes in their water component.[56] These wavelengths have sufficient photon energies (1 to 1.5 eV) to disrupt the protein/water order in the lens and give rise to sudden changes in refractive index resulting in localized opacities.

3. Mechanisms in Optical Radiation Cataractogenesis

In the ocular lens, free radicals have been implicated as participating in a number of the processes associated with aging and cataractogenesis.[15,57,58] Free radicals (i.e., species with unpaired electron spin) can be produced in biosystems in a variety of ways. Once generated, the radicals are capable of initiating and engaging in a variety of reactions, many of which, if uncontrolled, are detrimental to the function of both the molecular species in which the radical is generated and those species with which the radical interacts. Among the detrimental phenomena that have been related to free-radical generation are enzyme inactivation, membrane damage via lipid peroxidation, protein cross linking and aggregation, and deoxyribonucleic acid alteration. With respect to the ocular lens, a free-radical mechanism may be responsible for the observed increase in fluorescent chromophores that occurs with aging.[1,16] When lenticular levels of glutathione, a free-radical scavenger, are reduced by the addition of 3-aminotriazole to the incubation medium, the UV-induced development of nontryptophan fluorescent chromophores in whole-lens incubation experiments is enhanced.[15,43] Conversely, when D-penicillamine, another free-radical scavenger, is included in the medium, UV-induced fluorescent chromophore production is almost completely suppressed.[15,58] Several laboratories have reported the presence of free radicals in the lens nucleus and in the cortex.[15,57-60] The cortex contains high concentrations of glutathione which can prevent or abort free radical-induced processes while the nucleus contains much lower levels of glutathione.

Comparison of the action spectra for production of fluorescent material in the lens and for photochemical destruction of tryptophan in aqueous solution suggests that the tryptophan residues in lens proteins and/or free tryptophan are the initial light-absorbing, photochemically reactive species.[15] Accompanying the increase in fluorescent chromophores seen with in vitro experiments, and also as a consequence of aging, are increases in the yellow color of the lens and in insoluble protein levels, as well as a parallel decrease in both UV and some visible light transmission. Again, these changes are more pronounced in the nucleus (the extreme case being the brown nuclear cataract) than in the cortex and may be a consequence of the relative lack of reparative ability in the nucleus compared with the cortex.

Singlet oxygen may also be generated in the lens, as a consequence of the excitation of endogenous or exogenous photosensitizers in the presence of oxygen. The photosensitizers may be either certain drugs such as 8-methoxypsoralen or native components.[15,61] When human crystallins are exposed to a singlet oxygen-generating system in vitro, changes are induced in the proteins which closely mimic those occurring in human lens proteins during aging and in senile cataractogenesis.[62] These include covalent cross linking of the proteins, increased blue fluorescence, yellow pigmentation, and formation of heavy molecular weight aggregates.

The superoxide radical is also present in the ocular lens. It can be generated via photosensitized, enzymatic, and nonenzymatic pathways. The lens contains superoxide dismutase to catalyze the dismutation of superoxide and form H_2O_2. It also possesses catalase and peroxidases which can detoxify H_2O_2 formed in the dismutation processes. Despite the presence of these protective mechanisms, it has been postulated that under certain circumstances (i.e., if these enzyme systems are compromised in some way) superoxide radicals generated in the lens or anterior chamber may cause deterioration in the cation pump and peroxidative damage to membrane lipids.[63] When whole rat lenses were exposed to a riboflavin-photosensitized free radical-generating system, the carrier-mediated transport function in these lenses was decreased.[64] This was attributed to an H_2O_2 intermediate. It has been postulated that relatively high levels of ascorbate (a superoxide radical scavenger) in the aqueous humor may have an additional protective role.[65] With in vitro systems, levels of ascorbate comparable to those present in the aqueous give significant protection against exogenously produced superoxide radicals.

Despite the fact that the lens possesses a variety of mechanisms to protect itself against free radical-induced damage, under certain circumstances radical-induced damage to lens membranes, structural proteins, enzymes, and nucleic acids may occur. In a long-lived species such as man, the consequences of even small amounts of damage may be cumulative, contributing significantly to both aging and cataractogenesis. It has been postulated, in other tissues as well as the ocular lens, that the cell membrane is a primary site where significant cumulative radical effects may contribute to both aging and pathologic processes. Membrane polyunsaturated fatty acids are particularly susceptible to radical-initiated auto-oxidation processes which involve radical intermediates and are thus radical-propagation processes. Once initiated, the peroxidative process can alter the cells' permeability and cause fragility of the membranes. The initiating radical may be derived from a number of sources including sulfur and carbon-centered radicals generated in proteins. Since biologic membranes have both intrinsic and extrinsic proteins closely affiliated with lipid components, free radicals generated at this site may contribute to lipid peroxidative damage. Alternatively, radicals generated during lipid peroxidative processes may interact with associated proteins to induce cross-linking. Cross-linking occurring in either intrinsic or extrinsic membrane proteins can further contribute to membrane damage by altering membrane conformation. Aside from producing obvious alterations in membrane function strictly as a consequence of structural alteration, these changes could serve to potentiate further radical-induced damage.

4. Defense Systems of the Lens
a. Photo-Oxidative Damage

It has long been established that the human ocular lens contains very high levels of glutathione and ascorbic acid; the high glutathione (GSH) levels in the ocular lens are confined mainly to the cortex, with a much lower concentration present in the nuclear region.[1,15] It has also been demonstrated that the GSH content diminishes with age; this is particularly evident in the lens nucleus and may account for its susceptibility to the photochemically induced discoloration while the cortex, which has a much higher GSH level, remains transparent. It has been proposed that the lens is naturally endowed with high GSH and ascorbate levels since it is constantly exposed to UV radiation throughout a person's lifetime.[1] These two compounds are very effective free-radical scavengers and could abort radiation-induced free-radical reactions. The photodamage caused by a lifetime of cumulative UV radiation exposure (longer than 300 nm) has been attributed to photic mechanisms in which tryptophan acts as the initial absorbing chromophore, resulting in the eventual generation of free radicals which appear to be involved in the ensuing photochemical reactions.[57,58]

Recently, hydrogen peroxide has been implicated as a factor in the UV-induced formation of at least one of the fluorescent pigments.[66] It has been postulated that H_2O_2 formed within the lens, being a good electron scavenger, could withdraw an electron from the (UV) excited indole ring of tryptophan. This might lead to the eventual destruction of tryptophan, producing small amounts of anthranilic acid which may be involved in the production of one or more of the lens fluorogens.[31,42,66,67] H_2O_2 can itself be produced by near-UV radiation action on tryptophan.[68] Thus, a build up of H_2O_2 may also be significant in potential lenticular damage and the presence of adequate levels of GSH would also serve to protect the ocular lens in such a situation. Superoxide dismutase (SOD) and catalase are present in the normal lens in order to protect it from such oxidative damage.[69] H_2O_2 inhibits SOD activity in the lens extracts, and this inhibition is potentiated by 3-AT, while 3-AT alone has no effect on lens SOD; thus, it is postulated that endogenous catalase protects lens SOD from inactivation by H_2O_2.[69]

b. Singlet Oxygen

The photosensitizing action of the psoralen compounds has been correlated with the generation of cyclobutane photoaddition reactions with thymine in the DNA molecule.[70-72] A similar mechanism has been proposed for 8-methoxpsoralen (8-MOP) lens damage.[73] It has been demonstrated that 8-MOP can enter the lens, and following photic stimulation, it can bind to lens proteins thereby enhancing whatever UV damage is already occurring in that individual, i.e., an increase in lenticular fluorescence and phosphorescence.[74] 8-MOP can also exert a photodynamic action in lens proteins by forming new photoproducts with certain aromatic amino acids in which singlet oxygen is involved.[75-77] That is, the triplet state of 8-MOP can react with ground-state oxygen to generate $^1O_2$.[78] The recent demonstration of an oxygen requirement for the photoreaction of 8-MOP with proteins[75-80] indicates that this compound can undergo the Type-II reaction as well as the anaerobic Type-I reaction with DNA, resulting in its binding to lens proteins and the permanent retention of the photoproduct(s) which can also function as new longer wavelength-absorbing photosensitizers in the lens. Many reagents (antioxidants) are capable of quenching $^1O_2$ and doubtless the lens contains its share of them.[81]

One of the immediate effects of radiation on biologic tissue is the production of strongly oxidizing species such as the hydroxyl radical. In order to obtain significant biological effects from the OH radicals (or similar strongly oxidizing species such as a singlet oxygen, the peroxide, or the hydrogen peroxide radicals), they must be produced at or near the target, thereby directly inducing molecular damage; or there may be an energy transfer within the molecule (e.g., the OH radical attacks a protein and the energy is transferred along the peptide chain frequently terminating at an SH group in the chain); or the energy could migrate via lipid peroxidation. In all instances, the SH groups in biologic tissues play an important reparative as well as protective role. These groups may be small SH compounds (GSH) or part of a protein. Thus biologic reactions with strongly oxidizing agents appear to be involved with as well as determined by sulfhydryl groups. The GSH level within the lens is of extreme importance in ionizing radiation damage; a significant fall occurs almost immediately after an experimental animal is exposed,[82] while catalase and SOD may also play an important role in protecting the lens against H_2O_2 and the superoxide radicals.[83]

C. Vitreous

As previously noted, the vitreous is normally protected from UV radiation by the filtering action of the cornea (up to 295 nm) and by the lens as it ages (>295 nm). However, patients who have had their cataracts removed (aphakes and pseudophakes) have lost a significant and protective intraocular filter. The normal vitreous is a gel-like material composed mainly of water, collagenous protein, and long-chain carbohydrates. These compounds do not contain any significant chromophores absorbing above 250 to 260 nm, although a small number of aromatic amino acids are present.

In this respect, the cornea plays a much more significant role as a UV filter since it prevents UV radiation below 295 nm from entering the eye. However, the vitreous does contain some tryptophan residues and several cell types — the hyalocytes and fibrocytes. Thus, some chromophores are present that are capable of absorbing UV radiation longer than 295 nm, provided that the filtering action of the ocular lens is removed. There is some experimental evidence that exposure of the vitreous to UV radiation up to 320 nm results in shrinkage of the vitreous gel and denaturation of the collagen network.[84] There is also a decrease in the viscosity of hyaluronic acid preparations derived from UV-exposed vitreous which can be attributed mainly to a decrease in molecular weight. UV irradiation causes an increase in the reducing power of the polysaccharide solution due to a breakdown of the glucosidic linkages, an increase of the reducing end groups, and the formation of smaller fragments.[84] The absorption spectra of hyaluronic acid subjected to UV irradiation shows significant alterations with the development of new chromophores absorbing at approximately 267 nm. Other studies in which human vitreous gels were subjected to monochromatic UV radiation (280 to 300 nm) resulted in the generation of one or more fluorescent compounds. A 320- to 340-nm excitation and a 420-fluorescence emission peak could be demonstrated following 4 to 6 hr of irradiation, suggesting the possible photodegradation of certain amino acids.

It would thus appear that the cornea, which filters all UV radiation shorter than 295 nm, plays a major role in protecting the vitreous from UV damage. There is still insufficient experimental evidence to assess the effect of UV radiation longer than 295 nm, but there are indications that the vitreous is also sensitive to longer-wavelength UV radiation.[84] Thus the 295- to 400-nm filtering action of the ocular lens may also be of significance in protecting the vitreous.

D. Retina

The fact that visible light is required in the cyclic process of shedding and renewal of the outer membrane disks, which contain the visual pigments, might explain the finding that even moderate but prolonged exposure to visible light, at thresholds of illumination well below those capable of causing thermal damage to the retina, can result in retinal pathology in a variety of experimental animals.[85-93] Aging is known to be characterized by a loss of rod and cone cells.[94] The recent observation that photic trauma can damage the receptors suggests a potential cumulative action of light resulting in an enhanced loss of visual cells over a period of years. That is, phototoxic effects may be cumulative in the normal aging process of the retina. Photon energies in the electromagnetic spectrum increase as the wavelength decreases, from 1.6 eV at 750 nm to 3.3 eV at 400 nm and higher energies in the UV wavelengths capable of penetrating to the retina in the aphakic or pseudophakic eyes. One would anticipate that photic damage would be greatest for UV radiation (320 to 400 nm) and shortwave visible light in the blue region (400 to 475 nm), and decrease with increasing wavelengths of light, with the least photic damage occurring with red light. A variety of reports strongly implicate longwave UV and shortwave visible radiation (320 to 450 nm) as significant factors in retinal photodamage in primates as well as other experimental animals, and even in man.[1-6,95-100] These data are of particular concern in young patients as well as aphakes and pseudophakes who are on photosensitizing drugs and to all patients exposed to prolonged or above-ambient levels of UVA radiation (e.g., occupational-exposure industries where UV polymerization is employed, and certain activities such as sailing, snow skiing, etc.).

The spectral sensitivity of the human retina plays a role with respect to the efficiency of a specific wavelength in producing retinal damage. The ocular lens protects the retina from visible as well as UV radiation since it filters more of the shorter wavelengths of visible light (blue) compared with the longer wavelengths. Thus, the aging retina, which metabolically should be more susceptible to photic damage caused by visible light (as well as UV radiation), is in fact protected by the ocular lens which increasingly filters out the UV and shorter wavelengths of the visible spectrum as the person ages. This might explain why human retinas are normally capable of withstanding much higher thresholds of radiation intensity as compared with the retinas of other animals such as the rat, rabbit, and pigeon. The retinas of these animals can be damaged by levels of environmental light that are not damaging to the normal eye.

1. Photochemical Damage

Although it has long been recognized that visible as well as IR radiation is capable of causing thermal damage to the retina when the eye is exposed to sufficiently intense sources at these wavelengths (solar retinopathy, xenon arc, and laser photocoagulation), the potential for nonthermal light injury only recently has become apparent. During the past two decades, a growing body of literature has accumulated that attests to the deleterious effects of long-term exposures to low levels of visible light as well as UV radiation.[1-6,85-100] These investigations demonstrate that visible light at intensities well below levels that would cause thermal photocoagulation can damage retinal tissue in a variety of animals including man. This damage is manifested by electroretinographic and/or histopathologic changes.

Deleterious effects of long-term exposure of the growing chick eye to light were reported in 1961.[85] The effects on the photoreceptor cells could not be explained in terms of thermal injury alone. The following year it was demonstrated that light exposure accelerated the degeneration of the photoreceptor cells in rats afflicted with hereditary retinal degeneration.[86] In 1965, Noell[87] first demonstrated that the retinas of rats could be damaged by light of moderate intensity. This report was followed by a series of papers which established that long-term exposure of normal albino rats to visible light at levels well below possible thermal damage resulted in the degeneration and loss of rod photoreceptors.[88-92] The wavelength that produced maximum damage corresponded to the peak absorption of rat rhodopsin, and body temperature was noted to be an important factor in these photic effects. Photic damage to the retina after long-term exposure to low levels of visible light has now been reported in pigeons, rats, mice, rabbits, piglets, monkeys, and even humans.[93]

A schematic outline of a typical course of retinal damage following long-term exposure to light is shown in Figure 5. The initial effects involve the outer segments of the photoreceptor cells, in which the outer tip of the photoreceptor shows vacuole formation. The damage proceeds until the outer segment loses its normal lamellar structure and breaks off from the inner segment of the visual cell. As the outer segments are phagocytosed by the pigment epithelium, the inner segments develop pyknotic nuclei and also disappear. The final result is a retina in which most of the photoreceptor cells have disappeared but the remaining layers appear to be intact.

There is still a considerable amount of controversy regarding the effect of light on the pigment epithelium. Some workers believe that damage to the pigment epithelium occurs prior to the destruction of the photoreceptors; others believe that it occurs at the same time as photoreceptor cell destruction, and it has also been proposed that damage to the pigment epithelium occurs subsequent to the destruction of the receptor cells.[1] Some investigators believe that damage to the pigment epithelium plays a major and primary role, with outer-segment degeneration being a secondary response to this damage and subsequent repair processes (inflammatory response). There is, however, considerable evidence of direct photic damage to the photoreceptor cells of the retina which occurs very soon after the animal has been exposed to light. It appears that the relative emphasis on photoreceptor cell damage vs. pigment epithelial cell damage as

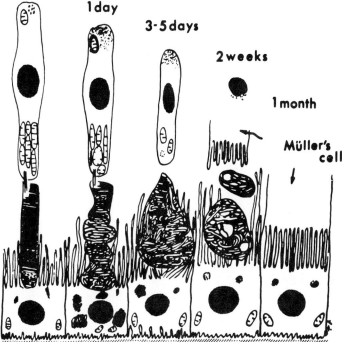

FIGURE 5. Schematic representation of retinal damage following exposure of albino rats to visible light. At a 3-hr exposure, only outermost tip of photoreceptor shows vacuoles. At 24 hr, photoreceptor outer segment is tortuous and swollen. Myelin membranes separate from each other and form vesicular and tubular structures. The synaptic end of photoreceptor cell shows pathologic changes. Pigment epithelium shows conspicuous increase in myeloid bodies. At 3 to 5 days, damaged outer segment is isolated from inner segment and becomes large, round, or pear-shaped body filled with tubular material, followed by cellular degeneration at 2 to 3 weeks and complete adhesion of pigment epithelium and Müller's cell in 1 month. (From Kuwabara, T. and Gorn, R. A., *Arch. Ophthalmol.*, 79, 69, 1968. With permission.)

the primary lesion, can be related to the use of pigmented vs. albino strains of experimental animals. Thus, the role of melanin in retinal photopathology may be significant and awaits further elucidation. Recent studies on melanin hematoporphyrin photobinding suggest such a role for this pigment.[101]

Although most of the work relating retinal damage to visible light comes from studies with experimental animals, there is increasing evidence indicating that the human retina can also be damaged by relatively low levels of visible light.[93] The normal dark-adaptation reaction requires 30 to 40 min; an individual's sensitivity to light begins to increase immediately after being placed in the dark and reaches its normal level after 30 to 40 min, at which time there is no further increase in sensitivity. However, several investigators have demonstrated that exposure to strong sunlight for 3 to 4 hr results in dark-adaptation thresholds that are elevated for 24 hr or more above normal levels, and that there is a chronic effect on night vision that may persist for up to 10 days.[95,96] Another study, involving patients suffering from solar retinopathy, reported that there was complete recovery in about half of the eyes 6 months after the injury.[97] This would not be expected if the damage was due to retinal coagulation caused by thermal injury.

It has been proposed that solar retinopathy in the rhesus monkey cannot be explained solely in terms of thermal injury; some type of thermally enhanced photochemical effect must also play a role. Some investigators believe that solar retinopathy can be accounted for almost entirely in terms of the photochemical effects of the shortwave visible (and UVA) components of the spectrum of the sun.[100,102-104]

A recent study has demonstrated that a simulated solar spectrum (400 to 1400 nm) with a predominant portion of the energy in the short visible wavelengths was more damaging to the retina than a long-wavelength spectrum (700 to 1200 nm), by a factor of 5.[100] These workers implied that for a continuous solar spectrum, as the retinal irradiance is reduced and exposure duration is prolonged, thermal insult becomes less pronounced while photochemical effects with thermal enhancement become more prominent. This reasoning is supported by theoretic considerations. Thermal damage to the retina would be expected for radiation in the near-IR region since the energy absorption takes place predominantly in the melanin granules of the pigment epithelium and choroid while the photoreceptors are not involved. The absorption of the near IR by the melanin involves wavelengths with photon energies (<1 eV) that would essentially induce vibrational changes in the molecule without adversely affecting its molecular structure; i.e., a thermal effect. However, the shorter the wavelength the greater the photon energy; in the UV and shortwave visible spectra (320 to 475 nm) the photon energies approach levels in which electronic excitation becomes the dominant mode of energy absorption (2.0 eV at 475 nm to 3.5 eV at 320 nm). Molecular systems in electronically excited states above the ground state are subject to photochemical reactions. Thus, overbleaching of the photoreceptor pigments results in a new chain of metabolic events that appears to be capable of leading to irreversible as well as reversible damage to the visual cells depending on the duration and intensity of exposure to light.

A variety of theories has been proposed to explain the mechanisms for the light effect on the retina.[1,93,106] These include the photodynamic action of visible light on the photoreceptor cells resulting in the production of free radicals, which can lead to chain reactions involving peroxidation of the lipid membrane portion of the outer segments. Under normal conditions of light exposure, new disc membranes are continuously being formed to replace the peroxidized disc membranes that are being shed from the tip of the outer segment. A second theory concerns the possible effects of light on specific metabolic pathways in the retina, particularly the observation that the oxygen consumption of the retina is suppressed by steady exposure to light. A third possibility is that bleaching results in the formation of a toxic photoproduct, which under normal conditions is rapidly eliminated; but with chronic bleaching (due to long-term exposure) it accumulates as a toxic agent. It has been proposed that the chronic bleaching of the photoreceptor pigments would eventually damage the membranes of the outer segments since the loss of too many of the retinal molecules from rhodopsin would result in the accumulation of the protein moiety of the molecule (opsin). The free opsin appears to be an unstable molecule and requires the chromophore, retinal, to form a stable compound. Thus, the destruction of the disc membranes could be due simply to the loss of the stabilizing chromophore, retinal, from the visual pigment that cannot be regenerated by the normal processes of dark adaptation due to chronic light exposure and overbleaching.

2. Recovery from Visible-Light Damage

It has now been shown that visible light plays a normal physiologic role in maintaining the health of the outer segments of the visual cells. Thus, in man and other diurnal animals, a certain amount of photic damage followed by repair and recovery of the receptor cells is a significant factor in the maintenance of the photoreceptor elements and normal visual acuity. One would also predict that diurnal animals should be less susceptible than nocturnal animals to the same intensity of visible light, since nature must have provided them with a more efficient recovery mechanism, because scotopic vision (daylight vision) plays such an important role in their daily lives.

The absorption characteristics of the ocular media (the cornea and lens) must be considered in determining the threshold level of visible light that is capable of causing retinal damage. As previously demonstrated, the human lens plays an increasingly important role with respect to its ability to filter UV radiation as it ages. The increasing yellow color of the lens nucleus with age also functions as a partial filter for visible radiation, particularly in the shorter wavelengths (in the blue region). Thus, the human ocular lens may serve an additional function in the older individual by virtue of its ability to filter out a significant portion of the visible radiation, particularly the shorter wavelengths (with the higher photon energy), thereby protecting the aging and metabolically less efficient retina from photic damage due to visible light.

It should be noted that the irradiance levels of energy incident on the retina (intensity measured as watts per square centimeter) is determined by the imaging properties (focusing properties) of the ocular media (the cornea and lens), the absorbing properties of the ocular media, and the size of the pupil. Utilizing these parameters, one can predict that the nocturnal animal should be more sensitive to the same threshold of light compared with the diurnal animal, and this appears to be borne out by experimental data.[1,93] Thus, the rat (particularly the albino rat) and rabbit appear to be the most sensitive animals to experimental retinal photodamage, with the diurnal animals (the monkey and human) displaying a decreasing order of sensitivity to the same intensity of visible light. There are as yet insufficient data available to determine the specific dose of photons absorbed, per receptor, for sustaining retinal damage. It is estimated that 1.5×10^3 to 1.5×10^4 photons per receptor per second continued for a relatively long period of time are necessary to cause retinal damage by visible light.[93] Although the early studies indicated that visible light damage to the retina was irreversible, there is now evidence that the retina is capable of recovering from a moderate amount of photic damage, particularly if the pigment epithelium of the retina and the photoreceptor cell body are preserved.[105] These studies demonstrate that retinas from albino rats exposed to 750 to 1000 fc (1.2 to 1.6×10^{-3} W/cm²) of light are capable of recovering within 3 to 6 weeks after such an exposure, as evidenced by a return of the electroretinogram to normal levels. The pathologic damage includes loss of the outer segments of the photoreceptor cells and moderate damage to the pigment epithelium. These damaged areas recover slowly, with the latter cells showing the first recovery response followed by regeneration of the membranes to form somewhat irregular outer segments.

3. Body Temperature and Light Damage

It is important to note that the body temperature of the animal plays an important role in determining whether the damage is reversible or irreversible. There is a direct relationship between an increase in body temperature and the degree of reversibility of photic damage to the retina; a rise in body temperature by 3 to 5°C above normal will significantly increase the photic damage to the retina at the same exposure threshold compared with an animal kept at normal body temperature.[107]

Most of the studies on retinal pathology have utilized fluorescent and incandescent light sources. As previously noted, the spectral output of the fluorescent light source more closely approximates daylight, particularly in the UV region, while the incandescent illumination has a large IR spectral output that serves as a heat source. Since even a relatively small increase in body temperature (approximately 3°C) can have a great influence on increasing the degree of light damage, it is important to differentiate experimental retinal photopathology from its purely photic vs. its thermal mechanism.

4. Ophthalmoscopy, the Operating Microscope, and Retinal Damage

One should also consider the potential problems with respect to indirect ophthalmoscopy and retinal damage. Several workers have demonstrated that indirect ophthalmoscopy is capable of producing retinal damage in primate eyes.[98,99] It should be noted that the standard method employed in indirect ophthalmoscopy involves the use of a 20-diopter convex lens placed between the light source and the patient's eye, which in effect will serve to act as an additional focusing element, thereby concentrating the light and energy per unit area onto the patient's retina (in addition to concentrating properties already inherent in the patient's own ocular media). It has been estimated that the amount of focal energy applied to the retina and choroid by the indirect ophthalmoscope is approximately 0.1 to 0.2 mW/cm^2, which approximates the amount of irradiance received at the retinal surface from the sun. However, it should also be noted that the indirect ophthalmoscope has 90% of its power in the IR region (longer than 750 nm). The retinal irradiance levels with an indirect vs. a direct ophthalmoscope have been measured and the data indicate a tenfold increase in retinal irradiance with the indirect ophthalmoscope.[108] It is estimated that at the patient's retina the total irradiance is composed of one third visible light to two thirds IR radiation (750 to 1400 nm). Some workers have proposed that IR filters should be incorporated into all ophthalmoscopes to prevent potential thermal damage from extensive indirect ophthalmoscopy. They also proposed that reasonably short exposures should be used when examining the posterior pole of the eye. Intense illumination and frequent re-examination at short intervals should be avoided. It should be pointed out that the energy delivered during indirect ophthalmoscopy is only 200 times less than the energy that is capable of producing a retinal burn.

Lesions resembling central serious retinopathy have been demonstrated in primate eyes exposed to long-wave UV radiation,[90,99] and recent reports have described clinically demonstrable retinal lesions in patients undergoing intraocular surgery with the operating microscope.[4,6] One must therefore consider the potential for retinal damage with these clinical techniques, particularly in certain conditions, such as retinitis pigmentosa, which might be accelerated by light exposure.[93] Photic damage has also been shown to result in pathologic changes in the pigment epithelium as well as the outer segments; this suggests the possibility that such damage would weaken the adhesions between the retina and pigment epithelium and potentiate retinal detachment.

5. Summary and Conclusions

Recent reviews have considered the possibility of ocular hazards resulting from ambient light exposure.[93,109,110] They indicate that ambient light levels are currently approaching the threshold level for permanent retinal damage (following chronic exposure). The levels of artificial illumination that we are exposed to at present vary between 20 and 50 fc (3.2 to 8.1 × 10^{-5} W/cm^2). Although these levels of irradiance are well below the levels that are capable of producing retinal photopathology in primates and man, they have been shown to be of sufficient intensity to produce permanent as well as reversible retinal damage in certain experimental animals, particularly albino rats. The trend by lighting engineers toward higher levels of illumination (e.g., 100 to 1000 fc) should be approached with extreme caution in view of the potential photic damage that could be incurred at these levels of illumination. It should also be noted that the lowest reported retinal damage threshold in primates occurs at wavelengths in the blue region of the spectrum, and the potential adverse effects of UV radiation on the retina must also be considered, particularly in the aphakic eye. Another point to bear in mind is the fact that the pigment epithelium is one of the major sites of primary photic damage; thus the melanosomes in the pigment epithelium may play a significant role as transducers of photic energy in the eye. These organelles seem to play a central role in both the thermal and chemical mechanisms of primary photic damage to the retina and may play a role in the pathogenesis of senile macular degeneration. One must also consider the role of photosensitizing agents in retinal photobiology. The fact that the psoralens absorb mostly in the longer-wavelength UV spectrum (between 320 and 360 nm) has allayed concern about the risk of these drugs to the retina. However, the ocular hazard from such photosensitizing drugs should be of concern in aphakic eyes that have lost their natural UV filter (the ocular lens), in pseudophakes, and in young children (whose own lens has yet to develop as an effective UV filter).

III. PHOTOSENSITIZED RADIATION EFFECTS ON OCULAR TISSUES

A photosensitizing agent can be defined as a compound whose chemical structure endows it with the ability to absorb optical radiation (UV and visible) and undergo a primary photochemical reaction resulting in the generation of highly reactive and relatively long-lived intermediates (triplets, radicals, and ions) that can cause chemical modifications in other (nearby) molecules of the biologic system. Regardless of subsequent events, the primary event of photosensitization in ocular tissues appears to be the absorption of light by the photosensitizer molecule, eventually resulting in a complex of photosensitizers with nucleic acid or protein. Only the pyrimidine bases in the nucleic acids are susceptible to photosensitization, and in the proteins, histidine is the most readily altered of all the amino acid residues (either alone or as part of the protein) followed by tryptophan, tyrosine, cystine, and methionine.[1] Sensitized photooxidation reactions in proteins generally do not involve disulfide and peptide bonds, with chemical alterations occurring most frequently in the aforementioned five amino acid residues. Hundreds of chemical compounds are capable of acting as photosensitizing agents.[1,111-116] Such compounds include a wide variety of drugs used in routine medical practice as well as in industry, agriculture, and the home. The most common photosensitizing reactions involve the skin, although internal organs are also susceptible to phototoxic reactions.

There are several parameters that could influence the possibility and extent of photosensitized damage in the eye. These include (1) the chemical structure of the drug in question and its absorption spectra, (2) the role of the blood-aqueous and blood-retinal barriers, (3) the age and/or the health of the patient, and (4) the oxygen concentration in the affected tissue. Certain drugs having a tricyclic (three fused aromatic rings), heterocyclic, or porphyrin ring system are known to be efficient photosensitizers. The reasons for this are (1) they have long-lived triplet states, (2) they have a low oxidation potential (Type I reaction), and (3) their triplet-state energy is such that transfer of energy to ground-state oxygen is possible (Type II reaction).

In addition to the demonstrated direct photochemical action of UV radiation on ocular tissues, particularly the cornea, lens, and retina, there is the possibility of photobiologic damage by means of photosensitized reactions due to the accumulation and retention of certain drugs within these tissues. For example, after the 13-mm stage of development, the ocular lens is completely encapsulated and never sheds its cells throughout life. Thus, photobinding a drug to the lens proteins and nucleic acids ensures its lifelong retention within the lens with the potential for enhanced photodamage if these compounds are capable of acting as photosensitizing agents. A similar situation exists in the neural retina which does not regenerate.

Only two groups of compounds (the phenothiazines and the psoralens) have been clearly identified as intraocular photosensitizing agents that are capable of causing photochemical damage to the choroid, the retina, and the lens in man as well as in experimental animals. This may be due to the screening effect of the blood-aqueous and the blood-retinal barriers. It is well known, for example, that it is difficult if not impossible to obtain an effective concentration of certain antibacterial, antimycotic, or antibiotic drugs in the interior of the normal eye. This has been attributed to the relative impermeability of the blood-aqueous and the blood-retinal barriers. Furthermore, it has already been demonstrated that the cornea, and particularly the lens as it ages, provide effective filters for UV radiation and the shorter wavelengths of the visible spectrum, thereby nullifying any potential photosensitizing action of drugs (that are activated at these wavelengths) which might accumulate in the posterior half of the globe. However, any photosensitizing agent that accumulates in the ocular lens or the retina might be a potential hazard if it becomes photobound to macromolecules within these tissues since it would now be permanently retained there.

The psoralen compounds are well-known photosensitizing agents and have been used (under controlled conditions) in many dermatology clinics to treat psoriasis and vitiligo.[72,117] This form of phototherapy, commonly referred to as PUVA therapy, involves the ingestion of 8-MOP or related compounds, followed by exposure to UVA radiation (320 to 400 nm) for short periods of time. 8-MOP can be found in a variety of ocular tissues within 2 hr after the animal (rat, dogfish, monkey, and human) is given a single dose (equivalent to a therapeutic level) and can become photobound to DNA and lens proteins if there is concurrent exposure to ambient levels of UVA radiation.[73-77] Since the mature ocular lens is a very effective filter for UVA radiation in most mammals (including man) there can be no photobinding of 8-MOP in the retina. However, UVA radiation can penetrate to the retina in aphakic and pseudophakic experimental animals and in young eyes (where the ocular lens still permits significant penetration of UVA radiation) and 8-MOP photobinding can occur in these retinas.

Psoralen-UVA (PUVA) therapy and cataract formation has now been documented in human cataracts as well as in experimental animals.[73,74,118-127] Cataracts from patients on PUVA therapy were subjected to high-resolution phosphorescence spectroscopy. The lens proteins from these patients showed phosphorescence peaks identical (in shape and lifetime) with the previously reported 8-MOP lens protein photoproduct seen in experimental rat PUVA cataracts.[126] These data provide objective proof that this drug can generate specific photoproducts in human lenses which have been shown to be associated with the formation of PUVA cataracts in experimental animals. However, this observation should not deter anyone from prescribing such therapy since simple and effective preventive measures are available. It should be noted that 8-MOP can be found in the lens *for only 24 hr,* provided that the eye is protected from UVA radiation. Thus, many dermatologists are now providing proper UV-filtering glasses to all their PUVA patients with instructions to put them on as soon as they ingest the drug and to continue to wear them for at least 24 hr. They must be worn indoors as well as outdoors, since there is sufficient UVA radiation in ordinary fluorescent lighting to photobind the 8-MOP.[74,125] A 2-year follow-up study utilizing UV slit-lamp densitography has proved the efficacy of this approach.[125,128] All the patients wore paper UV-filtering glasses for at least 24 hr following drug ingestion, and none developed enhanced or abnormal lens fluorescence levels. In contrast, patients whose eyes had not been properly protected (those treated prior to 1978) had anomalous and enhanced lens fluorescence and some developed PUVA cataracts. It should be noted that PUVA therapy could pose a potential hazard not only to the ocular lens but also to the retina in young people whose lenses are not effective UV absorbers and/or in aphakic or pseudophakic individuals, particularly if they are exposed to repeated PUVA treatments.[122,125-128] The intraocular lenses currently in use are excellent transmitters of UV radiation and thus provide less protection from UVA radiation than the natural lens or even ordinary glass (which absorbs UV radiation up to 320 nm). UV-absorbing intraocular lenses are now being tested by several manufacturers and should provide a simple solution for preventing potential UVA photodamage to the pseudophakic retina.

Studies on the effects of PUVA in albino and pigmented mice, where much of the UVA can be transmitted to the retina, demonstrate that there are several receptor organelles which can be damaged by such exposure.[129] These include the rod outer segments (ROS), the ellipsoid region of the rod inner segments, and the receptor nuclei. The damage involves vesiculation and disruption of the ROS, swelling of the ellipsoid as a whole with damage to the mitochondria, and necrosis of the nuclei. UVA by itself selectively causes more damage to the ROS, while 8-MOP in combination with UVA exposure results in far greater necrosis of the nuclei in addition to damaging the ROS and ellipsoids.[129,130]

The phenothiazines, especially chlorpromazine, have long been recognized as having adverse ocular side effects.[131] Chlorpromazine is reported to be cataractogenic with pigment deposits appearing in the lens as well as in the cornea and conjunctiva. The role of NP207 in retinopathy is well established while that of thioridazine and chlorpromazine is far less understood. There is a marked accumulation of chlorpromazine, prochlorperazine, and thioridazine in the uveal tract of pigmented animals. The phenothiazines, like other polycyclic aromatic compounds, have a high affinity for melanin.[113] The relationship between such an affinity and functional alterations in vision is as yet unclear. With NP207, the pigmentary pattern parallels the rod and cone disruptions. With other phenothiazines such as thioridazine, few side effects have been reported when they are administered in doses of less than 800 mg/day. Chlorpromazine has been used extensively as an antipsychotic. It also binds to melanin and causes relatively minor pigmentary changes of the fundus though some alterations in visual functions have been noted.

Allopurinol is a commonly used antihyperuricemic agent in treating gout. Scattered reports have appeared regarding the possible relationship between the development of lens opacities in relatively young patients (second to fourth decade) and chronic ingestion of this drug.[132-134] Cataracts obtained from 11 patients on chronic allopurinol therapy (>2 years) were subjected to high-resolution phosphorescence spectroscopy. The characteristic allopurinol triplet was demonstrated in all the cataracts. Identical spectra were obtained on normal human lenses incubated in media containing 10^{-3} M allopurinol and exposed to 1.2 mW/cm² UV radiation for 16 hr; control lenses (irradiated without allopurinol) were negative. Similar data were obtained on lenses from rats given one dose of allopurinol and exposed to UV radiation overnight. However, the allopurinol triplet could not be demonstrated in normal eye-bank lenses derived from patients who had been on chronic allopurinol therapy for more than 2 years without developing ocular problems.[134] These data suggest that allopurinol can act as a cataractogenic-enhancing agent in some patients when it is permanently photobound within their lenses (probably as an additional extrinsically derived photosensitizer). Thus, chronic allopurinol therapy (by itself) does not necessarily result in the retention of allopurinol unless it becomes photobound. The relationship between levels of UVA exposure, circulating allopurinol levels, (and renal function) in the genesis of photosensitized allopurinol cataracts will require further studies.

Experimental cataracts have been reported following tetracycline administration, an effect which may be due to photosensitization.[135] Fraunfelder[116] lists erythemal reactions of the eyelids and edema, photosensitivity, and erythema multiforme as other ocular side effects of this drug. Its action spectrum ranges between 350 to 420 nm. Since its mechanism of action is poorly understood, it is frequently labeled as phototoxic and possibly photoallergic.[111] Acute transient myopia, blurred vision, diplopia, and papilledema, though rare and for the most part reversible, also have been associated with the administration of tetracyclines.[111,116] The combined administration of tetracycline and minocycline can result in pseudotumor cerebri.[116] Since extraocular paresis and/or paralysis and papilledema can be caused by pseudotumor cerebri, these signs and symptoms are probably secondary to the pseudotumor and not directly related to any photosensitizing or toxic effects of the drug.

Griseofulvin is an antifungal agent which can cause severe allergic reactions with involvement of the eyelids and erythema multiforme-like rashes.[111] Though rare, these side effects can occur when the medication is given in heavy doses over extended periods of time, and are probably due to a photoallergic mechanism.[111] Transient macular edema has been reported with this drug.

Adriamycin is an anthracycline antibiotic that is also used as a chemotherapeutic agent in treating cancer. Adriamycin can affect cells by intercalating with DNA, membrane binding, and lipid peroxidation. The most thoroughly documented action of adriamycin is DNA intercalation.[136] The consequences of this intercalation include blockage of DNA, RNA, and protein synthesis, inhibition of DNA repair, and fragmentation of DNA. Adriamycin also binds to cell surfaces and alters membrane function at concentrations below those required for DNA intercalation. Adriamycin is reduced to a semiquinone free radical by cytochrome P_{450}. The semiquinone transfers an electron to molecular oxygen, producing the superoxide radical ion.[137] This leads to a free-radical chain reaction that results in peroxidation of unsaturated fatty acids. Superoxide generation may also lead to single-stranded scission of DNA.

Nalidixic acid therapy can also be associated with mild visual disturbances and changes in color perception, with reversible papilledema and sixth-nerve palsies.[116]

Other drugs with photosensitizing photoallergic and/or phototoxic properties include the sulfonamides, the oral hypoglycemic agents, antimalarial agents (chloroquine), and some of the oral contraceptives.[116]

The increasing interest in using HPD for phototherapy (and photodiagnostic procedures) merits careful evaluation with respect to their phototoxic (or sensitizing) potential. Because the HPD absorb over a wide range in the UV and visible region of the electromagnetic spectrum and the fact that they appear to be slowly metabolized (HPD can be retained for 3 months after injection)[138] necessitates that adequate precautions should be taken when such therapy is employed. These compounds can exert a photosensitizing action via the type-I and type-II reactions. The photodynamic action is mediated via singlet oxygen and has been shown to polymerize lens proteins in vitro.[139] The porphyrin-induced photochemical reactions also involve OH radicals and have been implicated in the generation of H_2O_2;[138] thus the potential for ocular damage certainly exists. Patients undergoing HPD therapy must be monitored for ocular side effects, and they should also be informed about the potential for severe sunburns, particularly within the first 3 months following therapy.

There has been a recent resurgence of interest in the therapeutic uses of topical vitamin A acid (retinoic acid) and closely related compounds[140-142] particularly for skin conditions such as acne and related disorders and psoriasis. In addition, such compounds have been tested as a method for treating corneal xerophthalmia, an ocular condition caused by a severe vitamin A deficiency.[143,144] Considerable success has been claimed with such a therapeutic regime, however, the oral administration of isotretinoin has resulted in some side effects; corneal opacities have been reported in a patient receiving this drug.[145] Topical retinoic acid in treating experimental corneal xerophthalmia has met with mixed results. While little is known about the specific mode of action of such drugs, the possibility of phototoxicity (and/or photosensitization) should be considered, particularly with respect to the eye. Patients undergoing clinical trials with these drugs should have careful ocular examinations prior to instituting therapy and be re-evaluated at specific intervals to assess their ocular status.

IV. CLINICAL LENS-FLUORESCENCE STUDIES

Since laboratory studies have demonstrated enhanced fluorescence in the ocular lens associated with aging and drug therapy, and human photosensitized cataracts have recently been reported, a method to monitor lens fluorescence in vivo has been developed.[146,147] A new slit lamp densitographic apparatus (based on the Scheimpflug principle) of accurately and reproducibly recording visible changes in lens density as the lens ages was recently introduced.[148,149] This apparatus has been modified to utilize UV radiation (300 to 400 nm) to measure and quantitate the age-related fluorescence levels in the normal lens in vivo and correlate them with in vitro data.[1,15,16,21,146,147] Visible and UV slit-lamp photographs taken with the Scheimpflug (Topcon SL45) camera on normal eyes and corresponding densitograms show increased lens fluorescence with age.[146,147] A series of UV and visible slit-lamp photographs of normal patients ranging in age from 5 to 82 years demonstrate a lack of fluorescence in the young lens and a progressive increase in fluorescence with age (Figures 6 to 8). These data can be expressed in graphic form (Figure 9) showing the normal age-related increase in lens fluorescence (in vivo) which corresponds well with the in vitro data (Figures 10 and 11) previously reported.[15,16,21] The in vitro studies were performed on lenses from normal eye bank eyes and represent two (nontryptophan) fluorescent peaks obtained by fluorescence spectroscopy.

Aside from demonstrating the normal age-related increase in lens fluorescence, abnormal enhanced fluorescence caused by occupational (or accidental) exposure to higher levels of UV radiation can also be detected. This is shown in Figure 12, obtained on a 40-year-old patient exposed to excessive UV radiation in his workplace. The increased fluorescence can easily be appreciated by comparing this lens with a normal 40-year-old eye (Figure 13). Enhanced fluorescence and/or abnormal fluorescence emission can also occur in patients on PUVA therapy and failure to properly protect such patients from all UV radiation exposure for at least 24 hr following ingestion of the drug can result in cataract formation as shown in Figure 14. This 52-year-old psoriatic patient received 4 years of intermittent PUVA treatment (without proper eye protection). Although many dermatology clinics now provide all PUVA patients with proper UV absorbing or reflecting spectacles, data obtained on a series of patients who were treated prior to 1977 (when the potential for photosensitized lens damage from psoralen therapy was first demonstrated)[74] show a significant elevation of one of the lens fluorescence peaks (Figure 15). In contrast, patients who have been on D-penicillamine therapy (for a variety of diseases) tend to have lower lens-fluorescence intensities (Figure 15). This is due to the fact that D-penicillamine (which is an excellent free-radical scavenger as well as a chelating agent) is capable of entering the lens, both in vivo as well in vitro.[43,58] As a free-radical scavenger, D-penicillamine aborts the UV photodamage.

These studies demonstrate the feasibility of obtaining in vivo lens-fluorescence data which are objective, reproducible, and which can be quantified. Thus UV slit-lamp densitography can be used to objectively monitor one parameter of lens aging (fluorescence), as well as photosensitized lens damage, at a molecular level months to years before visible opacities become manifest by conventional slit-lamp examination, and measures can be instituted to at least retard if not prevent such lens opacities.

In addition to performing in vivo lens-fluorescence measurements, the same photographs can also be utilized (with proper software) to obtain biometric measurements on these eyes including: (1) radius of curvature of the anterior and posterior cornea and corneal thickness, (2) depth of the anterior chamber, and (3) radius of curvature of the anterior and posterior lens surfaces and lens thickness. Thus the clinician can

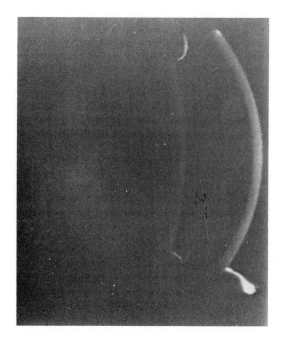

A

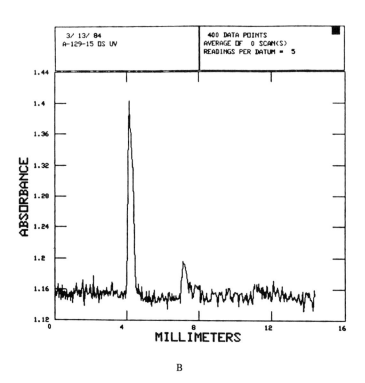

B

FIGURE 6.   (A) Visible (L) and UV (R) photos of a 5-year-old normal eye;
(B) UV (fluorescence) densitogram.

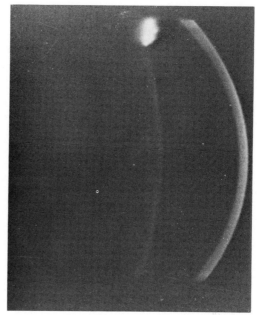

A

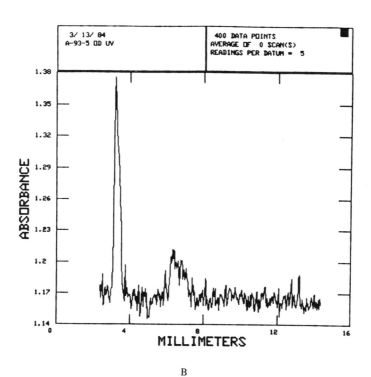

B

FIGURE 7.   (A) Visible (L) and UV (R) photos of a 28-year-old normal eye;
(B) UV (fluorescence) densitogram.

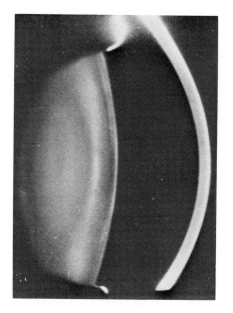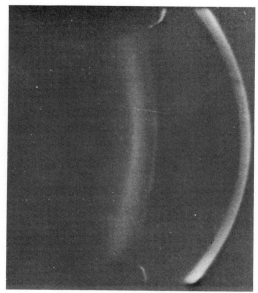

A

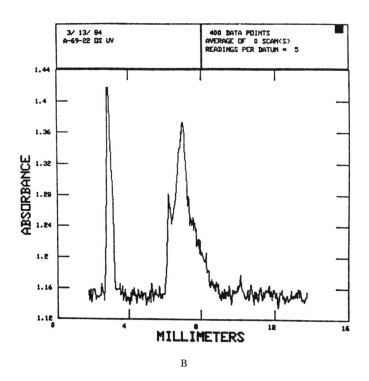

B

FIGURE 8.   (A) Visible (L) and UV (R) photos of a 65-year-old normal eye;
(B) UV (fluorescence) densitogram.

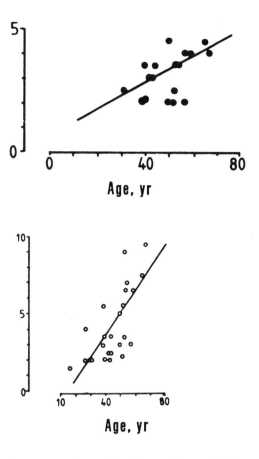

FIGURE 9. Normal age-related increase in two densitographic regions (derived from UV slit-lamp photos in vivo) which correspond to the 440-nm (Figure 10) and 520-nm (Figure 11) fluorescence emission levels obtained in vitro.

now obtain reproducible biometric data on the anterior-segment ocular tissues and structures by simply utilizing the Schiempflug slit-lamp photographic method. These data will provide an accurate method for monitoring age-related changes in the normal eye (e.g., A.C. diameter, lens thickness, lens density, growth of lens nucleus, and increased lens fluorescence). The progress of lenticular opacification can also be followed utilizing visible-light densitography[146] and lenticular and corneal fluorescence data can be obtained concurrently by substituting broadband UV radiation for the visible exciting light with appropriate filters.

Laser light scattering can also be employed as an in vivo method to monitor the development and progression of light-scattering elements within the lens before they become manifest with conventional slit-lamp examination.[150,151] Aside from the foregoing biophysical techniques already available, Raman and NMR spectroscopy will, in the near future, also become available for detecting and measuring molecular changes in the living lens at a very early stage in their development.

In NMR examinations, patients are subjected to long-wave radiation in a large chamber that exerts a magnetic field around them. Unlike radiation from a CT scan, NMR radiation is nonionizing and thus harmless. In essence, it energizes atomic nuclei in the patient's body. The nuclei do not remain energized but tend to relax back to their normal, less energetic ground state. In doing this they give off energy, or "reso-

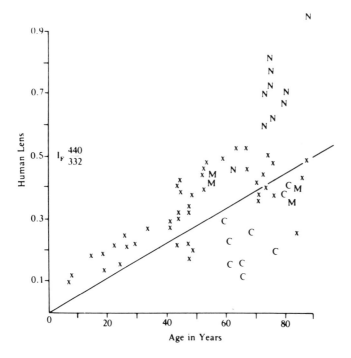

FIGURE 10. I_F 440/332 ratios representing whole-lens fluorescence intensity at 440 nm (360-nm excitation) divided by tryptophan intensity (in whole lens) at 332 nm (290-nm excitation). The I_F ratio shows age-related increase in the normal lens (X and solid line), a marked increase in brown nuclear cataracts (N), relatively normal or below-normal levels in cortical cataracts (C), and high normal values in mixed cortical and nuclear cataracts (M). Each point represents a single lens.

nate'' — thus the term nuclear magnetic resonance. Current studies utilizing ^{31}P NMR spectroscopy enable the investigator to monitor organophosphate metabolism in the lens in vivo (surface scanning) as well as in vitro.[152-156] Such data provide dynamic rather than static information about the general metabolic state of this organ and quickly reflect changes in high-energy phosphates (ATP, ADP, etc.), sugar phosphates, inorganic phosphates, and so forth. For example, in experimental sugar cataracts (glucose, galactose, xylose) one can measure the accumulation of sugar alcohols and the concomitant alterations in organophosphate levels as soon as these metabolic changes develop and well before any opacities become manifest. Other forms of NMR spectroscopy permit us to monitor changes in sodium and amino acids and detect very early changes in molecular aggregate formation as reflected by alterations in the lens water compartments.[157-159] Although such studies are still undergoing laboratory evaluation, sufficient data have accumulated to demonstrate the feasibility of applying one or more of these techniques to human studies in vivo. In essence, one will obtain a more sensitive type of CT scan capable of detecting molecular dysfunction within the eye without exposing it to ionizing radiation.

V. THE ROLE OF COMMERCIAL SUNGLASSES

Because of the confusion and controversial claims regarding the efficacy of commercially available sunglasses in protecting the eye from UV photodamage, a large series of such lenses have been analyzed to determine their transmission characteristics.

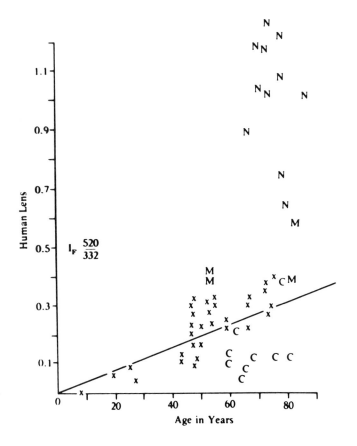

FIGURE 11. I_F 520/332 ratios representing fluorescence intensity of second fluorescent region in the lens at 520 nm (420- to 435-nm excitation) divided by tryptophan fluorescence intensity in the lens at 332 nm (295-nm excitation). Interference filters (295 and 435 nm) were employed in order to decrease the light scattering when cortical and mixed cataracts were examined. Each point represents a single lens.

These studies[160] are in general agreement with an earlier report[161] and demonstrate a wide variation in the UV-transmission characteristics of the sunglasses evaluated, ranging from 1.5 to 40%, with similar transmission values noted when tested for more discrete wavelengths (340 to 380 nm). Only the NOIR, Spectra-Shield, Silor, Univis, and UV 400 lenses were >99% effective in filtering all the UV radiation. It should also be noted that visible radiation is significantly decreased in darkly tinted sunglasses, while still permitting some long wavelength UV transmission. In patients with blue, gray, and hazel eyes, a 50% or more decrease in visible radiation can result in pupillary enlargement of 0.25 mm, thereby increasing the effective dose of radiation incident on the intraocular tissues.

VI. VDTs AND THE EYE

The recent controversy regarding ocular problems which have been reported in workers using VDTs may turn out to be beneficial and opportune. In contrast with the indifference and ignorance with which the development of the X-ray was embraced (in the not-too-distant past), the community at large, as well as the scientific specialists, are now well aware of possible dangers in misusing electromagnetic radiation. We now

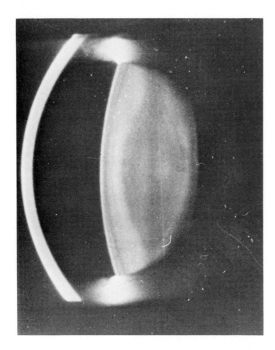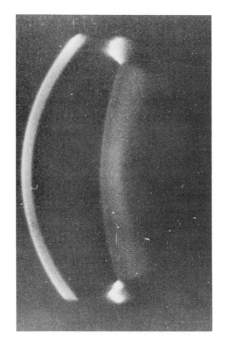

A

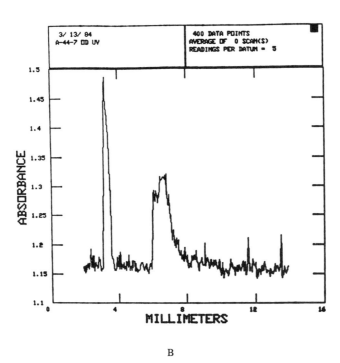

B

FIGURE 12.   (A) Visible (L) and UV (R) photos of a 40-year-old eye showing abnormal fluorescence due to occupational excessive UV exposure; (B) UV (fluorescence) densitogram. Note enhanced fluorescence compared with normal values (see Figure 13B).

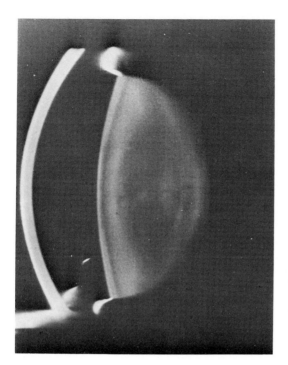
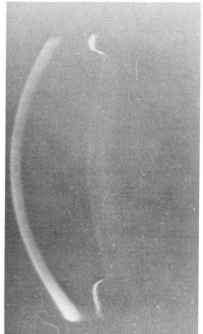

A

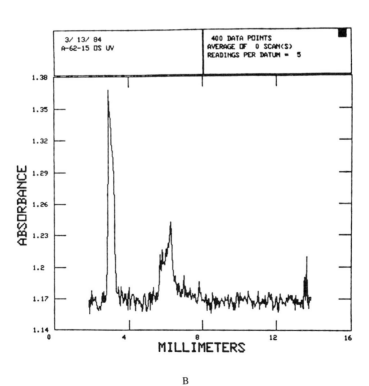

B

FIGURE 13. (A) Visible (L) and UV (R) photos of a normal 40-year-old eye; (B) UV (fluorescence) densitogram.

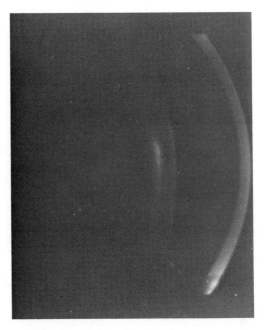

A

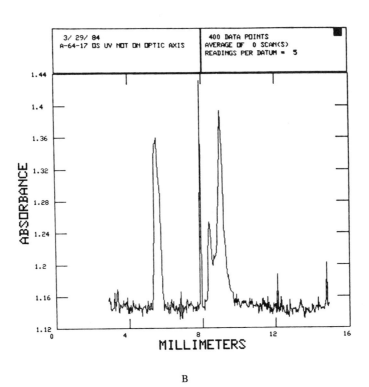

B

FIGURE 14.   (A) Visible (L) and UV (R) photos of a PUVA-induced cataract with abnormal fluorescence in a 52-year-old patient on PUVA therapy for 4 years; (B) UV (fluorescence) densitogram.

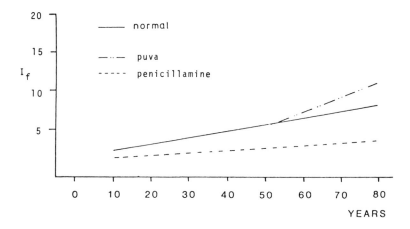

FIGURE 15.   Densitographic analyses from in vivo photos showing enhanced fluorescence in PUVA patients compared with normal individuals. Note decreased fluorescence level in patients on chronic D-penicillamine (over 1 year).

have the ability to monitor radiation emission levels from our technological marvels and obtain reasonably accurate measurements on most wavelength emissions of interest. We also have a considerable body of ever-expanding scientific knowledge which enables us to correlate specific radiation emission levels with threshold doses for possible photobiologic damage. Such measurements have recently been performed by scientists at the Bureau of Radiological Health (BRH), Bell Laboratories, and NIOSH.[162-164] Scientists at the BRH measured ionizing radiation (e.g., X-ray) emission levels on 125 VDTs; of these, 34 VDTs were also measured for nonionizing radiation emission (UV, visible, IR, microwave, and other radiofrequency [RF] emissions). A smaller number of VDTs were similarly evaluated by Bell Laboratory scientists. These data indicate that the VDTs "emit little or no harmful radiation under normal operating conditions".[162] The specific emissions that were detectable were all well below the current national and international safety standards.

Aside from "ocular fatigue", questions have been raised regarding a possible relationship between VDT radiation emission and "organic" ocular photodamage, particularly to the ocular lens. Of the various wavelengths in the electromagnetic spectrum, UV radiation and ocular photodamage have received considerable attention during the last two decades. The best current experimental and epidemiologic evidence does not indicate that the level of UV radiation emitted by the VDTs is capable of exerting any deleterious effects on the ocular lenses of personnel using these terminals. We should, however, pay more attention to the workplace with respect to the types of lighting (their UV emission levels) used in these environments and the reflectance level[165] of work surfaces (including reflectance of painted walls, desks, etc.) in order to maintain total ambient UV radiation exposure at minimum levels. Our own ocular lens serves us well as a natural filter for removing the UV radiation that penetrates into the eye, thereby protecting the underlying retina which has been shown to be quite sensitive to rather low levels of UV radiation. Thus, particular care must be taken to protect the aphakic and pseudophakic individuals from potential low-level UV radiation damage. A similar situation pertains to some patients who are receiving photosensitizing drugs. Fortunately, the levels of UV radiation emitted by the VDTs are approximately 1000-fold lower than the amount shown to cause retinal photodamage in experimental primate studies.

Further research should be encouraged, particularly in the areas relating to nonionizing photobiologic radiation damage in order to clarify and better define the molecular mechanisms resulting from exposure to UV, IR, microwave, and RF radiation. It is also important to determine whether damage can result from cumulative low-level exposure over a lifetime, and whether a synergistic effect could accrue from low-level exposure to broadband radiation (e.g., UV + microwave, ionizing + nonionizing).

Finally, it should be noted that we now have the capability of protecting the eye from potential UV photodamage by special eyeglasses and similar UV-absorbing materials could be employed at the manufacturing end to prevent UV radiation emission from our ever-increasing array of technological products.

VII. THERAPY

A. Radiation Filters

The section on the effect of UV and visible radiation on the aphakic or pseudophakic eye has considered the mechanisms involved in ocular photodamage caused by optical radiation, i.e., nonionizing radiant energy (280 to 1400 nm) which is present in our environment. As noted, the simplest and most effective preventive therapy for UV-induced cataracts involves the use of spectacles which are capable of filtering out 99+% of the UV radiation (300 to 400 nm) which penetrates through the cornea. The development of UV-visible slit-lamp densitography now enables us to detect lenticular UV photodamage at a molecular level, months to years before the opacities become manifest with conventional slit-lamp examination. Such a screening procedure will detect enhanced or abnormal lens fluorescence for any particular age group (by decade), thereby alerting the clinician that the patient has had excessive UV exposure. Studies indicate that any patient whose lens-fluorescence levels are >30% above the amount present for his age group (by decade), should be considered a potential candidate for the development of UV cataracts, particularly the brown nuclear cataract.[1,16,128] Such enhanced lens fluorescence can be caused by occupational or recreational exposure to prolonged solar UV radiation in those people living in the "sun belt" areas of the U.S., or by exposure in industries where UV radiation is employed in research and development or manufacturing procedures. Further progression of this type of lens fluorescence can easily be prevented by prescribing proper UV-filtering glasses to such patients.

Since a certain amount of ambient UV exposure exerts a positive photochemical influence on the developing lens during childhood, inducing the generation of pigments so that the lens becomes an effective filter for UV and short wavelength visible radiation (thereby protecting the aging and metabolically less efficient retina from potential photodamage), UV-protective spectacles are not recommended for the general population, nor are they required. Such spectacles are only required when enhanced or abnormal fluorescence is present. If the UV slit-lamp densitography screening procedure demonstrates abnormal lens fluorescence, it may be indicative of current or past ingestion of photosensitizing drugs or chemicals. Such patients should also be given UV-absorbing spectacles with sidepieces (to prevent reflected radiation from entering the eye) and, depending on the mode and frequency with which these patients are ingesting the photosensitizer, they may only need to wear them for 24 hr after ingesting the drug.

Since the aging retina is particularly sensitive to UV and shortwave visible radiation, such spectacles are also recommended for all aphakes and pseudophakes irrespective of their site of domicile (i.e., not just those living in sunbelt areas) or occupation. It is important to note that none of the contact lenses are capable of filtering UV radiation; in fact, all the plastic contact lenses transmit much more UV radiation shorter than 320 nm than does ordinary glass. The same applies to most of the intraocular lenses currently employed, although many manufacturers are now eagerly attempting to develop and market UV-filtering intraocular lenses. Once again, a word of caution is advisable. To be truly effective and protective, such intraocular lenses must filter 99+% of all UV radiation between 300 to 400 nm and at least 50 to 75% of the shortwave visible radiation between 400 to 475 nm.

B. Medication

Aside from the use of UV and shortwave visible radiation filters, the potential exists for a medical approach to protect the lens from direct and photosensitized optical radiation damage. A variety of investigators have noted that D-penicillamine exerts a significant protective action both in vivo and in vitro and prevents experimental UV radiation photodamage and/or cataracts from developing in spite of direct UV exposure.[15] This drug is an effective free-radical scavenger as well as chelating agent. Its latter action is the basis for its clinical use in treating Wilson's disease. It efficacy as a free-radical scavenger within the lens has been demonstrated by in vitro and in vivo experiments in animals[16,58] where it aborts radiation-induced free-radical damage and prevents the subsequent photochemical reactions from being promulgated. UV slit-lamp densitography studies on a series of patients who had been on 1 or more years of D-penicillamine therapy (for a variety of nonocular conditions) demonstrated that all had significantly decreased lens-fluorescence values compared with their control peer groups. This suggests that medical therapy to inhibit or prevent progression of radiation-induced lenticular photodamage is a distinct possibility in the future. Such therapy could be applied locally in the form of drops, ointment, or a prolonged-release form of medication, in much lower concentrations than are currently being employed for treating Wilson's disease or certain forms of arthritis (i.e., in microgram rather than milligram quantities) thereby diminishing if not obviating some of the side effects currently seen with D-penicillamine therapy. Aside from this specific drug, there are a significant number of other free-radical quenchers or scavengers which, at least in theory, should be effective as possible forms of medical therapy for radiation cataractogenesis. However, prior to such therapy becoming available, it must be proved effective as well as safe.

REFERENCES

1. Lerman, S., *Radiant Energy and the Eye,* Macmillan, New York, 1980.
2. Mainster, M. A., Solar retinitis, photic maculopathy and the pseudophakic eye, *Am. Intra-Ocular Implant Soc. J.,* 4, 84, 1978.
3. Mainster, M. A., Spectral transmittance of intraocular lenses and retinal damage from intense light sources, *Am. J. Ophthalmol.,* 85, 167, 1978.
4. Berler, D. K. and Peyser, R., Light intensity and visual acuity following cataract surgery, *Ophthalmology,* 90, 933, 1983.
5. Mainster, M. A., Ham, W. T., Jr., and Delori, F. C., Potential retinal hazards: instrument and environmental light sources, *Ophthalmology,* 90, 927, 1983.
6. Boldrey, E. E., Ho, B. T., and Griffith, R. D., Retinal burns occurring at cataract extraction, *Opthalmology,* 91, 1297, 1984.
7. Lerman, S., NMR and fluorescence spectroscopy on the normal, aging and cataractous lens, *Lens Res.,* 1, 175, 1983.
8. Lerman, S., Observations on the use of higher power lasers in ophthalmology, *IEEE J. Quantum Electron.,* 20, 1465, 1984.
9. Lerman, S., Thrasher, B., and Moran, M., Vitreous changes after posterior lens capsule or mid-vitreous Nd:YAG laser irradiation, *A. J. Ophthalmol.,* 97, 470, 1984.
10. Dougherty, T. J., Thoma, R. E., Boyle, D. G., and Weishaupt, K. R., Interstitial photoradiation therapy for primary solid tumors in pet cats and dogs, *Cancer Res.,* 41, 401, 1981.

11. Menon, I. A., Persad, S., Haberman, H. F., Kurian, C. J., and Basu, P. K., A qualitative study of the melanins from blue and brown human eyes, *Exp. Eye Res.,* 34, 531, 1982.

12. Maurice, D., The structure and transparency of the cornea, *J. Physiol. (London),* 136, 263, 1957.

13. Benedek, G. B., Theory of transparency of the eye, *Appl. Opt.,* 10, 459, 1971.

14. Miller, D. and Benedek, G., *Intraocular Light Scattering,* Charles C Thomas, Springfield, Ill., 1973.

15. Lerman, S. and Borkman, R. F., Photochemistry and lens aging, in *Interdisciplinary Topics in Gerontology,* Vol. 13, S. Karger, Basel, 1978, 154.

16. Lerman, S., Lens transparency and aging, in *Aging of the Lens,* Regnault, F., Hockwin, O., and Courtois, Y., Eds., Elsevier, Amsterdam, 1980, 263.

17. Cogan, D. G. and Kinsey, V. E., Action spectrum of keratitis produced by ultraviolet radiation, *Arch. Ophthalmol.,* 35, 670, 1946.

18. Bachem, A., Ophthalmic ultraviolet action spectra, *Am. J. Ophthalmol.,* 41, 969, 1956.

19. Sherashov, S. G., Spectral sensitivity of the cornea to ultraviolet radiation, *Biofizika,* 15, 543, 1970.

20. Jedziniak, J. A., Nicoli, D. F., Baram, H., and Benedek, G. B., Quantitative verification of the existence of high-molecular-weight protein aggregates in the intact normal human lens by light scattering spectroscopy, *Invest. Ophthalmol. Vis. Sci.,* 17, 51, 1978.

21. Lerman, S. and Borkman, R. F., Spectroscopic evaluation and classification of the normal, aging and cataractous lens, *Ophthalmic Res.,* 8, 335, 1976.

22. Teale, F. W. J., The ultraviolet fluorescence of proteins in neutral solution, *Biochem. J.,* 76, 381, 1960.

23. Burstein, E. A., Vedenkina, N. S., and Ivkova, M. N., Fluorescence and the location of tryptophan residues in protein molecules, *Photochem. Photobiol.,* 18, 263, 1973.

24. Grinwald, A. and Steinberg, I. A., The fluorescence decay of tryptophan residues in native and denatured proteins, *Biochim. Biophys. Acta,* 427, 663, 1976.

25. Lerman, S., Megaw, J. M., and Moran, M. N., NMR analyses of the cold cataract. III. ^{13}C acrylamide studies, *Invest. Ophthal. Vis. Sci.,* submitted, 1984.

26. Blundell, T. L., Lindley, P. F., Miller, L. R., Moss, D. S., Slingsby, C., Turnell, W. G., and Wistow, G. T., Interactions of gamma crystallin in relation to eye-lens transparency, *Lens Res.,* 1, 109, 1983.

27. Summers, L., Slingsby, C., White, H., Narebor, M., Moss, D., Miller, L., Mahadevan, D., Lindley, P., Driessen, H., Blundell, T., Den Dunnen, J., Moorman, R., Van Leen, R., and Schoenmaker, J., The molecular structures and interactions of bovine and human gamma crystallins, in *Ciba Foundation Symp. 106 Human Cataract Formation,* Nugent, J. and Whelen, J., Eds., Pitman Press, London, 1984, 219.

28. Regnauld, J., Sur la fluorescence des milieux de l'oeil chez l'homme et quelques mammiferes, *Institut,* 26, 410, 1958.

29. François, J., Rabaey, M., and Recoules, N., A fluorescent substance of low molecular weight in the lens of primates, *Arch. Ophthalmol.,* 65, 118, 1961.

30. Lerman, S., Tan, A. T., Louis, D., and Hollander, M., Anomalous absorptivity of lens proteins due to a fluorogen, *Ophthal. Res.,* 1, 338, 1970.

31. Lerman, S., Lens proteins and fluorescence, *Isr. J. Med. Sci.,* 8, 1583, 1972.

32. Spector, A., Roy, D., and Stauffer, J., Isolation and characterization of age-dependent polypeptide from human lens with non-tryptophan fluorescence, *Exp. Eye Res.,* 21, 9, 1975.

33. Pirie, A., Color and solubility of the proteins of human cataract, *Invest. Ophthalmol.,* 7, 634, 1968.

34. Pirie, A., Formation of *N'*-formylkynurenine in proteins from lens and other sources by exposure to sunlight, *Biochem. J.,* 125, 203, 1971.

35. van Heynigen, R., Fluorescent derivatives of 3-hydroxy-l-kynurenine in the lens of man, the baboon and the grey squirrel, *Biochem. J.,* 123, 30, 1971.

36. Pirie, A., Photo-oxidation of proteins and comparison of photo-oxidized proteins with those of the cataractous human lens, *Isr. J. Med. Sci.,* 8, 1583, 1972.

37. van Heyningen, R., The glucoside of 3-hydroxy-kynurenine and other fluorescent compounds in the human lens, *Exp. Eye Res.,* 15, 121, 1973.

38. Zigman, S., Griess, G., Yulo, T., and Schultz, J., Ocular protein alteration by near UV light, *Exp. Eye Res.,* 15, 255, 1973.

39. Satoh, K., Bando, M., and Nakajima, A., Fluorescence in human lens, *Exp. Eye Res.,* 16, 167, 1973.

40. Dilley, K. J. and Pirie, A., Changes to the proteins of the human lens nucleus in cataract, *Exp. Eye Res.,* 19, 59, 1974.

41. Augusteyn, R. C., Distribution of fluorescence in the human cataractous lens, *Ophthal. Res.,* 7, 217, 1975.

42. Dillon, J., Spector, A., and Nakanishi, A., Identification of *o*-carbolines isolated from fluorescent human lens proteins, *Nature (London),* 259, 422, 1976.

43. Lerman, S., Kuck, J. F., Borkman, R., and Saker, E., Induction, acceleration and prevention (in vitro) of an aging parameter in the ocular lens, *Ophthal. Res.,* 8, 213, 1976.

44. Ts'o, M. O. M., Fine, B. S., and Zimmerman, L. E., Photic maculopathy produced by indirect ophthalmoscope. I. Clinical and histopathic study, *Am. J. Ophthalmol.*, 73, 686, 1972.
45. Ham, W. T., Muller, H. A., Ruffolo, J. J., Guerry, D., and Guerry, R. K., Action spectrum for retinal injury from near ultraviolet radiation in the aphakic monkey, *Am. J. Ophthalmol.*, 93, 299, 1982.
46. Hochheimer, B., A possible cause of chronic cystic maculopathy: the operating microscopy, *Ann. Ophthalmol.*, 13, 153, 1981.
47. Berler, D. and Peyser, R., Light intensity and visual acuity following cataract surgery, *Ophthalmology*, Suppl. 89, 117, 1982.
48. Hiller, R., Giacometti, L., and Yuen, K., Sunlight and cataract: an epidemiologic investigation, *Am. J. Epidemiol.*, 105, 450, 1977.
49. Taylor, H. R., The environment and the lens, *Br. J. Ophthalmol.*, 64, 303, 1980.
50. Hollows, F. and Moran, D., Cataract — the ultraviolet risk factor, *Lancet*, 1, 1249, 1981.
51. Brilliant, L. B., Grasset, N. C., Pokhrel, R. P., Kolstad, A., Lepkowski, J. M., Brilliant, G. E., and Hawks, W. N., Associations among cataract prevalence, sunlight hours and altitude in the Himalayas, 1983 NEI Epidemiol. Symp., *Am. J. Ophthalmol.*, 113, 250, 1983.
52. Zigman, S. and Vaughn, W., Near UV light effects on the lenses and retinas of mice, *Invest. Ophthalmol.*, 13, 462, 1974.
53. Pitts, D., Hacker, P., and Parr, W. H., Ocular Ultraviolet Effects from 295 nm to 400 nm in the Rabbit Eye, Publication No. 77, National Institute for Occupational Safety and Health, U.S. Department of Health, Education and Welfare, Washington, D.C., 1977, 175.
54. Lerman, S., Human UV radiation cataracts, *Ophthal. Res.*, 12, 303, 1980.
55. Lerman, S., Gardner, K., Megaw, J., and Borkman, R., Prevention of direct and photosensitized UV radiation damage to the ocular lens, *Ophthal. Res.*, 13, 284, 1981.
56. Thomas, D. M. and Schepler, K. L., Raman spectra of normal and ultraviolet-induced cataractous rabbit lens, *Invest. Ophthalmol. Vis. Sci.*, 19, 904, 1980.
57. Kurzel, R. B., Wolbarsht, M. L., and Yamanashi, B. S., UV radiation effects on the human eye, *Photochem. Photobiol. Rev.*, 2, 133, 1977.
58. Borkman, R. F. and Lerman, S., Evidence for a free radical mechanism in aging and UV irradiated ocular lenses, *Exp. Eye Res.*, 25, 303, 1977.
59. Weiter, J. J. and Finch, E. D., Paramagnetic species in cataractous human lenses, *Nature (London)*, 254, 536, 1975.
60. Zigman, S., Groff, J., and Yulo, T., Enhancement of the non-tryptophan fluorescence of human lens proteins after near-UV light exposure, *Photochem. Photobiol.*, 26, 437, 1977.
61. Lerman, S., Ocular phototoxicity and PUVA therapy: an experimental and clinical evaluation, FDA Photochemical Toxicity Symp., *J. Natl. Cancer Inst.*, 69, 287, 1982.
62. Goosey, J. D., Zigler, S., Matheson, I. B. C., and Kinoshita, J. H., Effects of singlet oxygen on human lens crystallins, *Invest. Ophthalmol. Vis. Sci.*, 20, 679, 1981.
63. Varma, S. D., Superoxide and lens of the eye: a new theory of cataractogenesis, *Int. J. Quantum Chem.*, 20, 479, 1981.
64. Jernigan, H. M., Jr., Fukui, H. N., Goosey, J. D., and Kinoshita, J. H., Photodynamic effects of rose bengal or riboflavin on carrier-mediated transport systems in rat lens, *Exp. Eye Res.*, 32, 461, 1981.
65. Varma, S. D., Srivastava, V. K., and Richards, R. D., Photoperoxidation in lens and cataract formation: preventive role of superoxide dismutase, catalase and vitamin C, *Ophthal. Res.*, 14, 167, 1982.
66. van Haard, P. M. M., Hoenders, H. J., and Ketelaars, H. C. J., Human lens nuclear cataract: hydrogen peroxide action and anthranilic acid association with lens proteins, *Ophthal. Res.*, 12, 252, 1980.
67. Truscott, R. J. W., Faull, K., and Augusteyn, R. C., The identification of anthranilic acid in proteolytic digests of cataractous lens proteins, *Ophthal. Res.*, 9, 263, 1977.
68. McCormick, J. P., Fischer, J. R., Pachlatko, J. P., and Eisenstark, A., Characterization of a cell-lethal product from the photo oxidation of tryptophan: hydrogen peroxide, *Science*, 191, 468, 1976.
69. Bhuyan, K. C. and Bhuyan, D. K., Superoxide dismutase of the eye: relative functions of superoxide dismutase and catalase in protecting the ocular lens from oxidative damage, *Biochim. Biophys. Acta*, 542, 28, 1978.
70. Musajo, L. and Rodighiero, G., Mode of photosensitizing action of furocoumarins, in *Photophysiology*, Vol. 7, Giese, A. C., Ed., Academic Press, New York, 1972, 115.
71. Mantulin, W. W. and Song, P. S., Excited states of skin-sensitizing coumarins and psoralens. Spectroscopic studies, *J. Am. Chem. Soc.*, 95, 5112, 1973.
72. Parrish, J. A., Fitzpatrick, T. B., Tanenbaum, L., and Pathak, M. A., Photochemotherapy of psoriasis with oral methoxsalen and longwave ultraviolet light, *N. Engl. J. Med.*, 291, 1207, 1974.

73. Jose, J. J. and Yielding, K. L., Photosensitive cataractogens, chlorpromazine and methoxypsoralen, cause DNA repair synthesis in lens epithelial cells, *Invest. Ophthalmol. Vis. Sci.,* 17, 687, 1978.

74. Lerman, S., Jocoy, M., and Borkman, R. F., Photosensitization of the lens by 8-methoxypsoralen, *Invest. Ophthalmol. Vis. Sci.,* 16, 1065, 1977.

75. Lerman, S., Megaw, J., and Willis, I., The photoreaction of 8-MOP with tryptophan and lens proteins, *Photochem. Photobiol.,* 31, 519, 1980.

76. Lerman, S., Megaw, J., and Willis, I., Potential ocular complications of PUVA therapy and their prevention, *J. Invest. Dermatol.,* 74, 197, 1980.

77. Megaw, J., Lee, C., and Lerman, S., NMR analyses of tryptophan-8-methoxypsoralen photoreaction products, *Photochem. Photobiol.,* 32, 265, 1980.

78. Poppe, W. and Grossweiner, L. I., Photodynamic sensitization by 8 methoxypsoralen via singlet oxygen mechanism, *Photochem. Photobiol.,* 22, 217, 1975.

79. Yoshikawa, K., Mori, N., Sakakibara, S., Mizuno, N., and Song, P. S., Photo-conjugation of 8-methoxypsoralen with proteins, *Photochem. Photobiol.,* 29, 1127, 1979.

80. Dall'Acqua, S., Marciani, M., Zambon, F., and Rodighiero, G., Kinetic analysis of the photoreaction (365 nm) between psoralen and DNA, *Photochem. Photobiol.,* 29, 489, 1979.

81. Bessems, G. J. H., de Man, B. M., Hoenders, H. J., and Wollensak, J., Alpha-tocopherol in the normal and nuclear-cataractous human lens, *Lens Res.,* in press.

82. Hockwin, O., Early changes of lens metabolism after X-irradiation, *Exp. Eye Res.,* 1, 422, 1962.

83. Armstrong, D. A. and Buchanan, J. D., Reactions of O_2, H_2O_2 and other oxidants with sulfhydryl enzymes, *Photochem. Photobiol.,* 28, 741, 1978.

84. Balazs, E. A., Laurent, T. C., Howe, A. F., and Varga, L., Irradiation of mucopolysaccharides with ultraviolet light and electrons, *Radiat. Res.,* 11, 149, 1959.

85. Lauber, J. K., Schutze, J. B., and McGinnis, J., Effects of exposure to continuous light on the eye of the growing chicken, *Proc. Soc. Exp. Biol. Med.,* 106, 871, 1961.

86. Dowling, J. E. and Sidman, R. L., Inherited retinal dystrophy in the rat, *J. Cell Biol.,* 14, 73, 1962.

87. Noell, W. K., Aspects of experimental and hereditary retinal degeneration, in *Biochemistry of the Eye,* Graymore, C. N., Ed., Academic Press, New York, 1963, 51.

88. Noell, W. K., Delmelle, M. C., and Albrecht, R., Vitamin A deficiency effect on retina: dependence on light, *Science,* 172, 72, 1971.

89. Noell, W. K. and Albrecht, R., Irreversible effects of visible light on the retina: role of vitamin A, *Science,* 171, 76, 1971.

90. Ts'o, M. O. M., Photic maculopathy in Rhesus monkey: a light and electron microscopic study, *Invest. Ophthalmol. Vis. Sci.,* 12, 17, 1973.

91. Noell, W. K., Hereditary retinal degeneration and damage by light, in Estratto dagli Atti del Somposio di Oftalmologia Pediatrica, Parma, October, 1974, 332.

92. Organisciak, D. T. and Noell, W. K., The rod outer segment phospholipid/opsin ratio of rats maintained in darkness or cyclic light, *Invest. Ophthalmol. Vis. Sci.,* 16, 188, 1977.

93. Lanum, J., The damaging effects of light on the retina. Empirical findings, theoretical and practical applications, *Surv. Ophthalmol.,* 22, 221, 1978.

94. Marshall, J., Grindle, C. F. J., Ansell, P. L., and Borwein, B., Convolution in human rods: an aging process, *Br. J. Ophthalmol.,* 63, 181, 1979.

95. Clark, B., Johnson, M. L., and Dreher, R., The effect of sunlight on dark adaptation, *Am. J. Ophthalmol.,* 29, 828, 1946.

96. Hecht, S., Hendley, C. D., Ross, H., and Richmond, P. N., The effect of exposure to sunlight on night vision, *Am. J. Ophthalmol.,* 31, 1573, 1948.

97. Penner, R. and McNair, J. N., Eclipse blindness, *Am. J. Ophthalmol.,* 61, 1452, 1966.

98. Dawson, W. W. and Herron, W. L., Retinal illumination during indirect ophthalmoscopy: subsequent dark adaptation, *Invest. Ophthalmol.,* 9, 89, 1970.

99. Ts'o, M. O. M., Fine, B. S., and Zimmerman, L. E., Photic maculopathy produced by the indirect ophthalmoscope. I. Clinical and histopathic study, *Am. J. Ophthalmol.,* 73, 686, 1972.

100. Ham, W. T., Jr., Muller, H. A., Williams, R. C., and Geeraets, W. J., Ocular hazards from viewing the sun unprotected and through various windows and filters, *Appl. Opt.,* 12, 21, 1973.

101. Persad, S., Menon, A., and Haberman, H. F., Comparison of the effects of UV visible irradiation of melanins and melanin-hematoporphyrin complexes from human black and red hair, *Photochem. Photobiol.,* 37, 63, 1983.

102. Ham, W. T. and Mueller, H. A., Retinal sensitivity to damage from short wavelength light, *Nature (London),* 260, 153, 1976.

103. Ham, W. T., Ruffolo, J. R., Jr., Mueller, H. A., Clark, A. M., and Moon, M. E., Histologic analysis of photochemical lesions produced in rhesus retina by short-wavelength light, *Invest. Ophthalmol. Vis. Sci.,* 17, 1029, 1978.

104. Ham, W. T., Mueller, H. A., Ruffolo, J. R., Jr., Clarke, A. M., Sensitivity of the retina to radiation damage as a function of wavelength, *Photochem. Photobiol.,* 29, 735, 1979.

105. Kuwabara, T., Retinal recovery from exposure to light, *Am. J. Ophthalmol.,* 70, 187, 1970.
106. Lawwill, T., Three major pathologic processes caused by light in the primate retina: a search for mechanisms, *Trans. Am. Ophthalmol. Soc.,* 80, 517, 1982.
107. Noell, W. K., Walker, V. S., Kang, B. S., and Berman, S., Retinal damage by light in rats, *Invest. Ophthalmol.,* 5, 450, 1966.
108. Pomerantzeff, P., Govignon, J., and Schapens, C. L., Indirect ophthalmoscopy: is the illumination level dangerous?, *Trans. Am. Acad. Ophthalmol. Otolaryngol.,* 73, 246, 1961.
109. Sliney, D. H., The ambient light environment and ocular hazards, *Adv. Exp. Med. Biol.,* 77, 211, 1977.
110. Sliney, D. H., Biohazards of ultraviolet, visible and infrared radiation, *J. Occup. Med.,* 25, 203, 1983.
111. Baer, R. L. and Harber, L. C., Photosensitivity induced by drugs, *JAMA,* 192, 989, 1965.
112. Gallo, U. and Santa Maria, L., Eds., *Research Progress in Organic, Biological and Medicinal Chemistry,* Vol. 3, North-Holland, Amsterdam, 1972.
113. Meier-Ruge, W., Drug induced retinopathy, *CRC Crit. Rev. Toxicol.,* 352, 1972.
114. Grant, W. M., *Toxicology of the Eye,* Charles C Thomas, Springfield, Ill., 1974.
115. Hanna, C. and Fraunfelder, F. T., Drugs and toxins, in *Pathobiology of Ocular Disease: A Dynamic Approach,* Garner, A. and Klintworth, G. T., Eds., Marcel Dekker, New York, 1982, 1125.
116. Fraunfelder, F. T., *Drug-Induced Ocular Side Effects and Drug Interactions,* Lea & Febiger, Philadelphia, 1982.
117. Parrish, J. A., Fitzpatrick, T. B., Shea, C., and Pathak, M. A., Photochemotherapy of vitiligo. Use of orally administered psoralens and a high intensity longwave ultraviolet light (UV-A) system, *Arch. Dermatol.,* 112, 1531. 1976.
118. Cloud, T. M., Hakim, R., and Griffin, A. C., Photosensitization of the eye with methoxalen. I. Acute effect, *Arch. Ophthalmol.,* 64, 346, 1960.
119. Cloud, T. M., Hakim, R., and Griffin, A. C., Photosensitization of the eye with methoxsalen. II. Chronic effects, *Arch. Ophthalmol.,* 66, 689, 1961.
120. Freeman, R. G. and Troll, D., Photosensitization of the eye by 8-methoxypsoralen, *J. Invest. Dermatol.,* 53, 449, 1969.
121. Crylin, M. N., Pedvis-Leftick, A., and Sugar, J., Cataract formation in association with ultraviolet photosensitivity, *Ann. Ophthalmol.,* 12, 786, 1980.
122. Lerman, S., Megaw, J., Gardner, K., Takei, Y., and Willis, I., Localization of 8-methoxypsoralen in ocular tissues, *Ophthal. Res.,* 13, 106, 1981.
123. Wulf, H. C. and Andreasen, M. P., Distribution of ³H-8-MOP and its metabolites in rat organs after a single oral administration, *J. Invest. Dermatol.,* 76, 252, 1981.
124. Wulf, H. C. and Andreasen, M. P., Concentration of ³H-8-methoxypsoralen and its metabolites in the rat lens and eye after a single oral administration, *Invest. Ophthalmol. Vis. Sci.,* 22, 32, 1982.
125. Lerman, S., Psoralens and ocular effects in animals and man: in vivo monitoring of human ocular and cutaneous manifestations, in Photochemotherapeutic Aspects of Psoralens, Monogr. no. 66, National Cancer Institute, Bethesda, Md., 1984, 227.
126. Lerman, S., Megaw, J., and Gardner, K., P-UVA therapy and human cataractogenesis, *Invest. Ophthalmol. Vis. Sci.,* 23, 801, 1982.
127. Lerman, S., Takei, Y., Franks, Y., Megaw, J., Gardner, K., and Gammon, A., Photobinding of ³H-8-Methoxypsoralen to monkey intraocular tissues, *Invest. Ophthalmol. Vis. Sci.,* 25, 1267, 1984.
128. Lerman, S., Psoralens and ocular effects in animals and man: in vivo monitoring of human ocular and cutaneous manifestations, in Photochemotherapeutic Aspects of Psoralens, Monogr. no. 66, National Cancer Institute, Bethesda, Md., 1984, 227.
129. Dayhow-Barker, P. and Barker, F. M., II, Retinal effects of short term exposure to 8-MOP and UV-A, *Photochem. Photobiol.,* Suppl. 37, 283, 1983.
130. Dayhaw-Barker, P., Barker, F. M., II, and Diebert, K., Effects of three drugs on the retinal threshold to damage, *Am. J. Opt. Phys. Opt.,* 59, 10, 1982.
131. Potts, A. and Gonasum, L. M., Toxicology of the eye, in *Toxicology,* Casarett, J. J. and Doull, J., Eds., Macmillan, New York, 1975, 275.
132. Fraunfelder, F. T., Hanna, C., Dreis, M. W., and Cogrove, K. W., Possible lens changes associated with allopurinol therapy, *Am. J. Ophthalmol.,* 94, 137, 1982.
133. Lerman, S., Megaw, J., and Gardner, K., Allopurinol therapy and human cataractogenesis, *Am. J. Ophthalmol.,* 94, 141, 1982.
134. Lerman, S., Megaw, J., and Fraunfelder, F., Further studies on allopurinol and human cataractogenesis, *Am. J. Ophthalmol.,* 97, 205, 1984.
135. Krejci, L., Brettschneider, I., and Triska, J., Tetracycline hydrochloride and lens changes, *Ophthal. Res.,* 10, 30, 1978.
136. Zunino, F., Gambetts, R., and DiMarco, A., Interaction of daunomycin and its derivatives with DNA, *Biochim. Biophys. Acta,* 277, 489, 1972.

137. Berlin, V. and Haseltine, W. A., Reduction of adriamycin to a semiquione free radical by cytochrome P-450 reductase produces DNA cleavage in reaction modulated by molecular oxygen, *J. Biol. Chem.*, 256, 4747, 1981.
138. Dayhaw-Barker, P., Forbes, D., Fox, D., Lerman, S., Metgaw, S., McGinniss, J., Waxler, M., and Felten, R., Drug phototoxicity and visual health, in Long Term Visual Health Risks of Optical Radiation, U.S. Food and Drug Administration Symp., Bethesda, Md., September 24 to 27, 1983.
139. Roberts, J. E., The photodynamic effect of chlorpromazine, promazine and hematoporphrin on lens protein, *Invest. Ophthalmol. Vis. Sci.*, 25, 748, 1984.
140. Thomas, J. R., III, and Doyle, J. A., The therapeutic uses of topical vitamin A acid, *J. Am. Acad. Dermatol.*, 4, 505, 1981.
141. Ward, A., Brogden, R. N., Heel, R. C., Speight, T. M., and Avery, G. S., Etretinate, a review of its pharmacological properties and therapeutic efficacy in psoriasis and other skin disorders, *Drugs*, 26, 9, 1983.
142. Shalita, A. R., Cunningham, W. J., Leyden, J. J., Pochi, P. E., and Strauss, J. S., Isotretinoin treatment of acne and related disorders: an update, *J. Am. Acad. Dermatol.*, 9, 629, 1983.
143. Sommer, A., Treatment of corneal xerophthalmia with topical retinoic acid, *Am. J. Ophthalmol.*, 95, 349, 1983.
144. Hatchell, D. L., Faculjak, M., and Kubicek, D., Treatment of xerophthalmia with retinol, tretinoin, and etretinate, *Arch. Ophthalmol.*, 102, 926, 1984.
145. Weiss, J., Degnan, M., Leupold, R., and Lumpkin, L. R., Bilateral corneal opacities: occurrence in a patient treated with oral isotretinoin, *Arch. Dermatol.*, 117, 182, 1981.
146. Lerman, S. and Hockwin, O., UV-visible slit lamp densitography of the human eye, *Exp. Eye Res.*, 33, 587, 1981.
147. Lerman, S., Dragomirescu, V., and Hockwin, O., In vivo monitoring of direct and photosensitized UV radiation damage to the lens, *Acta 24th Int. Congr. Ophthalmol.*, 1, 354, 1983.
148. Dragomirescu, V., Hockwin, O., and Koch, H. R., Development of a new equipment for rotating slit image photography according to Scheimpflug's principle, in *Interdisciplinary Topics in Gerontology*, Vol. 13, S. Karger, Basel, 1978, 118.
149. Dragomirescu, V., Hockwin, O., and Koch, H. R., Photo-cell device for slit-beam adjustment to the optical axis of the eye in Scheimpflug photography, *Ophthal. Res.*, 12, 78, 1980.
150. Weiss, J. N., Rand, L. I., Gleason, R. E., and Soeldner, J. S., Laser light scattering spectroscopy of in vivo human lenses, *Invest. Ophthalmol. Vis. Sci.*, 25, 594, 1984.
151. Nishio, I., Weiss, J. N., Tanaka, T., et al., Early detection of in vivo cataractogenesis using laser light scattering spectroscopy, *Curr. Eye Res.*, in press.
152. Schleich, T., Matson, G. B., Acosta, G. et al., Surface coil ^{31}P NMR studies of the intact eye, *Exp. Eye Res.*, in press.
153. Schleich, T., Willis, G. A., and Matson, G. V., Longitudinal (T_1) relaxation times of the phosphorous metabolites in the bovine and rabbit lens, *Exp. Eye Res.*, 39, 455, 1984.
154. Lerman, S., Moran, M., and Megaw, J., The UV and acrylamide effect on the human lens, *Lens Res.*, in press.
155. Lerman, S., Megaw, J. M., and Moran, M. N., Further studies on the effects of UV radiation on the human lens, *Ophthal. Res.*, in press.
156. Schleich, T. and Willis, J. A., The effect of ultraviolet-A and visible light irradiation and the phosphorus metabolite levels of the rabbit lens in organ culture, *Lens Res.*, in press.
157. Gonzalez, R. G., Willis, J., Aguayo, J., Campbell, P., Chylack, L. T., Jr., and Schleich, T., ^{13}C-nuclear magnetic resonance studies of sugar cataractogenesis in the single intact rabbit lens, *Invest. Ophthalmol. Vis. Sci.*, 22, 808, 1982.
158. Lerman, S., Megaw, J., Gardner, K., Long, R., Ashley, D., and Goldstein, J. H., NMR analysis of the cold cataract: whole lens studies, *Invest. Ophthalmol. Vis. Sci.*, 23, 218, 1982.
159. Lerman, S., Megaw, J., Gardner, K., Ashley, D., Long, R., and Goldstein, J. H., NMR analyses of the cold cataract. II. Studies on protein solutions, *Invest. Ophthalmol. Vis. Sci.*, 24, 99, 1983.
160. Lerman, S. and Megaw, J., Transmission characteristics of commercially available sunglasses, *J. Ocular Cutaneous Toxicol.*, 2, 47, 1983.
161. Anderson, W. J. and Grabel, R. K. H., Ultraviolet windows in commercial sunglasses, *Appl. Opt.*, 16, 515, 1977.
162. Anon., An evaluation of radiation emission from video display terminals, in *Radiological Health*, Food and Drug Administration, U.S. Department of Health and Human Services, Washington, D.C., 1981.
163. Weiss, M. M. and Peterson, R. C., Electromagnetic radiation emitted from video computer terminals, Bell Telephone Laboratories, Inc., *Am. Ind. Hyg. Assoc. J.*, 40, 300, 1979.
164. Anon., Potential Health Hazards of Video Display Terminals, NIOSH Res. Rep. Publ. No. 81-129, National Institute for Occupational Safety and Health, U.S. Department of Health and Human Services, Washington, D.C., 1981.

165. Ulrich, O. A. and Evans, R. M., Ultraviolet reflectance of paints, American Welding Society Report, August 6, 1976.

Chapter 6

PHOTOIMMUNOLOGY

Warwick L. Morison

TABLE OF CONTENTS

I. INTRODUCTION

Photoimmunology is an old field of investigation with a new name. The first suggestions that nonionizing radiation might affect immune function were made early in the 20th century. Dermatologists were recognizing various types of photosensitivity and hypothesizing on the pathogenesis of these disorders. Solar urticaria, photoallergy, and lupus erythematosus (LE) were conditions produced or exacerbated by exposure to sunlight and in which a disturbance of immune function was considered central to the pathogenesis. Therefore, some interaction between sunlight and the immune system was thought to be involved in the development of these diseases. For two reasons it is not surprising that sunlight-induced immunologic effects were considered many years ago. First, it is obvious that sunlight penetrates deeply into the body. Any person who has held a flashlight in the palm of the hand and observed red light coming through the back of the hand is aware that nonionizing radiation penetrates to a considerable depth. More energetic UV radiation is less penetrating but still reaches the dermis and subcutaneous tissue. Second, it has long been known that the immune system is represented in skin in blood vessels and tissue spaces. Thus, the target was present within range of a known toxin, sunlight.

The name photoimmunology crept, or some people might say leapt, into usage about 10 years ago and is now generally used to encompass all phenomena involving interactions between nonionizing radiation and the immune system. Introduction of the name coincided with greatly increased interest in the field, which was the result of three stimuli. First, it was discovered that UV radiation, besides causing neoplastic transformation of cells in mice, also produced very specific alterations of immune function which played an integral role in photocarcinogenesis. This finding has revolutionized our approach to the pathogenesis of nonmelanoma skin cancer and has provided a focus for much of the recent investigation in photoimmunology. It also has resulted in much new information about immunosurveillance of cancer and has led to the use of UV radiation as a tool for unraveling immunoregulatory pathways in the mouse. The second stimulus for photoimmunology came from clinical observations. About 10 years ago a new treatment for certain skin diseases, in particular psoriasis, was introduced which involved oral ingestion of a photosensitizer called methoxsalen and subsequent exposure to UVA (320 to 400 nm) radiation, now usually referred to by the acronym PUVA therapy. It was soon found that this treatment was effective in a wide variety of skin diseases which appeared to be related only in possibly having an immunologic pathogenesis, and this suggested that PUVA therapy might be effective via a photoimmunologic mechanism. Much study of the effects of PUVA treatment on the immune system in humans and experimental animals ensued and this has in many ways meshed with studies of photocarcinogenesis, particularly since PUVA treatment appears to be carcinogenic in humans. Finally, the third stimulus to research in photoimmunology came from the greatly increased understanding of the skin as an immune organ. The demonstration that Langerhans cells have antigen-presenting (AP) cell function, that keratinocytes produce substances capable of modifying the function of lymphocytes, and that a population of lymphocytes is closely associated with the skin has revolutionized our approach to the integument. Obviously, since the skin is constantly bathed with nonionizing radiation, this has provided a great stimulus to photoimmunology.

Several motivations have prompted studies in photoimmunology. Some people have approached directly questions of how and why nonionizing radiation affects the immune system. An example of this approach is the study of interactions between UV radiation and immunity in photocarcinogenesis. Other people have used UV radiation as a tool for investigating immune function. An example of this approach is the early studies of the effects of UV radiation on Langerhans cells. Most recently, UV radiation has been used as a tool for deliberately manipulating immune function for possible therapeutic benefit. An example of this is the irradiation of islets of Langerhans prior to transplantation across a histocompatibility barrier in the treatment of experimental diabetes. One or two successes in this direction will probably provide a further stimulus for studies in photoimmunology.

II. EXPERIMENTAL STUDIES IN ANIMALS

Investigation of the effects of nonionizing radiation on immune function in animals has been confined largely to a narrow focus. Most work has concentrated on a few immune responses, in particular contact hypersensitivity (CHS) and rejection of UV-induced tumors. In addition, the fluorescent sunlamp bulb has been the source of radiation in most studies. By convention, radiation from this source is referred to as UVB (280 to 320 nm) radiation but its emission spectrum is continuous from the UVC (mainly 254-nm) region through the UVB region and includes much UVA radiation. It is important to remember that sunlight at the surface of the earth does not contain radiation shorter than 295 nm and is rich in UVA, visible, and IR radiation. Obviously the term "sunlamp bulb" is a misnomer.

A. Contact Hypersensitivity (CHS)

CHS is a term used to refer to an immune response in animals that is analogous to contact allergy or allergic contact dermatitis in humans; poison ivy dermatitis is probably the most common example. The response follows topical application to the skin of a chemical, called a hapten or contact sensitizer, which then binds to a protein or cell in the skin, called a carrier, to form the complete antigen. AP cells in the skin process the antigen and aid in stimulating the proliferation of T lymphocytes specifically sensitized to the antigen. Langerhans cells are a population of dendritic cells in the epidermis which act as AP cells, but there appear to be other populations of cells that also perform this function. These steps are the afferent limbs of the immune response and result in generation of a population of circulating, sensitized, long-lived T lymphocytes. This process takes 5 to 10 days. The state of sensitivity to the specific antigen can be adoptively transferred to another animal by injection of T lymphocytes from the sensitized animal. The efferent limb of the response is its expression in the skin upon further contact with the antigen and involves an influx of macrophages and T lymphocytes. In humans, the response is manifest as eczema while in animals the main features are swelling or edema of the skin with or without erythema, crusting, and scaling. The response reaches a peak 24 to 48 hr or later after exposure to the antigen.

Exposure of animals to UVB radiation suppresses the development of CHS, with two types of suppression being observed. So-called local suppression occurs when the sensitizing dose of hapten is applied to skin at the site of exposure to radiation. The suppression is called systemic when the sensitizing dose of hapten is applied to nonirradiated skin. In fact, both types of suppression are associated with the generation of circulating suppressor T lymphocytes that can be adoptively transferred, and therefore both can be systemic phenomena. However, the distinction between the two effects is important because the mechanisms leading to the generation of suppressor cells are probably quite different.

1. Local Suppression of CHS
Suppression of CHS in irradiated skin was first reported by Haniszko and Suskind[1]

FIGURE 1.   System for demonstrating local suppression of CHS by UV radiation in the mouse.

when they found that 14 daily exposures to UVB radiation suppressed the response to dinitrochlorobenzene (DNCB) in guinea pigs. The suppression was similar when the irradiation was given 2 weeks pre- or post-sensitization, which indicates that the effect was mediated on both the induction and elicitation phases of CHS. In a few subsequent studies, all in outbred guinea pigs, PUVA,[2] UVB,[3,4] and UVC[5] radiation have been found to suppress the elicitation of CHS in previously sensitized animals, but the mechanism of this effect is unknown. All other studies have focused on suppression of the induction of CHS.

Interest in local suppression of CHS by UV radiation was reawakened by studies of the function of epidermal Langerhans cells. Toews et al.[6] found that elimination of Langerhans cells in mice by exposure to UVB radiation was associated with suppression of CHS, which supported their hypothesis of Langerhans cells being an essential element in the development of this immune response. This local effect, in which the site of sensitization and irradiation are the same but the site of elicitation is not irradiated (Figure 1), requires only a low dose of UVB radiation. The site of elicitation is the ear and the response is evaluated by measuring specific swelling of the ear 24 hr after application of the hapten. The suppression is hapten-specific and is associated with the generation of hapten-specific Lyt-1[+] T cells that suppress the induction phase of the immune response.[7] Local suppression of CHS cannot be induced in all strains of mice that have been tested, but recently Glass et al.[8] found that suppressor cells are present in all strains, including those that do not exhibit suppression of CHS. Presumably, a positive immunoregulatory pathway is activated in nonsuppressible strains that overrides the tolerogenic signal elicited by UVB radiation. Local suppression of CHS by UV radiation is not restricted to mice; the phenomenon also occurs in hamsters following exposure to UVB radiation[9] and in guinea pigs following treatment with PUVA.[10] In both instances, there is some evidence that, as in the mouse, the suppression is active and associated with suppressor cells.

Several UV-induced alterations of cutaneous immune function have been identified and linked to the mechanism of local suppression of CHS. Initially, it was thought that UV-induced changes in the function of Langerhans cells might be the key to suppression of CHS. Langerhans cells are very sensitive to damage by UV radiation, and the AP cell function of the epidermis is impaired after exposure to this wave band of radiation.[11-13] However, although alterations in Langerhans cells are probably involved in local suppression of CHS, changes in other cells also play a role. Recent studies have shown that several other components of the epidermis are involved in immune function and are altered by exposure to radiation, and these alterations are possibly important in the mechanism of local suppression of CHS.

The findings of Granstein et al.[14] suggest that the UV-induced alteration of AP cell function may not involve a simple loss of function, but rather that it may involve an active process. Functional studies revealed that a UV-resistant population of I-J[+] AP cells in the epidermis is active in the generation of suppressor-cell pathways that lead to suppression of CHS rather than help after exposure to UV radiation. The I-J[+] cell has not been identified morphologically, and it may be a Langerhans cell or another

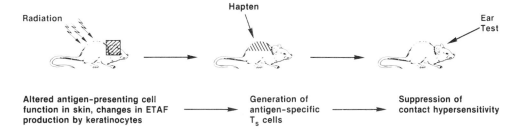

FIGURE 2.   Proposed mechanism of UV-induced local suppression of CHS in the mouse.

type of cell. Thus, it can be hypothesized that normal immunologic balance is disturbed after exposure to UV radiation because one population of AP cells, responsible for generation of helper cells, is UV-sensitive while a second population, responsible for generation of suppressor cells, is UV-resistant.

UV-induced changes in the function of keratinocytes may also be involved in local suppression of CHS. Keratinocytes produce epidermal cell-derived thymocyte-activating factor (ETAF),[15] which is functionally and biochemically very similar to interleukin-1 (IL-1), a nonspecific helper factor necessary for activation of T cells by antigen. Sauder et al.[16] found that epidermal cells from mice that had been exposed to monochromatic 270-nm radiation were defective in stimulating allogeneic T cells in vitro and that this defect could be partially corrected by the addition of ETAF. This finding was supported by in vitro studies in which a UV-induced impairment of AP cell function was partially restored by addition of IL-1[17,18] or partially purified ETAF.[19] Furthermore, Stingl et al.[19] found that after exposure to UV radiation, the time course for development of the AP cell defect in vitro matched the time course of reduction in ETAF production by epidermal cells. However, in two studies,[20,21] exposure of epidermal cells to broadband UV radiation from sunlamp bulbs either in vitro or in vivo resulted in increased production of ETAF. Differences in the radiation sources, the doses administered, and the model systems probably explain the discrepancies between the results of these studies. In either case, an alteration in ETAF production might be a key factor in UV-induced immunosuppression.

Finally, a population of dendritic cells in murine epidermis has been recently identified. These cells are Thy-1[+], are derived from bone marrow, and are distinct from Langerhans cells.[22,23] A preliminary study[24] found that these dendritic cells were morphologically altered by PUVA treatment, but their sensitivity to UVB radiation is unknown. The role of these cells in immune function and its suppression by UV radiation has not been determined.

In summary (Figure 2), the mechanism of local suppression of CHS in the mouse involves an alteration in AP cell function in the skin at the site of exposure to radiation. This altered function might be due to UV-induced damage to one cell population, possibly Langerhans cells, but may also involve defective function of another AP cell population and of keratinocytes. In either case, the result is preferential activation of a suppressor-cell pathway so that there is diminution of the normal immune response to the particular antigen.

2. Systemic Suppression of CHS

UVB radiation also produces suppression of the development of CHS to chemicals subsequently applied to nonirradiated areas of skin. In this model, illustrated in the mouse in Figure 3, the sites of sensitization and elicitation are both on skin that has not been exposed to radiation. Systemic suppression requires a much higher exposure

FIGURE 3.   System for demonstrating systemic suppression of CHS by UV radiation in the mouse.

dose of radiation for its induction as compared with local suppression. The phenomenon was first described in the mouse,[25,26] but it has also been observed recently in inbred guinea pigs.[27] In both species, the mechanism involves the generation of hapten-specific T lymphocytes which suppress the induction, but not the elicitation, of CHS. In the mouse, the phenotype of the T lymphocytes is Lyt-1$^+$2$^-$.[28]

Apart from UVB radiation, other wave bands can also affect CHS. PUVA treatment and sunlight produce suppression of CHS in mice and guinea pigs which is associated with generation of suppressor cells.[27,29,30] Large doses of visible radiation produce a small but consistent degree of suppression of CHS, while large doses of UVA radiation produce some enhancement of this immune response;[30] the mechanisms of these effects are unknown.

Attempts have been made to identify the chromophore molecule that absorbs radiation and leads to suppression of CHS. Urocanic acid is one candidate. In support of this possibility, DeFabo and Noonan[31] have presented evidence that the chromophore is superficially located in the epidermis, as is urocanic acid, and can be removed by stripping the epidermis with cellophane tape. They have also determined that wavelengths in the 260- to 270-nm region, which are within the absorption spectrum of urocanic acid, are most effective in producing systemic suppression of CHS. These findings would be strengthened by direct measurements of levels of urocanic acid to show that it has been removed from tape-stripped skin and followed by the demonstration that urocanic acid applied to the skin restores susceptibility to UV-induced suppression. In a recent study Morison and co-workers found in a different strain of mice that tape stripping did remove most of the urocanic acid from skin, but it did not abolish UV-induced suppression of CHS. Tape stripping itself produces much nonspecific immunosuppression which tends to make interpretation of data very difficult. Another candidate as the chromophore molecule is DNA. Its absorption spectrum also includes the relevant wavelengths. Furthermore, physicochemical agents that interact with DNA produce systemic suppression of CHS that resembles UVB-induced suppression in that it can be adoptively transferred to normal animals by injection of lymphoid cells obtained from suppressed animals.[32] Agents tested and found to have this ability include methoxsalen/UVA, 5-methyl isopsoralen/UVA, and superficial X-ray. In contrast, phototoxic treatments such as eosin/visible light and rose bengal/visible light that do not produce lesions in DNA also do not produce suppression of CHS that can be adoptively transferred. Of course, it is possible that DNA is involved in the pathway to suppression but is not the chromophore molecule.

There has been much interest in how UVB radiation causes systemic suppression of CHS. A first step in understanding the mechanism was the finding that exposure of mice to UVB radiation produces a defect in AP activity of splenic adherent cells and fewer Ia positive cells can be recovered from the spleens of these mice.[33,34] Furthermore, the impaired reactivity in these mice can be overcome by immunization of the irradiated animals with hapten coupled to normal AP cells.[26,33,35] These studies were interpreted to indicate that the UV-induced impairment of AP cell activity in the spleen was a central step in the suppression of CHS, and it was suggested that the splenic defect led to activation of a T suppressor cell pathway.[35] This may be true, but it is important to note that the immune response restored by immunization with hapten-coupled normal AP cells was delayed hypersensitivity and not CHS. The mechanisms of suppression of these two responses by UV radiation might be quite different, as will be discussed later. Suffice it to say that a defect of AP cell function is present in the spleens of irradiated mice and this defect might be causally related to the suppression of CHS.

The mechanism whereby absorption of radiation by skin leads to a systemic AP cell defect is unknown. One possible mechanism is that migration of damaged Langerhans cells from the irradiated skin to internal organs might give rise to the AP cell defect in the spleen and elsewhere. This possibility has been explored by asking whether alterations in Langerhans cells are essential for systemic suppression of CHS by UV radiation. Several pieces of evidence indicate that the answer is no. First, Langerhans cells are normal at the unirradiated sites of sensitization and challenge with hapten.[36-38] Second, elimination of Langerhans cells with high doses of UVA radiation is not associated with suppression of CHS and does not prevent the development of UVB-induced suppression.[38] Third, UV-induced suppression can be produced by doses of radiation of certain wavelengths that do not alter Langerhans cells.[36] Therefore, although migration of damaged Langerhans cells might occur after exposure to UV radiation, this is probably not an essential step in systemic suppression of CHS.

Circulating monocytes might be directly damaged by UVB radiation as they pass through cutaneous capillaries and then lodge in the spleen to give rise to the AP cell defect in that organ. This hypothesis has been tested by supplying alternative sources of precursors of splenic AP cells. UVB-irradiated mice were given exogenous bone marrow cells, spleen fragments, and splenic adherent cells in attempts to reconstitute the AP cell defect but none of these procedures restored normal CHS.[39] Furthermore, immunization of UVB-irradiated mice with hapten-coupled splenic adherent cells also failed to restore CHS.

A third possible mechanism could involve an alteration of cell trafficking that results in the AP cell defect and, through that, the systemic suppression of CHS. There is some evidence that lymphocyte trafficking is perturbed in UV-irradiated animals and that lymphocytes migrate preferentially to regional lymph nodes.[35,40] In contrast, treatment of lymphoid cells with UV radiation in vitro reduces their tendency to localize in lymph nodes after injection into normal animals.[40,41] An extension of this hypothesis is that the splenic AP cell defect is due to passive accumulation of inflammatory cells in the skin. The main points against this concept are that the splenic defect cannot be reconstituted by alternative sources of cells, and nonspecific trauma to the skin, which causes an influx of inflammatory cells, does not produce a specific suppression of CHS.[39]

Finally, factors may be released from irradiated skin and circulate to produce the AP cell defect and systemic suppression of CHS. A recent study suggests that this may occur. Serum obtained from mice 3 hr after exposure to UVB radiation produced suppression of the development of CHS in recipient mice that was associated with the generation of suppressor cells.[42] The factor in serum that produces this effect has not yet been identified, but certain of its properties indicate that it is not one of the known mediators of inflammation. This is supported by recent studies in which we have found that maximally tolerated doses of inhibitors of various mediators of inflammation are without effect on the suppression of CHS by UVB radiation. Inhibitors of histamine, serotonin, prostaglandins, and the leukotrienes had no effect, and complement-deficient animals exhibited suppression. In addition, corticosteroids did not inhibit the suppression. Gahring et al.[21] used a different approach and found that elevation of the level of ETAF/IL-1 activity in serum of UV-irradiated mice correlated with elevation

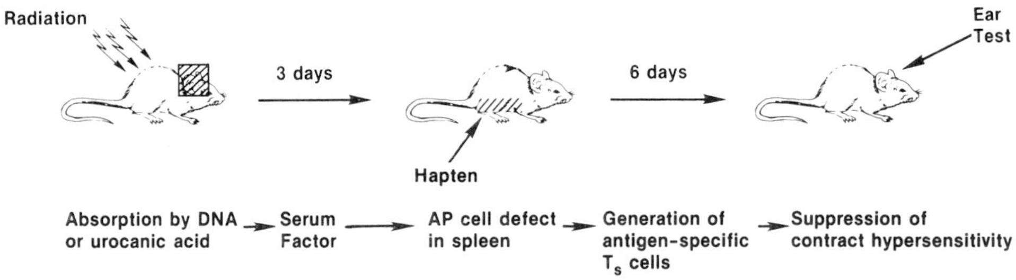

FIGURE 4.   Proposed mechanism of UV-induced systemic suppression of CHS in the mouse.

of the levels of the acute-phase reactants, amyloid, complement, and fibrinogen after a single exposure to radiation. However, after multiple exposures, the serum concentrations of acute-phase reactants were not elevated, despite sustained elevation of the serum level of ETAF/IL-1 activity. The authors suggest that these changes might at least partially explain UV-induced immunosuppression: the suppression after a single exposure could be mediated by acute-phase reactants and the suppression after multiple exposures could be due to lack of a necessary signal for effective immune function because of desensitization of target cells to the elevated levels of ETAF/IL-1. Somewhat at variance with these observations are those of Tominaga et al.[18] who found that UVB-induced systemic suppression of delayed hypersensitivity could be prevented by administration of IL-1.

In summary (see Figure 4), UVB radiation can produce systemic suppression of CHS in mice and guinea pigs and the suppression is due to generation of hapten-specific suppressor T lymphocytes. A defect of splenic AP cell function is associated with the suppression, but the mechanism by which this is produced is unknown. Furthermore, it is not known whether the two defects are interrelated. One possible scenario is that radiation is absorbed by a chromophore such as urocanic acid or DNA in skin, a mediator or photoproduct is released into the circulation and causes the AP cell defect in the spleen, and this results in preferential activation of a suppressor-cell pathway and consequent suppression of CHS.

B. Photocarcinogenesis

Much of the impetus for recent work in photoimmunology has come from observations of the role of the immune system in photocarcinogenesis. This interest began with the observation that tumors induced in mice by exposure to UV radiation have the unusual feature of being highly antigenic. Thus, when these tumors are transplanted in syngeneic, i.e., genetically identical, normal mice they fail to grow, but they do grow progressively in immunosuppressed mice (Figure 5).[43] Rejection of the tumors in normal mice is immunologic and mediated by T lymphocytes. This observation raised the obvious question of why such antigenic tumors were able to escape the normal immunologic surveillance mechanism and grow in the primary host. Investigation of the immune status of the primary host revealed susceptibility to growth of transplants of other UV-induced tumors but this defect was selective since most other immune responses in these animals were normal.[44-47] Furthermore, a subcarcinogenic dose of UV radiation was sufficient to produce susceptibility to the growth of transplanted UV-induced tumors, and this susceptibility only applied to UV-induced tumors since tumors produced by chemicals did not show accelerated growth in irradiated mice.[48]

Therefore, UV radiation in mice produces two alterations in the process of tumor development (Figure 6): (1) neoplastic transformation of cells in the skin, and (2) a specific, systemic, immunologic alteration which favors the growth of tumors. Subse-

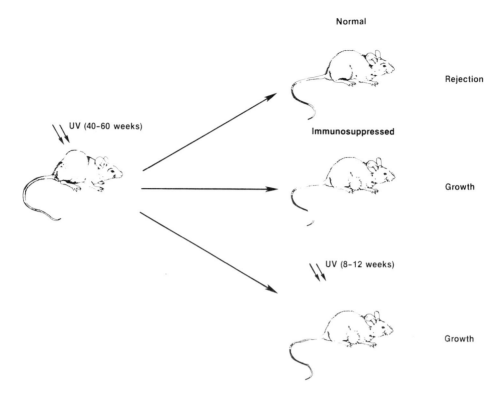

FIGURE 5. Transplantation and patterns of growth of UV-induced tumors in syngeneic mice.

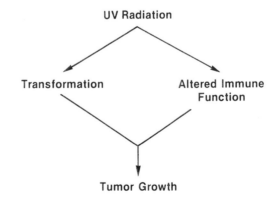

FIGURE 6. Mechanism of photocarcinogenesis in the mouse.

quent studies revealed that the immunologic alteration involved the generation of suppressor T lymphocytes which inhibit the rejection of UV-induced tumors.[49,50] The suppressor cells have the same phenotype as the CHS suppressor cells in that they are Lyt-1^+2^-, Ia$^-$.[28] The dose of radiation required to induce formation of the suppressor cells is much less than a carcinogenic dose, and they appear early in the development of neoplasia. The early and pivotal role of the suppressor cells was demonstrated by the finding that if suppressor cells are present at the time of commencement of irradiation, tumors appear earlier and in greater numbers.[51] This extended an observation that irradiation of one site markedly accelerated the induction of tumors by subsequent irradiation of another site.[52]

The stimulus for the formation of suppressor cells is unknown. However, presumably a putative tumor antigen appears on transformed cells and initiates the immune response. There is some evidence to support this concept. First, cells of the $10T_{1/2}$ mouse fibroblast line transformed in vitro by UV radiation are antigenically similar to those from skin cancers produced in vivo by UV radiation, and the transformed cells are recognized by UV-induced suppressor cells.[53] Second, UV-irradiated skin contains the elements necessary to induce a state of tumor susceptibility. Grafts of UV-irradiated skin measuring 5 × 2.5 cm transplanted onto normal mice induced tolerance to the growth of UV-induced tumors.[54] This observation suggests that the UV-associated antigen is present in skin at an early stage of neoplasia, but the possibility that the effect is due to the presence of passenger leukocytes in the grafted skin has not been excluded.

A further question is why the putative tumor antigen stimulates suppression and not help. Studies in the CHS system provide some clues to the answer. Exposure of mice to UV radiation alters antigen presentation in the skin so that an I-J$^+$ AP cell, which is resistant to damage, has a dominant influence and this I-J$^+$ cell preferentially activates a suppressor-cell pathway.[14] More direct evidence to support this concept comes from the finding that the function and/or development of tumor suppressor cells can be inhibited by administration of anti-I-J^k antibody.[55] Of course this finding is not only important for understanding the mechanism of neoplasia but also raises the possibility of specific therapy to prevent the development of skin cancer.

The FS40 sunlamp bulb has been the main source of radiation used in these studies of the immunobiology of skin cancer. Wavelengths between 275 and 315 nm from this source were most effective in producing suppression of tumor rejection.[56] Recently, sunlight has also been found effective in producing tumor susceptibility in mice.[57] The 295- to 320-nm wave band appears to be responsible for this effect of sunlight because it was prevented by filtering the radiation through Mylar® and by application of a sunscreen containing para-aminobenzoic acid.

Interestingly, PUVA-induced tumors in mice are not highly antigenic and do not show preferential growth in UVB-irradiated animals.[58] Furthermore, treatment of animals with PUVA does not prevent their normal immunologic rejection of UVB-induced tumors.[59]

C. Other Immune Responses

The finding that exposure of mice to UVB radiation suppressed the rejection of UV-induced tumors led to an investigation of other possible immunologic alterations in irradiated animals.

Delayed hypersensitivity to injected antigens is impaired in some circumstances. Both PUVA treatment and UVB radiation produce local and systemic impairment of delayed hypersensitivity to an injected antigen in the guinea pig.[60,61] UVB radiation also impairs delayed hypersensitivity in mice and this effect appears to involve the generation of antigen-specific T suppressor cells. However, the mechanism of this effect appears to be different from UV-induced suppression of CHS since it can be reconstituted with antigen-coupled, normal splenic adherent cells,[35] whereas these cells do not reconstitute suppression of CHS.[39]

The local graft vs. host reaction is also reduced in irradiated mice. There is less enlargement of the popliteal lymph node after injection of parental lymphocytes into the footpads of irradiated F_1 hybrid mice than occurs in unirradiated recipients.[45,62] This effect is due to a reduction in the host component of the reaction, possibly through diversion of cells from the site of the response, and there is no evidence that it involves activation of a suppressor-cell pathway.[62]

Allogeneic reactions are usually unaffected by UV radiation. Rejection of skin allografts in mice and rabbits is unaffected by UVB radiation,[45,63] although PUVA treatment of the donor and recipient sites produced some prolongation of allograft survival in rabbits.[63] Tumor allografts are rejected normally by irradiated mice,[44] and lymphocytes from such animals have normal cytotoxic responses against allogeneic cells in vitro.[46,47]

Obviously, further studies are required to fully define the effect of nonionizing radiation on various immune responses. The effect upon antibody responses and cell-mediated responses to microbial antigens are two areas awaiting study. However, with our present knowledge it is possible to say that the action of radiation is selective; only certain immune responses are affected while others are quite normal in the irradiated animal. Furthermore, it is becoming clear that the mechanisms by which UV radiation affects immune function are diverse, with formation of suppressor cells in some cases, alteration in the trafficking of cells in others, and selective cell killing in yet other cases. The selectivity and diversity of the effects of UV radiation may well have value for selective, targeted manipulation of immune function.

III. PHOTOIMMUNOLOGY IN HUMANS

Investigation of the effects of nonionizing radiation on immune function in humans has lagged far behind experimental studies in animals, but already enough is known to suggest that photoimmunology will be important in human health and disease. Only a few investigations have been designed to answer a specific question about the effects of radiation, and most studies have been directed toward determining the pathogenesis of various diseases. These two approaches will be discussed separately since they have quite different goals.

A. Experimental Studies
1. In Vivo Immune Responses
There are several reports of inhibition of contact allergy in humans by exposure to UV radiation. The response to DNCB was diminished in normal volunteers as compared with control subjects after daily exposures for 2 weeks in a solarium emitting mainly UVA but also a small amount of UVB radiation.[64] UVB radiation also delayed the development of contact allergy to mechlorethamine in patients being treated topically with this agent.[65,66] In these studies it is not possible to distinguish between an effect on the induction vs. the elicitation phase of the response. However, in several studies sunlight, UVB, or PUVA therapy inhibited the elicitation of contact allergy in previously sensitized subjects,[67-70] and in one study PUVA therapy possibly affected both induction and elicitation of contact allergy.[71]

The mechanism of suppression of contact allergy by UV radiation in humans is unknown, but since in all instances the effect has been detected locally at the site of exposure to radiation, it is reasonable to suspect it will be similar to the mechanism of local suppression in the mouse. Although the latter mechanism has not been completely defined, th early suggestion of a central involvement of Langerhans cells focused attention on the effect of UV radiation on these cells in humans. Langerhans cells are reduced in number in sun-damaged skin[72] following exposure to UVB and UVA radiation,[73,74] and after a course of PUVA therapy.[75-77] However, these cells are not completely eliminated by these treatments and a normal population is restored after a brief period of recovery. The relationship between the morphologic alteration in Langerhans cells and suppression of contact allergy has not been studied in humans.

2. Effect of UV Radiation on Lymphocytes
Alterations in the distribution and function of circulating lymphocytes can be detected after exposure to UV radiation. Two weeks of daily exposure in a solarium or

to sunlight produced a decrease in OKT8 suppressor/cytotoxic cells and of suppressor T-cell activity, and depression of natural killer-cell activity.[64,78] These changes were still evident in some subjects 2 weeks after completion of the exposures. A single whole-body exposure to UVB radiation or PUVA treatment also altered circulating lymphocytes with a decrease in identifiable T and B cells and an increase in null cells; these changes lasted less than 72 hr.[79,80] The mechanism of these changes is unknown, but possibly lymphocytes are damaged as they percolate through cutaneous capillaries and are then sequestered out of the circulation.

Apart from studies in normal subjects, there has also been much interest in the effect of radiation during treatment of various diseases of the skin. Lymphocytes from patients with psoriasis treated with PUVA therapy were found to have suppression of normal DNA synthesis[81] and some impairment of mitogen responses[82,83] early in the course of treatment, but after months of treatment, lymphocyte function was found to be normal.[84] Longer-term follow-up of patients who had been treated for years and who had evidence of aging of the skin as a result of treatment revealed a reduction of circulating helper/inducer T cells and impairment of the response of lymphocytes to mitogens.[85,86] Studies are required to determine if the patients with these changes are those most likely to develop skin cancer which can result from this treatment.

3. In Vitro Exposure of Lymphocytes to UV Radiation

In contrast to the paucity of literature on in vivo effects of radiation on immune function in humans, there are many studies of the effects on in vitro exposure of lymphocytes to various wave bands of radiation. Some of these effects are of more interest from a photobiologic rather than an immunologic viewpoint since they provide information about the relative toxicity of the various wave bands without indicating how this toxicity might be important in vivo. For example, when viability of lymphocytes or their response to a mitogen are tested after exposure, UVC is more toxic than UVB, which in turn is more toxic than UVA radiation, but the toxicity of UVA radiation is greatly increased by the addition of psoralen.[87-89]

In vitro treatment of lymphocytes with PUVA also inhibits the mixed-lymphocyte-culture reaction when either the stimulator or the responder cells are exposed,[90,91] and increases chromosomal aberrations and the frequency of sister-chromatid exchanges.[92,93] However, the frequency of sister-chromatid exchanges is not increased in lymphocytes obtained from patients during treatment.[94] The disparity between these findings after in vivo and in vitro exposure is probably due to the much higher exposure doses used in the in vitro model; this of course is one problem in the interpretation of most of the in vitro studies.

Although in vitro studies involving irradiation of human lymphocytes have not been very contributory to our understanding of photoimmunology, they could provide a good avenue for further studies. For example, development of in vitro correlates of in vivo immune responses is one way in which some of the limitations upon studies in humans can be overcome.

B. Nonmelanoma Skin Cancer

Demonstration of a central role of the immune system in the pathogenesis of non-melanoma skin cancer in mice has of course focused interest on whether sunlight-associated skin cancer in humans might involve similar immunologic alterations. At present the evidence is at best suggestive.

The strongest evidence for immune surveillance being important in human skin cancer is that the incidence of tumors on sun-exposed skin is greatly increased in renal transplant recipients treated with immunosuppressive drugs.[95-97] The incidence rises shortly after transplantation and reached 44% 9 years post-transplant in one study from a sunny climate.[98] Furthermore, the incidence appears to be dose-related and highest in patients exposed to most sunlight.[99] However, it must be noted that the drugs used in these patients have other effects apart from immunosuppression, and therefore this clinical observation is persuasive but by no means conclusive evidence of involvement of the immune system in the pathogenesis of skin cancer. Detection of human papillomavirus in skin cancers of an immunosuppressed renal transplant recipient raises the possibility that sunlight might be acting as a cofactor for the expression of viral oncogenesis in these patients.[100]

The number of circulating T lymphocytes and the degree of lymphocytic infiltration of nonmelanoma skin cancers were both found to be inversely proportional to the size of the tumor in one study.[101] These observations were interpreted as indicating that the extent of the immune response was important in determining the size of a tumor, but it is equally plausible that a reduced response is a consequence of the presence of a large tumor.

In another study, humoral and cell-mediated immunologic reactivity toward autologous tumor tissue was detected in most patients with squamous cell carcinoma that were tested.[102] The specificity and quantitation of the reactivity requires further study, but the results do suggest that human tumors are antigenic and can provoke an immunologic response.

A somewhat different approach was taken in a recent study which examined the ability of patients with xeroderma pigmentosum to develop contact allergy on sun-exposed skin.[103] The reasoning behind this study was that if immunologic abnormalities are important in human skin cancer then they should be most obvious in patients with the greatest susceptibility to the development of these tumors. It was found that in comparison to normal control subjects, most patients with xeroderma pigmentosum were grossly defective in their capacity to be sensitized to a common allergen, and the degree of this impairment was closely related to the severity of the cutaneous manifestations of the disease. These findings are consistent with the possibility that immunologic factors, presumably induced by exposure to sunlight, could be important in the development of skin cancer in these people. More direct evidence awaits the demonstration that human skin tumors are antigenic, that the patient does mount an immune response to the tumor, and that suppressor cells are important in blocking the expression of that response. A suitable in vitro model will be required for these studies.

C. Photosensitivity Disorders

Photoimmunology began with the investigation of several diseases which predominantly affect the skin and are characterized by photosensitivity. The term "photosensitivity" is used here in a clinical sense and may be defined as an altered reaction of the skin or other organs following exposure to nonionizing radiation. Immunologic mechanisms have been postulated to explain the pathogenesis of a number of these disorders, but strong evidence for this is only available in a few.

1. Solar Urticaria

Solar urticaria, which is simply the development of hives following exposure to sunlight, was the first photosensitivity disorder to be categorized as immunologic or "allergic" in nature. The suggestion arose because all types of hives were considered to have an immunologic pathogenesis. We now know that this is not true, and similarly, we now know that only some cases of solar urticaria have an immune basis. In other cases, although the pathogenesis is unknown, there is no evidence for an immune response. Solar urticaria usually develops in young adults without apparent cause and probably persists for life. Most clinicians consider it to be an uncommon disease, but it seems probable that it is fairly common in a mild form, so that most patients, instead of seeking medical advice, just avoid exposing themselves to the amount of sunlight which they know will trigger the problem.

The mechanism of development of solar urticaria in cases which have an immunologic basis appears to involve an antigen-antibody reaction in the skin at the site of exposure to sunlight. The putative antigen is a photoproduct and is either a molecule produced in normal skin or a molecule that is formed only in patients with solar urticaria. The nature of the antigen is unknown and the main evidence for an immune mechanism comes from serum-transfer tests. Two types of tests have been used in solar urticaria to study the nature of the reaction. The passive serum-transfer test is analogous to the Prausnitz-Kustner reaction in that the patient's serum is injected intradermally into a normal subject and the site is exposed to radiation within 24 hr. A positive response is indicated by an immediate wheal. In the reversed passive-transfer reaction, the serum is injected after exposure to radiation and a positive reaction eliminates the possibility of the response being due to a phototoxic agent in serum. When both tests are positive, the antigen presumably is a photoproduct formed in normal skin. In some patients, the passive-transfer test is positive but the reversed passive-transfer test is negative. A recent study of these patients found that a positive result in the reversed test was obtained when the patient's serum was irradiated, which suggests formation of a photoproduct that is unique to the patient.[104]

Certain properties of the serum factor, which is presumably an antibody, have been characterized: (1) it is thermolabile, (2) it progressively loses activity in a passively sensitized site after exposure to radiation, and (3) it retains reactivity in the sensitized site several days after injection.[105] These properties are consistent with the serum factor being an IgE reagenic antibody.

The mast cell is thought to be the target for the urticarial reaction and the source of mediators. Degranulation of mast cells has been observed after exposure to radiation.[106,107] The levels of histamine, eosinophil chemotactic factor, and neutrophil chemotactic factor are elevated in venous blood draining the site of the reaction.[106-108] These findings, combined with the results of serum-transfer tests, are all consistent with a pathogenesis for solar urticaria in which IgE antibody is bound to mast cells, exposure to radiation alters a component of skin to form an antigen, and mast cell degranulation and release of mediators is triggered by an antigen-antibody reaction on the cell surface.

2. Photoallergy

Photoallergy is a state of specifically altered reactivity toward an exogenous chemical in which photons play a role. Two types of photoallergy are recognized. Contact photoallergy follows epicutaneous application of a chemical and exposure to radiation, and the immunologic basis of this reaction is established. Systemic photoallergy involves oral or parenteral administration of the chemical, and there is no definite evidence that the pathogenesis of this disorder is immunologic; instead it is assumed to be immunologic by analogy to contact photoallergy.

The role of nonionizing radiation in contact photoallergy is in the formation of the antigen. The antigen is composed of a low molecular weight compound called a hapten which is conjugated to a carrier protein to form the complete antigen. There are three mechanisms by which radiation could be involved in production of the antigen: (1) formation of a photoproduct which then serves as the hapten, (2) photochemical conjugation of the photosensitizing compound to protein, and (3) photochemical alteration of a protein. Experimental evidence indicates that the first two mechanisms apply in different cases, but there is no evidence for the third mechanism being important.

Once the antigen has been formed, radiation plays no further part in the reaction.

The antigen triggers a cell-mediated immune response manifested as eczema and thus, apart from the early role of radiation, this immune response is very similar to ordinary contact allergy. The immunologic nature of the reaction has been established in guinea pigs[109] and mice[110-112] by adoptively transferring immune reactivity by injection of lymphoid cells from sensitized animals; the reaction is mediated by T lymphocytes. Contact photoallergy is much less common than ordinary contact allergy, and a recent study possibly has provided an explanation for the different frequencies of the reactions. To obtain a vigorous photoallergic response in mice, it is necessary to pretreat the animals with cyclophosphamide, and only a minimal response develops in the absence of this treatment. Granstein and co-workers[112] found considerable net splenic suppressor-cell activity in mice that were not pretreated with cyclophosphamide. Furthermore, these suppressor cells, which are antigen specific, inhibited the induction of the immune response. Thus, we may be protected from developing photoallergy to environmental agents by this immunoregulatory imbalance.

3. Lupus Erythematosus (LE)

Various diseases have been classified as autoimmune because responses to self-antigens appear to be involved in their pathogenesis. One of the most common of these diseases is LE which is a chronic inflammatory disease affecting multiple organs including skin. Photosensitivity is a feature of LE, and nonionizing radiation often precipitates or aggravates the disease. However, it is not clear whether this is a nonspecific effect of radiation or a specific effect due to a selective alteration of immune function.

LE is characterized by the appearance of a whole array of autoantibodies against individual constituents of cells, whole cells, and other proteins. The most important of these antibodies are directed against DNA and other nuclear constituents, and these appear to play a central role in the disease process. DNA is only weakly antigenic, but exposure to UV radiation results in the formation of a photoproduct, UV-DNA, which is antigenic and in animals stimulates the formation of antibodies that react with UV-DNA and native DNA.[113] UV-DNA is formed in vivo after exposure to UV radiation and it can be detected in skin[114] and serum.[115] When mice with high titers of anti-UV-DNA were exposed to UVC radiation, immunoglobulin and complement were deposited in the skin in a pattern similar to that seen in patients with LE,[116] suggesting that circulating antibody to UV-DNA may play a role in the pathogenesis of the skin lesions in LE. According to this theory, UV-DNA formed as a result of exposure to radiation is released from skin and immunizes the host, who then forms antibodies to UV-DNA. On subsequent exposure to radiation, the anti-UV-DNA reacts with the photoproduct in the skin, fixes complement, and gives rise to an inflammatory response. However, somewhat at variance with this theory is the finding that NZB mice, which spontaneously develop a disease resembling LE, do not show acceleration of the process when exposed to UV radiation.[117,118]

Antibodies to UV-DNA have been found in the serums of patients with LE.[119] These antibodies show immunologic specificity for UV-DNA and are distinct from antibodies that react with native DNA.[120] However, in the latter study, there was a poor correlation between the presence of antibodies to UV-DNA and a history of photosensitivity.

IV. THERAPEUTIC PHOTOIMMUNOLOGY

Photoimmunology is still very much in its infancy as a field of research, so at first glance it might appear premature to consider any practical applications, such as in therapy of disease. However, two considerations suggest this possibility might not be too far in the future. First, much interest in photoimmunology has resulted from the use of PUVA therapy in diseases thought to have an immunologic pathogenesis, and it is possible that we are already using an effect of nonionizing radiation on the immune system for therapeutic advantage. PUVA therapy for atopic eczema is one example.[121] Although the exact nature of the pathogenesis of this disorder has not been defined, there is good evidence to indicate that it does have an immunologic mechanism, and therefore it is quite possible the beneficial effect of PUVA therapy is due to suppression of an abnormal immune response. Second, the selectivity of the effects of nonionizing radiation on immune function is very striking. Studies in animals and other systems have shown that UV radiation selectively alters molecules, selectively changes the function of certain cells, and selectively suppresses only certain immune responses. Thus there is scope for selective manipulation of immune function for therapeutic advantage.

Two recent reports of the potential therapeutic value of UV-induced alterations of immunoregulatory pathways appear to take advantage of the selective sensitivity of Ia$^+$ dendritic cells to UV radiation. Lau et al.[122] have found that UV radiation could be of value in treating diabetes. Exposure of rat islets of Langerhans to UVB radiation in vitro prior to transplantation into diabetic rats across a major histocompatibility barrier resulted in prolonged survival of the grafts and a normoglycemic state in the recipients. The authors suggest that this effect was due to the inactivation by UV radiation of Ia$^+$ dendritic cells in the grafted islets, and that these dendritic cells are normally responsible for sensitization of the host and consequent rejection of the graft. In another study in rats, Glazier et al.[123] found that pretreatment of the host with UVB radiation prevented the development of graft vs. host (GVH) disease at the site of exposure to radiation after allogeneic bone marrow transplantation. There was evidence that this beneficial effect of UV radiation might be due to selective destruction of host Langerhans cells, which are Ia$^+$ dendritic cells in the epidermis. Another approach to cutaneous GVH is the use of PUVA therapy for established chronic disease.[124] Patients with the lichenoid type of disease respond to this treatment with a complete and apparently permanent remission. The mechanism of the effect appears to be elimination of the lymphoid cells that form the infiltrate in the dermis, and presumably these cells are responsible for the continuation of the disease process.

The potential therapeutic effects of UV radiation have also been studied in experimental allergic encephalomyelitis, an autoimmune disease in mice. This disease resembles multiple sclerosis in humans in that there is extensive demyelination in the CNS. T lymphocytes are an essential component of the pathophysiology of the condition. Hauser et al.[125] found that pretreatment with UVB radiation prevented the development of the disease, although such treatment had no effect on established disease. The mechanism of this effect is not clear; radiation did not induce suppressor cells that could be adoptively transferred. The authors suggest that a UV-induced alteration of AP cell function that is present in the mice might be involved in the mechanism.

These reports of successful manipulation of immune function by UV radiation for therapeutic effect are obviously preliminary, but they suggest considerable potential in the use of nonionizing radiation to selectively block immunological pathways that lead to certain diseases. The main hindrance to exploring this potential at present is our lack of understanding of both the pathophysiology of disease and the overall effects of nonionizing radiation on the immune system.

ACKNOWLEDGMENTS

This research was sponsored by the National Cancer Institute, U.S. Department of Health and Human Services, under contract No. N01-CO-23909 with Litton Bionetics, Inc. The contents of this publication do not necessarily reflect the views or policies of the Department of Health and Human Services, nor does mention of trade names, commercial products, or organizations imply endorsement by the U.S. Government.

REFERENCES

1. Haniszko, J. and Suskind, R. R., The effect of ultraviolet radiation on experimental cutaneous sensitization in guinea pigs, *J. Invest. Dermatol.*, 40, 83, 1963.
2. Morison, W. L., Parrish, J. A., Woehler, M. E., and Bloch, K. J., The influence of ultraviolet radiation on allergic contact dermatitis in the guinea-pig. II. Psoralen/UVA radiation, *Br. J. Dermatol.*, 104, 165, 1981.
3. Morison, W. L., Parrish, J. A., Woehler, M. E., and Bloch, K. J., The influence of ultraviolet radiation on allergic contact dermatitis in the guinea-pig. I. UVB radiation, *Br. J. Dermatol.*, 104, 161, 1981.
4. Austad, J., and Mork, N., Effects of short-wave ultraviolet light (UVB) on delayed hypersensitivity in the guinea pig, *Acta Derm. Venerol.*, 62, 133, 1982.
5. Austad, J. and Mork, N., Effects of short-wave ultraviolet radiation (UV-C) on delayed hypersensitivity in the guinea-pig, *Br. J. Dermatol.*, 108, 63, 1983.
6. Toews, G. B., Bergstresser, P. R., and Streilein, J. W., Epidermal Langerhans cell density determines whether contact hypersensitivity or unresponsiveness follows skin painting with DNFB, *J. Immunol.*, 124, 445, 1980.
7. Elmets, C. A., Bergstresser, P. R., Tigelaar, R. E., Wood, P. J., and Streilein, J. W., Analysis of the mechanism of unresponsiveness produced by haptens painted on skin exposed to low dose ultraviolet radiation, *J. Exp. Med.*, 158, 781, 1983.
8. Glass, M. J., Bergstresser, P. R., Tigelaar, R. E., and Streilein, J. W., *In vivo* low dose ultraviolet B (UVB) radiation universally induces contact hypersensitivity (CH) suppressor cells in mice, *J. Invest. Dermatol.*, 82, 397, 1984.
9. Streilein, J. W. and Bergstresser, P. R., Langerhans cell function dictates induction of contact hypersensitivity or unresponsiveness to DNFB in Syrian hamsters, *J. Invest. Dermatol.*, 77, 272, 1981.
10. Horio, T. and Okamoto, H., Immunologic unresponsiveness induced by topical application of hapten to PUVA-treated skin in guinea pigs, *J. Invest. Dermatol.*, 80, 90, 1983.
11. Stingl, G., Gazze-Stingl, A., Aberer, W., and Wolff, K., Antigen presentation by murine epidermal Langerhans cells and its alteration by ultraviolet B light, *J. Immunol.*, 127, 1707, 1981.
12. Perry, L. L. and Greene, M. I., Antigen presentation by epidermal Langerhans cells: loss of function following ultraviolet (UV) irradiation *in vivo*, *Clin. Immunol. Immunopathol.*, 24, 204, 1982.
13. Gurish, M. F., Lynch, D. H., Yowell, R., and Daynes, R. A., Abrogation of epidermal antigen-presenting cell function by ultraviolet radiation administered *in vivo*, *Transplantation*, 36, 304, 1983.
14. Granstein, R. D., Lowy, A., and Greene, M. I., Epidermal antigen-presenting cells in activation of suppression: identification of a new functional type of ultraviolet radiation-resistant epidermal cell, *J. Immunol.*, 132, 563, 1984.
15. Sauder, D. N., Carter, C. S., Katz, S. I., and Oppenheim, J. J., Epidermal cell production of thymocyte activating factor (ETAF), *J. Invest. Dermatol.*, 79, 34, 1982.
16. Sauder, D. N., Noonan, F. P., DeFabo, E. C., and Katz, S. I., Ultraviolet radiation inhibits alloantigen presentation by epidermal cells: partial reversal by the soluble epidermal cell product epidermal cell-derived thymocyte-activating factor (ETAF), *J. Invest. Dermatol.*, 80, 485, 1983.
17. Granstein, R. D., Tominaga, A., Mizel, S. B., Parrish, J. A., and Greene, M. I., Molecular signals in antigen presentation. II. Activation of cytolytic cells *in vitro* after ultraviolet radiation or combined gamma and ultraviolet radiation treatment of antigen-presenting cells, *J. Immunol.*, 132, 2210, 1984.
18. Tominaga, A., Lefort, S., Mizel, S. B., Dambrauskas, J. T., Granstein, R., Lowy, A., Benacerraf, B., and Greene, M. I., Molecular signals in antigen presentation. I. Effects of interleukin 1 and 2 on radiation-treated antigen-presenting cells *in vivo* and *in vitro*, *Clin. Immunol. Immunopathol.*, 29, 282, 1983.
19. Stingl, L. A., Sauder, D. N., Iijima, M., Wolff, K., Pehamberger, H., and Stingl, G., Mechanism of UV-B-induced impairment of the antigen-presenting capacity of murine epidermal cells, *J. Immunol.*, 130, 1586, 1983.
20. Ansel, J. C., Luger, T. A., and Green, I., The effect of *in vitro* and *in vivo* UV irradiation on the production of ETAF activity by human and murine keratinocytes, *J. Invest. Dermatol.*, 81, 519, 1983.
21. Gahring, L., Baltz, M., Pepys, M. B., and Daynes, R., Effect of ultraviolet radiation on production of epidermal cell thymocyte-activating factor/interleukin 1 *in vivo* and *in vitro*, *Proc. Natl. Acad. Sci. U.S.A.*, 81, 1198, 1984.
22. Bergstresser, P. R., Tigelaar, R. E., and Streilein, J. W., Thy-1 antigen-bearing dendritic cells in murine epidermis are derived from bone marrow precursors, *J. Invest. Dermatol.*, 83, 83, 1984.
23. Breathnach, S. M. and Kata, S. I., Thy-1⁺ dendritic cells in murine epidermis are bone marrow-derived, *J. Invest. Dermatol.*, 83, 74, 1984.
24. Aberer, W. and Stingl, G., Effects of physicochemical agents on Ia⁻ and Thy-1 positive epidermal cells, *J. Invest. Dermatol.*, 82, 417, 1984.

25. Jessup, J. M., Hanna, N., Palaszysnki, E., and Kripke, M. L., Mechanisms of depressed reactivity to dinitrochlorobenzene and ultraviolet-induced tumors during ultraviolet carcinogenesis in BALB/c mice, *Cell. Immunol.,* 38, 105, 1978.
26. Noonan, F. P., Kripke, M. L., Pedesen, G. M., and Greene, M. I., Supression of contact hypersensitivity in mice by ultraviolet irradiation is associated with defective antigen presentation, *Immunology,* 43, 527, 1981.
27. Morison, W. L. and Kripke, M. L., Systemic suppression of contact hypersensitivity by ultraviolet b radiation or methoxsalen/ultraviolet a radiation in the guinea pig, *Cell. Immunol.,* 85, 270, 1984.
28. Ullrich, S. E. and Kripke, M. L., Mechanisms in the suppression of tumor rejection produced in mice by repeated UV irradiation, *J. Immunol.,* 133, 2786, 1984.
29. Kripke, M. L., Morison, W. L., and Parrish, J. A., Systemic suppression of contact hypersensitivity in mice by psoralen plus UVA radiation (PUVA), *J. Invest. Dermatol.,* 81, 87, 1983.
30. Morison, W. L., Pike, R. A., and Kripke, M. L., Effect of sunlight and its component wavebands on contact hypersensitivity in mice and guinea pigs, *Photodermatology,* 2, 195, 1985.
31. DeFabo, E. C. and Noonan, F. P., Mechanism of immune suppression by ultraviolet irradiation *in vivo*. I. Evidence for the existence of a unique photoreceptor in skin and its role in photoimmunology, *J. Exp. Med.,* 157, 84, 1983.
32. Morison, W. L., Systemic suppression of contact hypersensitivity associated with suppressor lymphocytes: is a lesion in DNA an essential step in the pathway?, *J. Invest. Dermatol.,* 82, 421, 1984.
33. Greene, M. I., Sy, M. S., Kripke, M., and Benacerraf, B., Impairment of antigen-presenting cell function by ultraviolet radiation, *Proc. Natl. Acad. Sci. U.S.A.,* 76, 6591, 1979.
34. Letvin, N. L., Nepom, J. T., Greene, M. I., Benacerraf, B., and Germain, R. N., Loss of Ia-bearing splenic adherent cells after whole body ultraviolet irradiation, *J. Immunol.,* 125, 2550, 1980.
35. Fox, I. J., Sy, M., Benacerraf, B., and Greene, M. I., Impairment of antigen-presenting cell function by ultraviolet radiation, *Transplantation,* 31, 262, 1981.
36. Noonan, F. P., Bucana, C., Sauder, D. N., and DeFabo, E. C., Mechanism of systemic immune suppression by UV irradiation *in vivo*. II. The UV effects on number and morphology of epidermal Langerhans cells and the UV-induced suppression of contact hypersensitivity have different wavelength dependencies, *J. Immunol.,* 132, 2408, 1984.
37. Lynch, D. H., Gurish, M. F., and Daynes, R. A., The effects of high-dose UV exposure on murine Langerhans cell function at exposed and unexposed sites as assessed using *in vivo* and *in vitro* assays, *J. Invest. Dermatol.,* 81, 336, 1983.
38. Morison, W. L., Bucana, C., and Kripke, M. L., Systemic suppression of contact hypersensitivity by UVB-radiation is unrelated to the UVB-induced alterations in the morphology and number of Langerhans cells, *Immunology,* 52, 299, 1984.
39. Kripke, M. L. and Morison, W. L., Modulation of immune function by UV-radiation, *J. Invest. Dermatol.,* 85, 625, 1985.
40. Spangrude, G. J., Bernhard, E. J., Ajioka, R. S., and Daynes, R. A., Alterations in lymphocyte homing patterns within mice exposed to ultraviolet radiation, *J. Immunol.,* 130, 2974, 1983.
41. Milton, J. D., The effect of ultraviolet irradiation on the localization of syngeneic and allogeneic lymphoid cells and on alloimmunogenicity, *Immunology,* 44, 281, 1981.
42. Swartz, R. P., Role of UVB-induced serum factor(s) in suppression of contact hypersensitivity in mice, *J. Invest. Dermatol.,* 83, 305, 1984.
43. Kripke, M. L., Antigenicity of murine skin tumors induced by ultraviolet light, *J. Natl. Cancer Inst.,* 53, 1333, 1974.
44. Kripke, M. L. and Fisher, M. S., Immunologic parameters of ultraviolet carcinogenesis, *J. Natl. Cancer Inst.,* 57, 211, 1976.
45. Kripke, M. L., Lofgreen, J. S., Beard, J., Jessup, J. M., and Fisher, M. S., *In vivo* immune responses of mice during carcinogenesis by ultraviolet irradiation, *J. Natl. Cancer Inst.,* 59, 1227, 1977.
46. Spellman, C. W., Woodward, J. G., and Daynes, R. A., Modification of immunological potential by ultraviolet radiation, *Transplantation,* 24, 112, 1977.
47. Norbury, K. C., Kripke, M. L., and Budmen, M. B., *In vitro* reactivity of macrophages and lymphocytes from ultraviolet-irradiated mice, *J. Natl. Cancer Inst.,* 59, 1231, 1977.
48. Kripke, M. L., Thorn, R. M., Lill, P. H., Civin, C. I., Pazmino, N. H., and Fisher, M. S., Further characterization of immunological unresponsiveness induced in mice by ultraviolet radiation, *Transplantation,* 28, 212, 1979.
49. Fisher, M. S. and Kripke, M. L., Systemic alteration induced in mice by ultraviolet light irradiation and its relationship to ultraviolet carcinogenesis, *Proc. Natl. Acad. Sci. U.S.A.,* 74, 1688, 1977.
50. Spellman, C. W. and Daynes, R. A., Modification of immunological potential by ultraviolet radiation. II. Generation of suppressor cells in short-term UV-irradiated mice, *Transplantation,* 24, 120, 1977.
51. Fisher, M. S. and Kripke, M. L., Suppressor T lymphocytes control the development of primary skin cancers in ultraviolet-irradiated mice, *Science,* 216, 1133, 1982.

52. De Gruijl, F. R. and van der Leun, J. C., Systemic influence of pre-irradiation of a limited skin area on UV-tumorigenesis, *Photochem. Photobiol.,* 35, 379, 1982.
53. Fisher, M. S., Kripke, M. L., and Chan, G. L., Antigenic similarity between cells transformed by ultraviolet radiation *in vitro* and *in vivo, Science,* 223, 593, 1984.
54. Palaszynski, E. W. and Kripke, M. L., Transfer of immunological tolerance to ultraviolet-radiation-induced skin tumors with grafts of ultraviolet-irradiated skin, *Transplantation,* 36, 465, 1983.
55. Granstein, R. D., Parrish, J. A., McAuliffe, D. J., Waltenbaugh, C., and Greene, M. I., Immunologic inhibition of ultraviolet radiation-induced tumor suppressor cell activity, *Science,* 224, 615, 1984.
56. Fabo, E. C. and Kripke, M. L., Wavelength dependence and dose-rate independence of UV radiation-induced immunologic unresponsiveness of mice to a UV-induced fibrosarcoma, *Photochem. Photobiol.,* 32, 183, 1980.
57. Morison, W. L. and Kelley, S. P., Sunlight suppresses the rejection of UVB-induced skin tumors in mice, *J. Natl. Cancer Inst.,* 74, 525, 1985.
58. Kripke, M. L., Morison, W. L., and Parrish, J. A., Induction and transplantation of murine skin cancers induced by methoxsalen plus ultraviolet (320—400 nm) radiation, *J. Natl. Cancer Inst.,* 68, 685, 1982.
59. Kripke, M. L., Morison, W. L., and Parrish, J. A., Differences in the immunologic reactivity of mice treated with UVB or methoxsalen plus UVA radiation, *J. Invest. Dermatol.,* 76, 4445, 1981.
60. Briffa, D. V., Parker, D., Tosca, N., Turk, J. L., and Greaves, M. W., The effect of photochemotherapy (PUVA) on cell mediated immunity in guinea pig, *J. Invest. Dermatol.,* 77, 377, 1981.
61. Morison, W. L., Parrish, J. A., Woehler, M. E., Krugler, J. I., and Bloch, K. J., Influence of PUVA and UVB radiation on delayed hypersensitivity in the guinea pig, *J. Invest. Dermatol.,* 76, 484, 1981.
62. Morison, W. L. and Pike, R. A., Suppression of graft-versus-host reactivity in the mouse popliteal nody by UVB radiation, *J. Invest. Dermatol.,* 84, 483, 1985.
63. Morison, W. L., Parrish, J. A., Woehler, M. E., and Bloch, K. J., The influence of PUVA and UVB radiation on skin-graft survival in rabbits, *J. Invest. Dermatol.,* 75, 331, 1980.
64. Hersey, P., Hasic, E., Edwards, A., Bradley, M., Haran, G., and McCarthy, W. H., Immunological effects of solarium exposure, *Lancet,* 1, 548, 1983.
65. Halprin, K. M., Comerford, M., Presser, S. E., and Taylor, J. R., Ultraviolet light treatment delays contact sensitization to nitrogen mustard, *Br. J. Dermatol.,* 105, 71, 1981.
66. Nusbaum, B. P., Edwards, E. K., Horwitz, S. N., and Frost, P., The effect of UV radiation on sensitization to mechlorethamine, *Arch. Dermatol.,* 119, 117, 1983.
67. Volden, G., Molin, L., and Thomsen, K., PUVA-induced suppression of contact sensitivity to mustine hydrochloride in mycosis fungoides, *Br. Med. J.,* 2, 865, 1978.
68. O'Dell, B. L., Jessen, R. T., Becker, L. E., Jackson, R. T., and Smith, E. B., Diminished immune response in sun-damaged skin, *Arch. Dermatol.,* 116, 559, 1980.
69. Kalimo, K., Koulu, L., and Jansen, C. T., Effect of a single UVB or PUVA exposure on immediate and delayed skin hypersensitivity reactions in humans, *Arch. Dermatol.,* 275, 374, 1983.
70. Strains, G. H., Greaves, M., Price, M., Bridges, B. A., Hall-Smith, P., and Vella-Briffa, D., Inhibition of delayed hypersensitivity reaction in skin (DNCB test) by 8-methoxypsoralen photochemotherapy, *Lancet,* 2, 556, 1980.
71. Moss, C., Friedmann, P. S., and Shuster, S., Impaired contact hypersensitivity in untreated psoriasis and the effects of photochemotherapy and dithranol/UV-B, *Br. J. Dermatol.,* 105, 503, 1981.
72. Thiers, B. H., Maize, J. C., Spicer, S. S., and Cantor, A. B., The effect of aging and chronic sun exposure on human Langerhans cell populations, *J. Invest. Dermatol.,* 82, 223, 1984.
73. Gilchrest, B. A., Murphy, G. F., and Soter, N. A., Effect of chronologic aging and ultraviolet irradiation on Langerhans cells in human epidermis, *J. Invest. Dermatol.,* 79, 85, 1982.
74. Aberer, W., Schuler, G., Stingl, G., Honigsmann, H., and Wolff, K., Ultraviolet light depletes surface markers of Langerhans cells, *J. Invest. Dermatol.,* 76, 202, 1981.
75. Friedmann, P. S., Disappearance of epidermal Langerhans cells during PUVA therapy, *Br. J. Dermatol.,* 105, 219, 1981.
76. Friedman, P. S., Ford, G., Ross, J., and Diffey, B. L., Reappearance of epidermal Langerhans cells after PUVA therapy, *Br. J. Dermatol.,* 109, 301, 1983.
77. Ree, K., Reduction of Langerhans cells in human epidermis during PUVA therapy: a morphometric study, *J. Invest. Dermatol.,* 78, 488, 1982.
78. Hersey, P., Haran, G., Hasic, E., and Edwards, A., Alteration of T cell subsets and induction of suppressor T cell activity in normal subjects after exposure to sunlight, *J. Immunol.,* 31, 1, 1983.
79. Morison, W. L., Parrish, J. A., Bloch, K. J., and Krugler, J. I., *In vivo* effect of UV-B on lymphocyte function, *Br. J. Dermatol.,* 101, 513, 1979.
80. Morison, W. L., Parrish, J. A., Bloch, K. J., and Krugler, J. I., *In vivo* effect of PUVA on lymphocyte function, *Br. J. Dermatol.,* 104, 405, 1981.

81. Kraemer, K. H. and Weinstein, G. D., Decreased thymidine incorporation in circulating leukocytes after treatment of psoriasis with psoralen and long-wave ultraviolet light, *J. Invest. Dermatol.,* 69, 211, 1977.

82. Cormane, R. H., Hamerlinck, F., and Siddiqui, A. H., Immunologic implications of PUVA therapy in psoriasis vulgaris, *Arch. Dermatol. Res.,* 265, 245, 1979.

83. Morison, W. L., Parrish, J. A., Bloch, K. J., and Krugler, J. I., Transient impairment of peripheral blood lymphocyte function during PUVA therapy, *Br. J. Dermatol.,* 101, 391, 1979.

84. Harper, R. A., Tam, D. W., Vonderheid, E. C., and Urbach, F., Normal T-lymphocyte function in psoriatic patients undergoing methoxsalen photochemotherapy, *J. Invest. Dermatol.,* 72, 323, 1979.

85. Moscicki, R. A., Morison, W. L., Parrish, J. A., Bloch, K. J., and Colvin, R. B., Reduction of the fraction of circulating helper-inducer T cells identified by monoclonal antibodies in psoriatic patients treated with long-term psoralen/ultraviolet-A radiation (PUVA), *J. Invest. Dermatol.,* 79, 205, 1982.

86. Morison, W. L., Wimberly, J., Parrish, J. A., and Bloch, K. J., Abnormal lymphocyte function following long-term PUVA therapy for psoriasis, *Br. J. Dermatol.,* 108, 445, 1983.

87. Morison, W. L., Parrish, J. A., Anderson, R. R., and Bloch, K. J., Sensitivity of mononuclear cells to UV radiation, *Photochem. Photobiol.,* 29, 1047, 1979.

88. Morison, W. L., Parrish, J. A., McAuliffe, D. J., and Bloch, K. J., Sensitivity of mononuclear cells to UV radiation: effect on subsequent stimulation with phytohemagglutinin, *Photochem. Photobiol.,* 32, 99, 1980.

89. Morison, W. L., Parrish, J. A., McAuliffe, D. J., and Bloch, K. J., Sensitivity of mononuclear cells to PUVA: effect on subsequent stimulation with mitogens and on exclusion of trypan blue dye, *Clin. Exp. Dermatol.,* 6, 273, 1981.

90. Morhenn, V. B., Benike, C. J., and Engleman, E. G., Inhibition of cell mediated immune responses by 8-methoxypsoralen and long-wave ultraviolet light: a possible explanation for the clinical effects of photoactivated psoralen, *J. Invest. Dermatol.,* 75, 249, 1980.

91. Kraemer, K. H., Levis, W. R., Cason, J. C., and Tarone, R. E., Inhibition of mixed leukocyte culture reaction by 8-methoxypsoralen and long-wavelength ultraviolet radiation, *J. Invest. Dermatol.,* 77, 235, 1981.

92. Carter, D. M., Wolff, K., and Schnedl, W., 8-methoxypsoralen and UVA promote sister-chromatid exchanges, *J. Invest. Dermatol.,* 67, 548, 1976.

93. Swanbeck, G., Thyresson-Hök, M., Bredberg, A., and Lambert, B., Treatment of psoriasis with oral psoralens and longwave ultraviolet light, *Acta Derm. Venereol.,* 55, 367, 1975.

94. Wolff-Schreiner, E. C., Carter, D. M., Schwarzacher, H. G., and Wolff, K., Sister chromatid exchanges in photochemotherapy, *J. Invest. Dermatol.,* 69, 387, 1977.

95. Marshall, V. C., Skin tumours in immunosuppressed patients, *Aust. N.Z. J. Surg.,* 43, 214, 1973.

96. Koranda, F. C., Dehmel, E. M., Kahn, G., and Penn, I., Cutaneous complications in immunosuppressed renal homograft recipients, *JAMA,* 229, 419, 1974.

97. Hoxtell, E. O., Mandel, J. S., Murray, S. S., Schuman, L. M., and Goltz, R. W., Incidence of skin carcinoma after renal transplantation, *Arch. Dermatol.,* 113, 436, 1977.

98. Hardie, I. R., Strong, R. W., Hartley, L. C. J., Woodruff, P. W., and Clunie, G. J. A., Skin cancer in caucasian renal allograft recipients living in a subtropical climate, *Surgery,* 177, 1980.

99. Boyle, J., Briggs, J. D., MacKie, R. M., and Junor, B. J. R., Cancer, warts, and sunshine in renal transplant patients, *Lancet,* 1, 702, 1984.

100. Letzner, M. A., Orth, G., Detronquay, V., Ducasse, M., Kreis, H., and Crosnier, J., Detection of human papillomavirus type 5 DNA in skin cancers of an immunosuppressed renal allograft recipient, *Lancet,* 2, 422, 1983.

101. Dellon, A. L., Potvin, C., Chretien, P. B., and Rogenntine, C. N., The immunobiology of skin cancer, *Plast. Reconstr. Surg.,* 55, 343, 1975.

102. Nairn, R. C., Nind, A. P. P., Guli, E. P. G., Muller, H. K., Rolland, J. M., and Minty, C. C. J., Specific immune response in human skin carcinoma, *Br. Med. J.,* 2, 702, 1971.

103. Morison, W. L, Bucana, C., Hashem, N., Kripke, M. L., Cleaver, J. E., and German, J. L., III, Impaired immune function in patients with xeroderma pigmentosum, *Cancer Res.,* 45, 3929, 1985.

104. Horio, T. and Minami, K., Solar urticaria, photoallergen in a patient's serum, *Arch. Dermatol.,* 113, 157, 1977.

105. Sams, W. M., Jr., Solar urticaria: studies of the active serum factor, *J. Allergy,* 45, 295, 1970.

106. Hawk, J. L. M., Eady, R. A. J., Challoner, A. V. J., Kobza-Black, A., Keahey, T. M., and Greaves, M. W., Elevated blood histamine levels and mast cell degranulation in solar urticaria, *Br. J. Clin. Pharmacol.,* 9, 183, 1980.

107. Keahey, T. M., Lavker, R. M., Kaidbey, K. H., Atkins, P. C., and Zweiman, B., Studies on the mechanism of clinical tolerance in solar urticaria, *Br. J. Dermatol.,* 110, 327, 1984.

108. Soter, N. A., Wasserman, S. I., Pathak, M. S., Parrish, J. A., and Austen, K. F., Solar urticaria: release of mast cell mediators into the circulation after experimental challenge, *J. Invest. Dermatol.,* 72, 282, 1974.

109. Harber, L. C. and Baer, R. L., Mechanisms of drug photosensitivity reactions, *Toxicol. Appl. Pharmacol. Suppl.,* 3, 58, 1969.
110. Maguire, H. C. and Kaidbey, K., Experimental photoallergic contact dermatitis: a mouse model, *J. Invest. Dermatol.,* 79, 147, 1982.
111. Takigawa, M. and Miyachi, Y., Mechanisms of contact photosensitivity in mice. I. T cell regulation of contact photosensitivity of tetrachlorosalicylanilide under the genetic restrictions of the major histocompatibility complex, *J. Invest. Dermatol.,* 78, 108, 1982.
112. Granstein, R. D., Morison, W. L., and Kripke, M. L., The role of suppressor cells in the induction of murine photoallergic contact dermatitis and in its suppression by prior UVB irradiation, *J. Immunol.,* 130, 2099, 1983.
113. Levine, L., Seaman, E., Hammerschlag, E., and van Vunakis, H., Antibodies to photoproducts of deoxyribonucleic acids irradiated with ultraviolet light, *Science,* 153, 1666, 1966.
114. Tan, E. M. and Stoughton, R. B., Ultraviolet light alteration of cellular deoxyribonucleic acid *in vivo,* *Proc. Natl. Acad. Sci. U.S.A.,* 62, 708, 1969.
115. Tan, E. M., Production of potentially antigenic DNA in cells, in *Immunopathology 6th Int. Symp.,* Miescher, P. A., Ed., Grune & Stratton, New York, 1971, 346.
116. Natali, P. G. and Tan, E. M., Experimental skin lesions in mice resembling systemic lupus erythematos, *Arthritis Rheum.,* 16, 579, 1973.
117. Davis, P. and Percy, J. S., Effect of ultraviolet light on disease characteristics of NZB/W mice, *J. Rheumatol.,* 5, 126, 1978.
118. Strickland, P. T., Photocarcinogenesis and influence of UV radiation on autoimmune disease in NZB/N mice, *J. Natl. Cancer Inst.,* 73, 537, 1984.
119. Tan, E. M., Antibodies to deoxyribonucleic acid irradiated with ultraviolet light: detection by precipitins and immunofluorescence, *Science,* 161, 1353, 1968.
120. Davis, P., Russell, A. S., and Percy, J. S., Antibodies to UV light denatured DNA in systemic lupus erythematosus: detection by filter radioimmunoassay and clinical correlations, *J. Rheumatol.,* 3, 375, 1976.
121. Morison, W. L., Parrish, J. A., and Fitzpatrick, T. B., Oral psoralen photochemotherapy of atopic eczema, *Br. J. Dermatol.,* 98, 25, 1978.
122. Lau, H., Reemtsma, K., and Hardy, M. A., Prolongation of rat islet allograft survival by direct ultraviolet irradiation of the graft, *Science,* 223, 607, 1984.
123. Glazier, A., Morison, W. L., Bucana, C., Hess, A. D., and Tutschka, P. J., Suppression of epidermal graft-versus-host disease with ultraviolet radiation, *Transplantation,* 37, 211, 1984.
124. Hymes, S. R., Morison, W. L., Farmer, E. V., Walters, L. L., Tutschka, P. J., and Santos, G. W., Methoxysalen and ultraviolet a radiation in the treatment of chronic cutaneous graft-versus-host reaction, *J. Am. Acad. Dermatol.,* in press, 1984.
125. Hauser, S. L., Weiner, H. L., Che, M., Shapiro, M. E., Gilles, F., and Letvin, N. L., Prevention of experimental allergic encephalomyelitis (EAE) in the SJL/J mouse by whole body ultraviolet irradiation, *J. Immunol.,* 132, 1276, 1984.

Chapter 7

PHOTOSENSITIVITY TO DRUGS

John H. Epstein and Bruce U. Wintroub

TABLE OF CONTENTS

I. INTRODUCTION

Photosensitivity reactions have become increasingly common in the past several decades due not only to the general public's desire to develop a "good sun tan" but also due to the increasing amounts of photosensitizing chemicals in our environment. A significant number of these chemicals are therapeutic agents, and these will be the primary concern of this discussion.

Before we examine the problems of photochemical toxicity in human skin, however, perhaps a brief discussion of certain basic concepts might be in order. Let us start with the basic law of photobiology. This law states that nonionizing radiation must be absorbed to produce a photochemical, and thus the resultant photobiological, reaction. This law then stipulates that the photosensitizer, chromophore, radiation absorber, or whatever term one wishes to use must be present at the time of radiation for a reaction to occur.

The action spectrum of a photochemical reaction and the resultant photobiological reaction consists of the wavelengths absorbed by a molecule which leads to a specific response. The action spectrum usually, but not always, simulates the absorption spectrum of a molecule. However, it must always be included in the absorption spectrum, since this radiation must be absorbed to produce a reaction.

"Photosensitivity" is the broad term used to connote adverse reactions to this radiation.[1] Two types of reactions may occur — phototoxic or photoallergic. The phototoxic response can be divided into 2 subgroups — photodynamic and nonphotodynamic. Simplistically, the differentiation relates to the need of oxygen in the photodynamic process, though the process is much more complex.[2]

Phototoxicity is common. It will occur in everybody if enough of the chromophore or photosensitizers are present and the skin is exposed to a sufficient amount of the appropriate wavelengths. Clinically, the responses usually are comprised of a delayed erythema with or without edema, followed by hyperpigmentation and desquamation. Thus they resemble the ordinary UVB radiation (between 280 or 290 nm and 315 or 320 nm) sunburn response. In fact, the ordinary UVB sunburn is by far the most common phototoxic reaction that is seen.

In contrast, photoallergy is uncommon.[3-5] It is an acquired, altered reactivity, presumably dependent on an antigen-antibody or a cell-mediated hypersensitivity. Clinically, it is characterized by unusual reactions. These reactions include immediate urticarial responses and delayed papular to eczematous lesions.

Almost all of the well-documented photobiological events that occur in the skin are induced by UVB radiation. Such radiation can inhibit DNA, RNA, and protein synthesis and mitosis formation; labilize lysosomal membranes; stimulate formation or release of vasoactive substances such as prostaglandins and kinins; induce a delayed erythema and new pigment formation; cause cancer; and produce vitamin D precursors in the epidermis. For practical purposes, this radiation does not pass through window glass. Thus, a good sturdy piece of window glass will eliminate all of these cutaneous responses.

UVA radiation (315 or 320 to 400 nm) also produces a few minor photobiological events, such as immediate pigment darkening, due to photo-oxidation of melanin, new pigment formation, and a transient immediate and a delayed erythema response. In addition, UVA radiation is important for two reasons. UVA radiation markedly accentuates the injury produced by the UVB radiation and is responsible for the vast majority of exogenously photosensitized reactions that occur in the skin.

It is with this last issue (i.e., chemical photosensitivity) that this chapter is concerned.

II. EXOGENOUS PHOTOSENSITIZERS

Exogenous chemical photosensitizers may arrive on the skin topically or systemically through the vascular system.

The topical exogenous photosensitizers may be placed in the following categories:

1.   Cosmetics: perfumes, creams, soaps, etc.
2.   Medications
      A. Advertent: psoralens, tars
      B. Inadvertent: phenothiazines, sulfonamides, halogenated salicylanilides (and related compounds), sunscreens, etc.
3.   Plants: gas plant, lime rinds, celery, carrots, etc.

Topical exogenous photosensitizers may be applied to the skin in the form of cosmetics, perfumes, moisturizing creams, soaps, and the like. Certain medications, some of which are intended to produce photoreactions, e.g., the psoralen compounds and occasionally tar, are applied to the skin.

Other medications arrive on the skin without the intent to photosensitize. These include phenothiazines, sulfonamides, antibacterial agents such as the halogenated salicylanilides and related compounds, and sunscreens.

A number of plants contain photosensitizing chemicals, primarily psoralen compounds, which can and do induce photosensitive reactions. These plants include carrots, celery (especially celery infected with pink rot disease), gas plant, lime rinds, and the like. The primary photosensitizers in these plants are psoralen compounds, though other photosensitizers are found in other plants.[6]

Industrial emissions constitute another source of topical photoactive chemicals. These agents are primarily polycyclic hydrocarbons that can act as photosensitizers as well as additive carcinogens.[2,7] In addition, potential promoters of photocarcinogenesis may be found in industrial emissions.

The commonly used systemic photosensitizers may be placed in the following categories:

1.   Antibacterial sulfonamides
2.   Thiazide diuretic medications
3.   Sulfonylurea antidiabetic medications
4.   Phenothiazines
5.   Antibiotics — especially demeclocycline

Photosensitizing chemicals that reach the skin through the vasculature are generally medications. The number of systemic photosensitizers is immense. They include potent photosensitizers such as the psoralen compounds that are usually employed to produce photoreactions, to weak photosensitizers such as the antihistamine Benadryl®. Included in this list of commonly used systemic photosensitizers are antibacterial sulfonamides and their relatives, the thiazide diuretics, and the sulfonylurea antidiabetic drugs. The phenothiazines, especially chlorpromazine and certain antibiotics, are also included in this group. More complete lists of potential topical and systemic photosensitizers are available.[8,9]

III. PHOTOTOXICITY

As noted, the most common photosensitivity reactions to exogenous chemicals are phototoxic in nature. A significant number of these chemicals are therapeutic agents, i.e., drugs. Drug-induced phototoxic reactions can occur in 100% of people following the first exposure to the chemical and a dose response can be demonstrated with the incidence of phototoxicity being related to the concentration of the sensitizers and the amount of the appropriate radiation. This section will focus on the clinical expression and mechanism of phototoxicity due to topically or systemically administered drugs and will consider only briefly phototoxicity associated with certain metabolic disorders, such as the porphyrias, in which a product with photosensitizing properties accumulates in the skin as a result of an inborn error of metabolism.

A. Clinical Reactions

Acute phototoxic responses are by far the most common reactions to these agents. These responses are usually characterized by a delayed erythema and edema followed by hyperpigmentation and desquamation or peeling. If the chemical is applied to the skin, the epidermis may be severely damaged, such as is seen in topical psoralen photosensitization. In contrast, if the agent reaches the skin through the vasculature, the primary site of injury may be in the dermis with little or no visible epidermal change. In both instances, the inflammatory cellular response is very slight in the dermis of human skin.[8]

This is similar to the lack of cellular infiltration noted in human cutaneous acute UVB sunburn reactions. When the tissue is examined at the submicroscopic level, vascular injury can be detected in responses to systemic photosensitizers such as protoporphyrins.[10,11]

Host effects may influence the natural history of drug-induced phototoxic reactions. Several factors, including hair, pigment, and thickness of the stratum corneum, influence radiation penetration. Topical photosensitizers are dependent on percutaneous absorption and metabolism in the skin.[12] Systemic chromophores are influenced by gastrointestinal absorption, distribution, and metabolism of the chemicals. In addition, increased humidity, temperature, and wind may also enhance phototoxic responses.[13,14] However, recent studies suggest that heat may inhibit phototoxic reactions.[15,16] The reasons for these discrepancies are unknown.

Certain exogenous chemicals such as tetracycline hydrochloride, nalidixic acid, and the sulfones can produce low-grade phototoxic injuries that are expressed as blistering, fragility, denudation, scarring, and milium formation.[17,18] These changes are identical (clinically and microscopically) with those found in a number of the porphyrias.[19]

Chronic actinic damage and skin cancer formation are induced primarily by the UVB rays from the sun. In general, this process in humans has not been associated with drugs. However, such a relationship with certain forms of photochemotherapy has recently been established. In a large series of psoriatic patients treated with psoralens and UVA radiation, Stern et al.[20] noted a definite increase in cutaneous cancer formation. This increase was even more clinically significant because the cancers were found primarily on parts of the body usually not chronically exposed to the sun. In addition, there is histologic evidence of focal dystrophy of epidermal cells, atypical changes in melanocytes, and deposition of colloid bodies and amyloid at the dermoepidermal junction.[21]

Stern et al.[22] also reported an increased skin cancer incidence in psoriatic patients who had received very extensive treatments with coal tar and UVB radiation (the Goeckerman regimen). This may represent an additive carcinogenic effect between the tar and UVB radiation energy, since the action spectrum for coal tar photosensitization is in the UVA radiation range. Thus, patients with psoriasis may be at increased risk of developing skin cancer because of certain treatment modalities in wide use at the present time.

B. Mechanisms

The interactions of light, phototoxic chemicals, and their biologic targets may result from several types of photochemical reactions. In each case, damage to biological substrates is initiated by the absorption of light energy by a phototoxic compound. Historically, phototoxic reactions have been divided into two categories: oxygen-dependent (photodynamic) and oxygen-independent (nonphotodynamic).[2,8] In the case of drug phototoxicity, recent studies have resulted in a more detailed understanding of the various mechanisms of phototoxicity.

The action spectrum for these reactions usually includes at least the UVA range, though certain molecules such as porphyrins and a number of dyes photosensitize to visible light.[2] In addition, a limited number of chemicals are activated by UVB rays.[23,24]

Photodynamic processes appear to be responsible for reactions to certain dyes, coal tar, polycyclic hydrocarbons, and porphyrin molecules.[2] Photodynamic reactions may induce an excited triplet state which reacts with oxygen, forming a singlet oxygen or superoxide anion.[25-27] This activated oxygen can then damage cell components. The available evidence indicates that this process occurs in the endothelial cells of the superficial dermal blood vessels of the skin in the porphyrias.[10,11,19,28] In addition, there is evidence that porphyrin photosensitization can lead to activation of the classical complement pathway and generate chemotactic activity derived from the fifth component of complement.[29,30] It should be noted that demethylchlortetracycline photosensitization can also cause complement activation and generate chemotactic factors.[31]

Nonphotodynamic reactions have been described for psoralen photosensitization.[32-34] In this instance, certain psoralen compounds intercalate into the DNA helix. On photoactivation with UVA radiation, mono- and bifunctional adducts may be formed in the DNA, depending on the structure of the psoralen molecule and the wavelengths utilized for irradiation. Photoreactions with proteins may also occur. It should be noted that psoralens can produce photodynamic responses as well.[34] Psoralen photoinduced singlet oxygen formation has been correlated with erythema production by several psoralens, suggesting that these photodynamic responses may be responsible for some of the effects of psoralen photosensitization in human skin.

Photoinduced DNA cross-links have been reported with coal-tar extracts and anthracene.[32] Also, lysosomal labilization has been noted with anthracene as well as porphyrins.[28] How this injury translates into erythema, edema, and eventual hyperpigmentation remains to be determined. Another established mechanism concerns the production of toxic photoproducts which can cause membrane damage and result in erythematous cutaneous responses. Recent studies indicate that photoreactions to certain chemicals, such as chlorpromazine and protryptyline, may be due at least in part to this type of mechanism.[35]

The erythrogenic mediators of these reactions are not well understood. Unlike UVB phototoxicity, prostaglandins do not appear to be involved in 8-methoxypsoralen (8-MOP) and UVA photoreactions. Anthracene phototoxic-induced hyperemia in mouse skin appears to be mediated by histamine.[36] Recently, phototoxic-induced immediate erythema and edema reactions to hematoporphyrin[37] and benoxaprofen[38] have been shown to be related to mast-cell degranulation. In the case of benoxaprofen, the degranulation appears to be due to photosensitization of the membrane by a lipophilic photoproduct of the parent chemical.[39] How these findings relate to the erythematous responses to photoinjury induced by other molecules remains to be determined. In general, much more information is needed to clarify the mechanisms which lead to the changes we see during phototoxic cutaneous responses.

C. Phototoxic Agents of Special Interest

Certain frequently used orally and topically administered agents are known to produce phototoxicity. In certain cases phototoxicity is employed for therapeutic benefit, as in the case of psoralen and tar, while in other cases, phototoxicity is a distinctly adverse event. In this section, those drugs which are commonly used will be reviewed with respect to clinical problems and mechanisms of phototoxicity.

1. Psoralen Phototoxicity

Furocoumarins are a class of compounds to which psoralens belong, and these compounds consist of a double-ringed coumarin moiety to which a furan ring is attached. At least 28 different furocoumarins have been isolated from natural sources, but only 4 are clinically useful: psoralen, 8-MOP, 5-methoxypsoralen, and 4,5,8-trimethylpsoralen. The absorption maximums of psoralens range between 210 and 330 nm, but the erythema action spectrum is in the UVA range from 320 to 370 nm.

Psoralens combined with sun exposure have been used to treat vitiligo for centuries. The availability of high intensity, artificial, UVA light sources in the past decade has permitted the use of psoralens in combination with controlled doses of UVA light.[40] The acronym PUVA (psoralen and UVA) photochemotherapy is used to indicate this form of dermatologic therapy. Three major dermatologic diseases are frequently treated with PUVA — vitiligo, psoriasis, and mycosis fungoides.

The mechanism of psoralen photosensitization has been intensively studied. Non-photodynamic reactions have been described for psoralen photosensitization.[32] In this instance, certain psoralen compounds intercalate into the DNA helix.[33,34]

On photoactivation with UVA radiation, mono- and bifunctional adducts may be formed in the DNA, depending on the structure of the psoralen molecule and the wavelengths utilized for irradiation.[32-34] Photoreactions with proteins may also occur. It should be noted that psoralens can produce photodynamic responses as well.[34] Psoralen photoinduced singlet oxygen formation has been correlated with erythema production by several psoralens, suggesting that these photodynamic responses may be responsible for some of the effects of psoralen photosensitization in human skin.[34]

2. Chlorpromazine Phototoxicity

Chlorpromazine is a major tranquilizer frequently utilized in psychiatric patients. Clinical photosensitivity to chlorpromazine was reported in the 1950s[41] and the drug is now known to be phototoxic in a variety of in vitro systems including RBC, bacteria, mammalian cells, bacteriophage, and viruses.[42] Chlorpromazine causes several photodermatoses when taken systemically. An exaggerated sunburn reaction (phototoxicity) and a hyperpigmentation of purple or slate-gray tone in light-exposed skin have been described. The wavelength range required to elicit a clinical reaction has been a topic of controversy. Chlorpromazine has an absorption maximum at 305 nm in aqueous solution, but the action spectrum for phototoxicity has been reported to be below[41] and above 320 nm in man.[43] For phototoxicity in mice, the action spectrum has been reported to be 320 to 340 nm with a maximum of 330 nm.[44]

The mechanisms of the chlorpromazine phototoxicity have been studied extensively and at least two possible mechanisms have been demonstrated in vitro. Photoaddition of chlorpromazine to protein, DNA, and cell membranes has been reported.[45] In addition, it appears that stable photoproducts of chlorpromazine elicit cutaneous toxicity in animals and hemolyse RBC.[35]

In both systems, toxicity was detected after induction by preirradiated chlorpromazine. In the case of red cell hemolysis, the stable lysis-producing product did not require oxygen for activity nor cause lipid oxidation in the presence of oxygen. Thus, chlorpromazine has been shown to be phototoxic in many systems, but the route of translation of these in vitro effects to human phototoxicity is unclear.

3. Tetracycline Phototoxicity

Of the tetracyclines, demethylchlortetracyline (Declomycin®), is the most potent phototoxic agent. It causes immediate and delayed phototoxic reactions in most individuals, according to dose.[46,47] Human studies indicate that the action spectrum for demethylchlortetracycline phototoxicity is above 320 nm, and studies in mice demonstrated an effective radiation range of 350 to 450 nm with greatest response at 400 nm. Recent experiments clearly have demonstrated a requirement for complement and polymorphonuclear leukocytes as amplifiers or effectors of demethylchlortetracycline phototoxicity.[31]

4. Nalidixic Acid Phototoxicity

Nalidixic acid is a bacteriostatic antibiotic frequently used to treat urinary tract infections. In association with extensive sun exposure, nalidixic acid caused a characteristic bullous eruption, fragility, scarring, and milium formation in light-exposed areas, particularly the lower legs and feet.[17] Similar reactions have been noted for tetracycline hydrochloride and sulfones.[18] While the mechanisms of phototoxicity are not known, the clinical and histopathologic changes are identical with those found in a number of the porphyrias.[19] Recently Keane et al.[48] reported inducing such lesions in CF-1 female mice with repeated UVA exposures following photosensitization by nalidixic acid.

5. Phototoxicity due to Nonsteroidal Anti-Inflammatory Agents

In the past 10 years, many new nonsteroidal anti-inflammatory drugs have been introduced and are widely used to treat a variety of inflammatory and symptomatic musculoskeletal disorders. Though photosensitivity reactions have been reported to a number of these agents,[49,50] two of these agents, benoxaprofen (Oraflex®) and piroxicam (Feldene®) commonly produce phototoxic reactions.

Benoxaprofen is a proprionic-acid derivative which was introduced into European and U.S. markets for treatment of rheumatoid arthritis, osteoarthritis, ankylosing spondylitis, and psoriasis. The drug was suspended because it caused fatal cholestatic hepatitis, especially in the elderly. Unlike other nonsteroidal anti-inflammatory drugs which act principally by inhibiting prostaglandin synthetase, benoxaprofen is a 5-lipoxygenase inhibitor. Benoxaprofen caused side effects in 65% of patients, and cutaneous reactions were the most common, accounting for 70% of all side effects.[51] The most common cutaneous side effect was photosensitivity, which occurred in 29% of patients on drug. The action spectrum of the phototoxic reaction is 310 to 340 nm. The reaction is manifested as immediate itching, burning, and erythema.[52] The mechanism of this phototoxicity is unknown; however, mast-cell degranulation is a prominent feature of this process.[38,39]

Piroxicam (Feldene®) is an oxicam which inhibits prostaglandin synthetase and is used for treatment of rheumatoid arthritis, osteoarthritis, gout, and ankylosing spondylitis. While the incidence of cutaneous side effects is approximately 2.4%, a unique photosensitivity due to piroxicam has been reported in 23 patients.[50] The photosensitivity reaction is usually vesiculobullous and is often pruritic. The mechanism of piroxicam photosensitivity is unknown.

D. Assays for Phototoxicity to Drugs

Agents capable of producing phototoxic effects have been identified by use of a variety of in vitro and in vivo systems. However, the ultimate issue concerns the effect these molecules have on human tissue in vivo.[53,54] In general, the following four techniques have been utilized: systemic administration, topical application with occlusion, topical application after the stratum corneum is stripped off, and intradermal injection of the molecules. Each of the techniques has disadvantages, among which are lack of distribution to the skin of the active photosensitizing molecule, metabolism of the chemical to a nonphotosensitizing structure, lack of metabolism to an active photosensitizing structure, lack of penetration to the appropriate target tissue, lack of irradiation with the appropriate wavelengths, and lack of irradiation at the appropriate time.

IV. PHOTOALLERGY

A. Clinical Expression

Photoallergic reactions are uncommon and are acquired altered reactivities dependent on antibody-dependent or cell-mediated hypersensitivity. Clinically, photoallergic reactions present as an immediate wheal and flare or a delayed papular to eczematous dermatitis.[3,4,8,55,56] Delayed reactions are microscopically characterized by a dense dermal perivascular round-cell infiltrate similar to that seen in allergic contact dermatitis. Though vasodilitation and edema are present in the immediate reaction, these are difficult to discern histologically.

B. Photoallergy to Exogenous Chemicals

The skin is the site of photoallergic reactions to exogenous chemicals which may be applied topically or administered systemically. As with phototoxicity, in the photoallergic reactions to these chemicals the action spectrum usually falls in the UVA range. The immunologic basis for these reactions is supported primarily by studies on contact photoallergy. Photoallergic reactions to drugs and other exogenous chemicals are almost always of a cell-mediated type.

1. Photoallergic Contact Dermatitis
a. Clinical Description

Photoallergic contact reactions are clinically identical to any other type of allergic contact dermatitis. Though the most common picture is eczematous in nature, the spectrum of the possible responses may range from a simple erythema to a severe vesiculobullous eruption. When the process is chronic, lichenification results from repeated mechanical trauma (rubbing and scratching). The sun-exposed areas of the skin are involved primarily, as would be expected. However, the eruption may extend to unexposed parts of the body and even become generalized. Even when this occurs, the dermatitis is most marked in light-exposed sites.

Adults are affected much more commonly than children, and reactions occur in populations that are exposed to sunlight and photocontactants. For example, reactions to the optical brighteners more likely would be seen in persons who use them, and those to chlorpromazine more likely would occur in people who work in mental institutions. The most extensive statistical data have been compiled on the photocontact reactions induced by the halogenated salicylanilides and related antibacterial compounds because of the large number of people photosensitized by these agents between 1960 and 1970.[57] For unknown reasons, reactions occurred predominantly in men past the age of 40 years. Skin color and race apparently have little influence on the problem, which occurs readily in blacks and Asians as well as in Caucasians.

b. Persistent Light Reactions

In general, removal of the offending photosensitizer and related compounds will eliminate the problem. A small percentage of patients continue to develop the dermatitis on sun-exposed areas without apparent further contact with the offending agent or related structures. These patients are persistent light reactors.[58] Up to 25% of patients with photocontact reactions to the halogenated salicylanilides have become persistent light reactors. In studies with antibacterial halogenated salicylanilides, two types of persistent light reactors were found: a mild variety that loses its reactivity within 1½ years and a severe type that persists indefinitely.[59]

Chemicals other than the antibacterial halogenated salicylanilides induce persistent light reactions. These include the antifungal compounds buclosamide (Jadit),[60,61] chlorpromazine,[62-64] promethazine,[65] musk ambrette,[66] and epoxy resins.[67]

The mechanism or mechanisms of persistent light reactivity are not clear. Cross reaction to unknown photocontactants has been considered. Willis and Kligman[68,69] presented evidence suggesting that the reactions could result from the retention of small amounts of the photosensitizer in the dermis. Photoinduced covalent binding of the halogenated salicylanilide to albumin has been demonstrated.[5] Other possibilities include the persistence of a sensitized mononuclear infiltrate in the dermis, which will react on minimal antigenic exposure; hypersensitivity to the protein component of the complete antigen, which then becomes an independent photoallergen; or the development of clones of cells that are persistently sensitive to a number of photoallergens.[57] A possible relationship of persistent light reaction to the chronic eczematous type of polymorphous light eruption (PMLE) has been reported.[59] The histology of persistent light reactions is nonspecific and resembles allergic contact dermatitis.

c. Differential Diagnosis

The differential diagnosis includes any eruption that may involve the sun-exposed skin. These include allergic contact dermatitis, the eczematous type of polymorphous light reactions, and phototoxic reactions. Airborne allergens contact exposed skin, but unlike photocontactant reactions, the airborne contact eruption will be accentuated in skin-fold areas such as the upper eyelids, antecubital fossae, and flexural areas of the wrist. Differentiation from eczematous polymorphous light reactions and allergic contact reactions to sunscreens, "sun tanning" lotions and creams, and medications used to relieve the discomfort of a sunburn is more difficult since the reactions are confined to the sun-exposed areas and are indistinguishable clinically and histologically. Therefore, the most useful diagnostic tools are the patch, photopatch, and phototesting procedures.

The diagnosis of photocontact dermatitis is suspected by the clinical picture, and confirmation and identification of the offending chemical depend on photopatch testing. This is accomplished by the application in duplicate of nonirritating concentrations of the potential photosensitizers in appropriate vehicles (i.e., a 1% concentration of the halogenated salicylanilides in petrolatum). The use of an extra layer of black paper over the patches will help prevent a "masked" positive reaction to the photopatch test.[70] This is unnecessary with the use of aluminum patches. Twenty-four hours after application one set of patches is irradiated with the UVA light. Any light source that emits sufficient amounts of UVA light can be utilized.[71] Window-glass filtration is necessary if there is a significant amount of UVB emitted by the lamp, as in the case of the hot-quartz source. Twenty-four hours after irradiation, the unexposed and exposed sites are compared. A positive reaction to the photopatch tests reproduces the clinical lesions morphologically and histologically.

Difficulties with patch testing may occur. If the patient is contact allergic to a chemical, it may be difficult to determine if he or she is photocontact allergic as well. However, in general, the photopatch test site will be much more reactive than the patch-test area in a patient with dual sensitivity. Another problem is identification of the potential photoallergen. Although the history may be helpful in this determination, the patients often are not aware of the contact (except for suntan oils or the like). This is often true of preservatives or ingredients in soaps. Therefore, clinicians use the following series of compounds which commonly cause photocontact allergy, and add whatever can be determined from the history: 5% amyl dimethyl para-aminobenzoic acid

(PABA), glyceryl PABA, 5% musk ambrette, octyl dimethyl PABA, oxybenzone, dioxybenzone, 0.25% tetrachlorosalicylanilide (TCSA) and 1% TBS. They also routinely patch test with the screening materials suggested by the North American Contact Dermatitis Groups (NACDG)[72] to evaluate other potential contactants and phototest to examine for PMLE.[73]

d. Photocontactants

Photoallergic reactions to many topically contacted chemicals have been reported. These include sulfonamides,[55,56,74] phenothiazines,[43,56,62,63,65,75-79] sulfonylcarbamides,[80] men's colognes and aftershave lotions,[81] blankophores (optical brighteners),[82] Persian lime rind,[83] ragweed,[84] sunscreens,[85-93] diphenhydramine,[94] psoralens,[95,96] epoxy resins,[67] and quindoxin.[97,98] The halogenated salicylanilides and related antibacterial and antifungal compounds represented the most important group of allergic contact photosensitizers. In the 1960s, these chemicals were responsible for numerous photoallergic reactions. Perhaps TCSA was the most potent photosensitizer of this group. Between 1960 and 1961 it was responsible for an estimated 10,000 cases in England,[99] and it was therefore removed from general use. Subsequently, a number of related phenolic compounds were incorporated into soaps and other vehicles to combat infection, reduce body odor, act as preservatives, and destroy fungi. Photocontact reactions were induced by many of these agents, including bithionol, the brominated salicylanilides, hexachlorophene, dichlorophene, fentichlor (bis [2-hydroxy-5-chlorophenyl] sulfide), Multifungin (bromochlorosalicylanilide), Jadit (a mixture of buclosamide and salicylic acid),[3,57] and chloro-2-phenylphenol.[100]

There has been a rapid decline in the induction of photocontact dermatitis by the halogenated salicylanilides and related compounds since 1968.[101] This is due to the removal of the more potent of these photosensitizers from general use. However, within the past 5 years, there have been two new contactants which appear to produce photoallergic responses. These are the two widely used fragrance compounds 6-methylcoumarin[102,103] and musk ambrette.[66,104,105] In addition, musk ambrette has been reported to be responsible for the induction of a persistent light-reactor state similar to that noted with the halogenated salicylanilides.[66] The action spectrum for the photoallergic reactions to these fragrances falls in the UVA range.[102,103,106]

e. Mechanism

The clinical appearance, histology, and photopatch test responses suggest that the photoreactions are dependent on cell-mediated immunity (CMI). Experimental studies utilizing animal and human models support this concept.

Photoallergic reactions in human skin characteristic of CMI responses have been induced using multiple agents including sulfonamides,[107] phenothiazines,[63] and the halogenated salicylanilides.[69] Perhaps the most extensive studies have been accomplished with the halogenated salicylanilides. Willis and Kligman[69] utilized UVB as well as UVA exposures plus the chemicals to induce photosensitivity, but only UVA and the halogenated salicylanilides elicited the photocontact allergy. No evidence of antibody-mediated hypersensitivity has been detected in patients with photocontact reactions.

Animal and human studies have confirmed the CMI mechanism for photocontact allergy reactions; however, the nature of the antigen has not been settled. Two mechanisms are possible, and both may be correct. The studies of Burckhardt and Schwarz-Speck,[80] Jung and Schwarz,[108] and Schwarz and Speck[74] with sulfonamide and related compounds; Epstein and Enta,[109] Jung and Schultz,[110] and Willis and Kligman[69,111] with the halogenated salicylanilides; and Fulton and Willis[95] with methoxypsoralen suggested that the haptens were stable photoproducts of these chemicals. An alternative concept is that the photoproducts might well be shortlived free radicals, which attach the protein carrier within microseconds to form the complete antigen.[112] Support for this theory has developed from clinical observations.[3,57,113] In addition, Jung's studies of postirradiation free-radical formation and subsequent binding to albumin and β-globulin of chlorpromazine,[114] and triplet-state induction by radiation of triacetyldiphenolisatin (TDI) with deactivation by binding to albumin, β-globulin, and skin protein,[115] present further evidence in favor of the latter concept. The studies of Jung et al.[116,117] with Jadit were even more supportive. These workers demonstrated protein binding in vitro after irradiation. The protein complex then acted as a full antigen on plain patch testing of Jadit-photosensitive patients.

f. Experimental Predictive Testing Studies

Determination of the potential for a chemical to induce allergic photocontact sensitization has depended on demonstration of such reactions in patients who clinically have developed photocontact allergies to the chemical. Though animal models are readily available for phototoxicity studies, their use in evaluation of possible photoallergic reactions has presented a complicated problem. In fact, no animal models have proved to be valuable for predictive screening of photoallergic potential of chemicals.

Animal models are of great value in the study of photocontact reactions. Schwarz and Speck[74] first reported the induction of photoallergic contact dermatitis to sulfanilamide in guinea pigs. Subsequently, photoallergic contact reactions in guinea pigs have been induced in TCSA and related compounds, chlorpromazine, musk ambrette, and 6-methylcoumarin.[118,119] In vitro and in animals, immunologic studies have supported the cell-mediated nature of the hypersensitivity.[57,116,117,120] More recently, mouse models have been shown to be most efficient for experimentally examining this problem.[121,122] Using such animals, demonstration of the necessity of Langerhans cells, apparently to process the photoallergen appropriately; the need for genetically dependent T cells for the development of the reactivity; and the inhibiting influence of UVB-induced suppressor T cells have been established under experimental conditions.[123-125]

g. Human Experimental Model

Predictive testing in human skin is not definitive. In the 1960s, identification of TCSA and related phenolic compounds was accomplished by photopatch testing clinically involved patients. Subsequently Willis and Kligman[69] induced contact photoallergy to certain of these agents in normal human subjects using a modification of the maximization test which was developed for evaluating the potential for chemicals to produce contact dermatitis.[126] Recently, Kaidbey and Kligman[127,128] further modified the photomaximization procedure, and were able to photoallergic contact sensitize normal human volunteers to certain methylated coumarin derivatives, TCSA, 3.5-DBS, chlorpromazine, and sodium omadine. A lesser number of positive-induction responses were noted with TBS contaminated with 47% DBS, 4,5-DBS, Jadit, and bithionol. However, using the same test, negative results were noted with PABA and musk ambrette which have produced photoallergic contact reactions clinically. The authors considered them weak photosensitizers. Thus, to date, there is no proven effective predictive testing model for photoallergic contact dermatitis.

2. Systemic Drug Photoallergy

Photoallergic reactions to systemic photosensitizers are less common than those induced by contactants, and they are less well understood. However, a few apparent photoallergic reactions have been reported to a number of agents including the antibacterial sulfonamides,[74,107,129-131] quinethazone (Hydromox),[132] sulfonylurea antidiabetic agents,[133] the chlorothiazide diuretics,[134] phenothiazines,[135,136] oral contraceptive hormones,[137] griseofulvin,[138] chlordiazepoxide hydrochloride (Librium®),[139] several antihistamines,[140] triacetyldiphenolisatin,[141] the artificial sweetener calcium cyclamate,[142-144] chloroquine,[145] quinidine,[146,147] carprofen[148] and 5-fluorocytosine.[149,150]

The reaction time of these responses is delayed in nature, and the clinical eruptions range from lichenoid papules to eczematous changes. Though the problems are generally short-term, occasionally persistent light reactivity may be induced by systemic photosensitizers.[55]

V. THERAPY OF DRUG-INDUCED PHOTOSENSITIVITY

Therapy of acute photoallergic or phototoxic responses is identical to that used for any such inflammatory reactions. This includes the use of topical cool wet dressings, soothing shake lotions, topical corticosteroids, and systemic antipruritus agents. If the process is severe enough, systemic corticosteroids may be indicated. As with any topical or systemic drug-induced eruption, removal of the offending agent is essential to the cure of the allergic process. In case of photoallergy or phototoxicity, either the sun or the chemical could be removed. Because exposure to radiant energy is difficult to control, removal of the chemical is the most appropriate approach. Rarely, the medication is indispensible and in such cases avoidance of the sun is essential.

Some patients develop persistent light eruptions which persist after discontinuing use of the offending agent. When this occurs, the patient usually becomes markedly photosensitive. Long-term anti-inflammatory therapy and avoidance of any sun exposure may be necessary to control such a process.

REFERENCES

1. Epstein, J. H., Phototoxicity and photoallergy, in *Sunlight and Man,* Pathak, M. A., Harber, L. C., Seiji, M., and Kukita, A., Eds., University of Tokyo Press, Tokyo, 1974, 459.
2. Blum, H. F., *Photodynamic Action and Diseases Caused by Light,* Reinhold, New York, 1941.
3. Epstein, J. H., Photoallergy. A review, *Arch. Dermatol.,* 106, 741, 1972.
4. Morison, W. L., Parrish, J. A., and Epstein, J. H., Photoimmunology, *Arch. Dermatol.,* 115, 350, 1979.
5. Kochevar, I. E., Photoallergic responses to chemicals, *Photochem. Photobiol.,* 30, 437, 1979.
6. Pathak, M. A., Phytophotodermatitis, in *Sunlight and Man,* Pathak, M. A., Harber, L. C., Seiji, M., and Kukita, A., Eds., University of Tokyo Press, Tokyo, 1974, 495.
7. Epstein, J. H., Photocarcinogenesis, skin cancer and aging, *J. Am. Acad. Dermatol.,* 9, 487, 1983.
8. Epstein, J. H., Advances in cutaneous reactions to the sun, in *Yearbook of Dermatology,* Malkinson, F. D. and Pearson, R. W., Eds., Year Book Medical Publishing, Chicago, 1971, 5.
9. Parrish, J. A. and Pathak, M. A., Photomedicine, in *Dermatology in General Medicine,* 2nd ed., Fitzpatrick, T. B., Eisen, A. Z., Wolff, K., Freedberg, I. M., and Austen, K. F., Eds., McGraw-Hill, New York, 1979, 942.
10. Honigsman, H., Scnait, G. S., Konrad, R. A., Stingl, G., and Wolff, K., Mouse model for protoporphyria, *J. Invest. Dermatol.,* 66, 188, 1976.
11. Schnait, F. G., Wolff, K., and Konrad, K., Erythropoietic protoporphyria — submicroscopic events during the acute photosensitivity flare, *Br. J. Dermatol.,* 92, 545, 1975.
12. Anderson, R. R. and Parrish, J. A., Optics of human skin, *J. Invest. Dermatol.,* 77, 13, 1981.
13. Levine, G. M. and Harber, L. C., The effect of humidity on the phototoxic response to 8-methoxypsoralen in guinea pigs, *Acta Derm. Venereol.,* 49, 82, 1969.
14. Owens, D. W. and Knox, J. M., Influence of heat, wind, and humidity on ultraviolet radiation injury, in *Ultraviolet Carcinogenesis,* Natl. Cancer Institute Monogr. no. 50, Kripke, M. L. and Sass, E. R., Eds., NCI, Bethesda, Md., 1978, 161.
15. Kaidbey, K. H., Witkowski, T. A., and Kligman, M. A., The influence of infrared radiation on short-term ultraviolet-radiation-induced injuries, *Arch. Dermatol.,* 118, 315, 1982.
16. Walter, J. F., Gange, R. W., and Mendelson, I. R., Psoralen-containing sunscreen induces phototoxicity and epidermal ornithine decarboxylase activity, *J. Am. Acad. Dermatol.,* 6, 1022, 1982.

17. Ramsay, C. A. and Obreashkova, E., Photosensitivity from nalidixic acid, *Br. J. Dermatol.,* 91, 523, 1974.
18. Epstein, J. H., Tuffanelli, D. I., Seibert, J. S., and Epstein, W. L., Porphyria-like cutaneous changes induced by tetracycline hydrochloride photosensitization, *Arch. Dermatol.,* 112, 661, 1976.
19. Epstein, J. H., Tuffanelli, D. L., and Epstein, W. L., Cutaneous changes in the porphyrias: a microscopic study, *Arch. Dermatol.,* 107, 689, 1973.
20. Stern, R. S., Laird, N., Melskin, J., Parrish, J. A., Fitzpatrick, T. B., and Bleich, H. L., Cutaneous squamous cell carcinoma in patients treated with PUVA, *N. Engl. J. Med.,* 310, 1156, 1984.
21. Abel, E. A. and Farber, E. M., Photochemotherapy, in *Recent Advances in Dermatology,* Rook, A. and Savin, J., Eds., Churchill Livingstone, Edinburgh, 1980, 259.
22. Stern, R. S., Zibler, S., and Parrish, J. A., Skin carcinoma in patients treated with topical tar and artificial ultraviolet radiation, *Lancet,* 1, 732, 1980.
23. Breza, T. S., Halprin, K. M., and Taylor, J. R., Photosensitivity to vinblastine, *Arch. Dermatol.,* 111, 1168, 1975.
24, Kunse, J., Roeber, H., and Kollakowski, M., Phototoxic dermatitis with DTIC treatment, *Z. Hautkr.,* 55, 100, 1979.
25. Stratigos, J. D. and Magnus, I. A., Photosensitivity by demethylchlortetracycline and sulphanilamide, *Br. J. Dermatol.,* 80, 391, 1968.
26. Foote, C. S., Photosensitized oxidation and singlet oxygen: consequences in biological systems, in *Free Radicals in Biology,* Pryor, W. A., Ed., Academic Press, New York, 1976, 85.
27. Ito, T. and Kobayashi, K., A survey of in vivo photodynamic activity of xanthenes, thiazines and acridines in yeasts cells, *Photochem. Photobiol.,* 26, 591, 1978.
28. Harber, L. C. and Bickers, D. R., The porphyrias: basic science aspects, clinical diagnosis and management, in *Year Book of Dermatology,* Malkinson, F. D. and Pearson, R. W., Eds., Year Book Medical Publishing, Chicago, 1975, 9.
29. Lim, H. W., Perez, H. D., Poh-Fitzpatrick, M., and Gigli, I., Generation of chemotactic activity in serum from patients with erythropoietic protoporphyria and porphyria cutanea tarda, *N. Engl. J. Med.,* 304, 212, 1981.
30. Lim, H. W., Perez, H. D., Goldstein, I. M., and Gigli, I., Complement-derived chemotactic activity is generated in human serum containing uroporphyrin after irradiation with 405 nm light, *J. Clin. Invest.,* 67, 1072, 1981.
31. Lim, H. W., Novotny, H., and Gigli, I., Role of complement and polymorphonuclear cells in demethylchlortetracycline-induced phototoxicity in guinea pigs, *J. Clin. Invest.,* 71, 1326, 1983.
32. Pathak, M. A., Kramer, D. M., and Fitzpatrick, T. B., Photochemistry and photobiology of furocoumarins (psoralens), in *Sunlight and Man,* Pathak, M. A., Harber, L. C., Seiji, M., and Kukita, A., Eds., University of Tokyo Press, Tokyo, 1974, 335.
33. Song, P. S. and Tapley, K. J., Jr., Photochemistry and photobiology of psoralens, *Photochem. Photobiol.,* 29, 1177, 1979.
34. Ben-Hur, E. and Song, P. S., The photochemistry and photobiology of furocoumarins (psoralens), *Adv. Radiat. Biol.,* 11, 131, 1984.
35. Kochevar, I. and Lamola, A. A., Chlorpromazine and protriptyline phototoxicity: photosensitized, oxygen-independent red cell hemolysis, *Photochem. Photobiol.,* 29, 1177, 1979.
36. Argenbright, L. W., Forbes, P. D., and Steward, G. J., Quantitation of phototoxic hyperemia and permeability. II. Inhibition of histamine (H_1 and H_2) receptor antagonists in mouse skin, *J. Invest. Dermatol.,* 75, 417, 1980.
37. Kamide, R., Gigli, I., and Lim, H. W., Participation of mast cells and complement in the immediate phase of hematoporphyrin-induced photosensitivity, *J. Invest. Dermatol.,* 82, 485, 1984.
38. Sik, R. H., Paschall, C. S., and Chignell, C. F., The phototoxic effect of benoxaprofen and its analogs on human erythrocytes and rat peritoneal mast cells, *Photochem. Photobiol.,* 38, 411, 1983.
39. Kochevar, I. E., Hoover, K. W., and Grulenouski, M., Benoxaprofen photosensitization of cell membrane disruption, *J. Invest. Dermatol.,* 82, 214, 1984.
40. Parrish, J. A., Fitzpatrick, T. B., Pathak, M. A., and Tanenbaum, L., Photochemotherapy of psoriasis with oral methoxsalen and longwave ultraviolet light, *N. Engl. J. Med.,* 291, 1207, 1974.
41. Epstein, J. H., Brunsting, L. A., Petersen, M. C., and Schwarz, B. E., A study of photosensitivity occurring with chlorpromazine therapy, *J. Invest. Dermatol.,* 28, 329, 1957.
42. Kochevar, I. E., Phototoxicity mechanisms: chlorpromazine photosensitized damage to DNA and cell membranes, *J. Invest. Dermatol.,* 77, 59, 1981.
43. Epstein, S., Chlorpromazine photosensitivity, phototoxic and photoallergic reactions, *Arch. Dermatol.,* 98, 354, 1968.
44. Hunter, J. A., Bhutani, L. K., and Magnus, I. A., Chlorpromazine photosensitivity in mice: its action spectrum and effect of anti-inflammatory agents, *Br. J. Dermatol.,* 82, 157, 1970.
45. Rosenthal, I., Ben-Hur, E., Prager, A., and Riklis, E., Photochemical reactions of chlorpromazine: chemical and biochemical implications, *Photochem. Photobiol.,* 28, 591, 1978.

46. Kligman, A. M., Declomycin Compendium, Lederle Laboratories, Division of American Cyanamide Company, New York, 1962.
47. Maibach, H. I., Sams, N. M., Jr., and Epstein, J. H., Screening for drug toxicity by wavelengths greater than 310 nm, *Arch. Dermatol.,* 95, 12, 1967.
48. Keane, J. T., Pearson, R. W., and Malkinson, F. D., Nalidixic acid-induced photosensitivity in mice: a model for pseudoporphyria, *J. Invest. Dermatol.,* 82, 210, 1984.
49. Diffey, B. L., Daymond, T. J., and Fairgreaves, H., Phototoxic reactions to piroxicam, maproxen and tiaprofenic acid, *Br. J. Rheumatol.,* 22, 239, 1983.
50. Stern, R. S. and Bigby, M., An expanded profile of cutaneous reactions to nonsteroidal anti-inflammatory drugs, *JAMA,* 252, 1433, 1984.
51. Halsey, J., Benoxaprofen: side-effects profile in 300 patients, *Br. J. Med.,* 284, 1365, 1982.
52. Ferguson, J., A study of benoxaprofen-induced photosensitivity, *Br. J. Dermatol.,* 107, 429, 1982.
53. Emmett, E. A., Phototoxicity from exogenous agents, *Photochem. Photobiol.,* 38, 429, 1979.
54. Kligman, A. M. and Kaidbey, K. H., Human models for identification of photosensitizing chemicals, *J. Natl. Cancer Inst.,* 69, 264, 1982.
55. Epstein, S., Photoallergy versus phototoxicity, in *Dermatoses Due to Environmental and Physical Factors,* Rees, R. B., Ed., Charles C Thomas, Springfield, Ill., 1962, 119.
56. Storck, H., Photoallergy and photosensitivity: due to systemically administered drugs, *Arch. Dermatol.,* 91, 469, 1965.
57. Herman, P. and Sams, W. M., Jr., *Soap Photodermatitis,* Charles C Thomas, Springfield, Ill., 1972.
58. Jillson, V. F. and Baughman, R. D., Contact dermatitis from bithionol, *Arch. Dermatol.,* 88, 409, 1963.
59. Epstein, J. H., Wuepper, K. D., and Maibach, H. I., Photocontact dermatitis to halogenated compounds and related compounds, *Arch. Dermatol.,* 97, 236, 1968.
60. Burry, J. N., Persistent light reactions from buclosamide, *Arch. Dermatol.,* 101, 95, 1970.
61. Burry, J. N. and Hunter, G. A., Photocontact dermatitis from Jadit, *Br. J. Dermatol.,* 82, 244, 1970.
62. Amblard, P., Beani, J. C., and Raymond, J. L., Persistent light reaction due to phenothiazines in atopic disease, *Ann. Dermatol. Venereol.,* 109, 225, 1982.
63. Burdick, K. H., Prolonged sensitivity to intradermal chlorpromazine, *Cutis,* 5, 1113, 1969.
64. Wiskemann, A. and Wulf, K., Untersuchungen über den auslosenden Spektralbereich und die direkte Lichtpigmentierung bei chronischen und akuten Lichtauschlagen, *Arch. Klin. Exp. Dermatol.,* 209, 443, 1959.
65. Sidi, E., Hincky, M., and Gervais, A., Allergic sensitization and photosensitization to Phenergan cream, *J. Invest. Dermatol.,* 24, 345, 1955.
66. Giovinazzo, V. J., Harber, L. C., Bickers, D. R., Armstrong, R. B., and Silvers, D. N., Photoallergic contact dermatitis to musk ambrette, *J. Am. Acad. Dermatol.,* 3, 384, 1980.
67. Allen, H. and Kaidbey, K. H., Persistent photosensitivity following occupational exposure to epoxy resin, *Arch. Dermatol.,* 115, 1307, 1979.
68. Willis, I. and Kligman, A. M., The mechanism of the persistent light reactor, *J. Invest. Dermatol.,* 51, 385, 1968.
69. Willis, I. and Kligman, A. M., The mechanism of photoallergic contact dermatitis, *J. Invest. Dermatol.,* 51, 378, 1968.
70. Epstein, S., "Masked" photopatch tests, *J. Invest. Dermatol.,* 41, 369, 1963.
71. Harber, L. C., Bickers, D. R., Epstein, J. H., Pathak, M. A., and Urbach, F., Report on ultraviolet light sources, *Arch. Dermatol.,* 109, 833, 1974.
72. North American Contact Dermatitis Group of the National Program for Dermatology, The Role of Patch Testing in Allergic Contact Dermatitis, Johnson & Johnson, New Brunswick, N.Y., 1974.
73. Epstein, J. H., Polymorphus light eruption, *Ann. Allergy,* 24, 397, 1966.
74. Schwarz, K. and Speck, M., Experimentelle Untersuchungen zun Frage der Photoallergie der Sulfonamide, *Dermatologica,* 114, 232, 1957.
75. Epstein, S., Allergic photocontact dermatitis from promethazine (Phenergan), *Arch. Dermatol.,* 81, 175, 1960.
76. Epstein, S. and Rowe, R. J., Photoallergy and photocross-sensitivity to Phenergan, *J. Invest. Dermatol.,* 29, 319, 1957.
77. Ertle, T., Work-related contact and photocontact allergy in a farmer caused by chlorpromazine, *Derm. Beruf. Umwelt.,* 30, 120, 1982.
78. Polano, J. K., Photosensitivity due to drugs, *Excerpta Med. Int. Congr. Ser.,* 85, 102, 1964.
79. Torinuki, W., Kumai, N., and Miura, T., Chronic photosensitive dermatitis due to phenothiazines, *Tohoku J. Exp. Med.,* 138, 223, 1982.
80. Burckhardt, W. and Schwarz-Speck, M., Photoallergische Ekzeme durch Nadisan, *Schweiz. Med. Wochenschr.,* 87, 954, 1954.
81. Epstein, E., Persome dermatitis in men, *JAMA,* 209, 911, 1969.

82. Burckhardt, W., Photoallergy eczema due to blankophores (optic brightening agents), *Hautarzt*, 8, 486, 1957.

83. Epstein, S., Discussion of Reference 92, 1956.

84. Epstein, S., Role of dermal sensitivity in ragweed contact dermatitis, *Arch. Dermatol.*, 82, 48, 1960.

85. Davies, M. G., Hawk, J. L., and Rycroft, R., Acute photosensitivity from the sunscreen 2-ethoxy-ethyl-*p*-methoxycinnamate, *Contact Dermatitis*, 8, 190, 1982.

86. Fagerlund, V. L., Kalimo, K., and Hansen, C., Photocontact allergy from sunscreens, *Duodecin*, 99, 146, 1983.

87. Fitzpatrick, T. B., Pathak, M. A., Magnus, I. A. et al., Abnormal reactions of man to light, *Annu. Rev. Med.*, 14, 195, 1963.

88. Goldman, G. C. and Epstein, E., Jr., Contact photosensitivity dermatitis from sun-protective agent, *Arch. Dermatol.*, 100, 447, 1969.

89. Holzle, E. and Plewig, G., Photoallergic contact dermatitis by benzophenone containing sunscreening preparations, *Hautarzt*, 33, 391, 1982.

90. Kaidbey, K. H. and Allen, H., Photocontact allergy to benzocaine, *Arch. Dermatol.*, 117, 77, 1981.

91. Mathias, C. G. T., Maibach, H. I., and Epstein, J. H., Allergic contact photodermatitis to para-aminobenzoic acid, *Arch. Dermatol.*, 114, 1665, 1978.

92. Sams, W. M., Contact photodermatitis, *Arch. Dermatol.*, 73, 142, 1956.

93. Satulsky, E. M., Photosensitization induced by monoglyceron para-aminobenzoate, *Arch. Dermatol.*, 62, 711, 1950.

94. Emmett, E. A., Diphenydramine photoallergy, *Arch. Dermatol.*, 110, 249, 1974.

95. Fulton, J. E. and Willis, I., Photoallergy to methoxsalen, *Arch. Dermatol.*, 98, 445, 1968.

96. Sidi, E. and Bourgeois-Cavardin, J. Mise au point due traitement du vitiligo par l'Ammi Majus, *Presse Med.*, 61L, 436, 1953.

97. Scott, K. W. and Dawson, T. A. J., Photocontact dermatitis arising from the presence of quindoxin in animals feeding stuffs, *Br. J. Dermatol.*, 90, 543, 1974.

98. Zanoun, S., Johnson, B. E., and Frain-Bell, W., The investigation of quindoxin photosensitivity, *Contact Dermatitis*, 2, 342, 1976.

99. Wilkinson, D. S., Photodermatitis due to tetrachlorosalicylanilide, *Br. J. Dermatol.*, 73, 213, 1961.

100. Adams, R. M., Photoallergic contact dermatitis to chloro-2-phenyl-phenol, *Arch. Dermatol.*, 106, 711, 1972.

101. Smith, S. Z. and Epstein, J. H., Photocontact dermatitis to halogenated salicylanilides and related compounds, *Arch. Dermatol.*, 113, 1372, 1977.

102. Jackson, R. T., Nesbit, L. T., and DeLeo, V. A., 6-Methyl coumarin photocontact dermatitis, *J. Am. Acad.. Dermatol.*, 2, 124, 1980.

103. Kaidbey, K. H. and Kligman, A. M., Contact photoallergy to 6-methyl coumarin in proprietary sunscreens, *Arch. Dermatol.*, 114, 1709, 1978.

104. Galosi, A. and Plewig, G., Photoallergic eczema caused by musk ambrette, *Hautarzt*, 33, 589, 1982.

105. Raugi, G. J., Storrs, F. J., and Larsen, W. G., Photoallergic contact dermatitis to men's perfume, *Contact Dermatitis*, 5, 251, 1979.

106. Giovinazzo, V. J., Harber, L. C., Bickers, D. R., and Armstrong, R. B., Photoallergic contact dermatitis to musk ambrette: action spectrum in guinea pigs and man, *Photochem. Photobiol.*, 33, 773, 1981.

107. Epstein, S., Photoallergy and primary phototoxicity to sulfanilamide, *J. Invest. Dermatol.*, 2, 43, 1939.

108. Jung, E. G. and Schwarz, K., Photoallergy to "Jadit" with photocrossreactions to derivatives of sulfanilamide, *Int. Arch. Allergy Appl. Immunol.*, 27, 313, 1965.

109. Epstein, S. and Enta, T., Photoallergic content dermatitis, *JAMA*, 194, 1016, 1965.

110. Jung, E. G. and Schultz, R., Kontakt und Photoallergien durch Desinfizien, *Dermatologica*, 137, 216, 1968.

111. Willis, I. and Kligman, A. M., Photocontent allergic reactions: elicitation by low dose ultraviolet rays, *Arch. Dermatol.*, 110, 535, 1969.

112. Jenkins, F. P., Welti, D., and Baines, D., Photochemical reactions of tetrachlorosalicylanilide, *Nature (London)*, 210, 827, 1964.

113. Osmundsen, P. E., Contact photoallergy to tribromsalicylanide, *Br. J. Dermatol.*, 81, 429, 1969.

114. Jung, E. G., In vitro-Untersuchungen zur Chlorpromazine (CPZ) Photoallergie, *Arch. Klin. Exp. Dermatol.*, 237, 501, 1970.

115. Jung, E. G., Photoallergic durch Triacetyldiphenolisatin (TDI). II. Photochemische Untersuchungen zur Pathogenese, *Arch. Klin. Exp. Dermatol.*, 231, 39, 1967.

116. Jung, E. G., Dummler, U., and Immich, H., Photoallergie durch 4-chlor-2-hydroxy-benzoesaure-*n*-butylmid. I. Lichtbiologische Untersuchungen zur Antigenbildung, *Arch. Klin. Exp. Dermatol.*, 232, 403, 1968.

117. Jung, E. G., Hornke, J., and Hajede, P., Photoallergic durch 4-chlor-2-hydrobenzoesaure-*n*-butyl-mid. II. Photochemische Untersuchungen, *Arch. Klin. Exp. Dermatol.,* 233, 287, 1968.
118. Harber, L. C., Current status of mammalian and human models for predicting drug photosensitivity, *J. Invest. Dermatol.,* 77, 65, 1981.
119. Jordan, W. P., Jr., The guinea pig model for predicting photoallergic contact dermatitis, *Contact Dermatitis,* 8, 109, 1982.
120. Harber, L. C., Targovnik, S. E., and Baer, R. L., Contact photosensitivity patterns to halogenated salicylanilides in man and guinea pigs, *Arch. Dermatol.,* 96, 646, 1967.
121. Maguire, H. C., Jr. and Kaidbey, K. H., Experimental photoallergic contact dermatitis: a mouse model, *J. Invest. Dermatol.,* 79, 147, 1982.
122. Miyachi, Y. and Takigawa, M., Mechanisms of contact photosensitivity in mice. III. Predictive testing of chemicals with photoallergic potential in mice, *Arch. Dermatol.,* 119, 736, 1983.
123. Granstein, R. D., Morison, W. L., and Kripke, M. L., The role of suppressor cells in the induction of murine photoallergic contact dermatitis and in its suppression by prior UVB irradiation, *J. Immunol.,* 130, 2099, 1983.
124. Miyachi, Y. and Takigawa, M., Mechanisms of contact photosensitivity in mice. II. Langerhans cells are required for successful induction of contact photosensitivity to TCSA, *J. Invest. Dermatol.,* 78, 363, 1982.
125. Takigawa, M. and Miyachi, Y., Mechanisms of contact photosensitivity in mice. I. T cell regulation of contact photosensitivity to tetrachlorsalicylanilide under genetic restrictions of the major histocompatibility complex, *J. Invest. Dermatol.,* 79, 108, 1982.
126. Kligman, A. M., Identification of contact allergens by human assay. III. The maximization test: a procedure for screening and rating contact sensitizers, *J. Invest. Dermatol.,* 47, 393, 1966.
127. Kaidbey, K. H. and Kligman, A. M., Photo-maximization test for identifying photoallergic contact sensitizers, *Contact Dermatitis,* 6, 161, 1980.
128. Kaidbey, K. H., The evaluation of photoallergic contact sensitizers in humans, in *Dermatotoxicology,* 2nd ed., Marzulli, F. N. and Maibach, H. I., Eds., Hemisphere Publishers, Washington, D.C., 1983, 405.
129. Blum, H. F., Studies of photosensitivity due to sulfanilamide, *J. Invest. Dermatol.,* 4, 159, 1941.
130. Burkhardt, W., Untersuchungen über die Photoaktivitat einiger Sulfanilamide, *Dermatologica,* 83, 63, 1941.
131. Stevanovic, D. V., Photosensitivity due to certain drugs, *Br. J. Dermatol.,* 73, 233, 1961.
132. Miller, R. C. and Beltrani, V. S., Quinethazone photosensitivity dermatitis, *Arch. Dermatol.,* 93, 346, 1966.
133. Hitselberger, J. F. and Foxnaugh, R. P., Photosensitivity due to chlorpropamide, *JAMA,* 180, 142, 1962.
134. Harber, L. C., Lashinsky, A. M., and Baer, R. L., Photosensitivity due to chlorothiazide and hydrochlorothiazide, *N. Engl. J. Med.,* 261, 1378, 1959.
135. Calnan, C. D., Frain-Bell, W., and Cuthbert, W. I., Occupational dermatitis from chlorpromazine, *Trans. St. John's Hosp. Dermatol. Soc.,* 48, 49, 1962.
136. Schultz, K. H., Wickemann, A., and Wulf, K., Kliniche und experimentelle Untersuchungen über die photodynamiche Wirksamkeit von Phinothiazin Derivaten, insbesondere von Magaphen, *Arch. Klin. Exp. Dermatol.,* 202, 285, 1956.
137. Erickson, L. R. and Peterka, E. S., Sunlight sensitivity from oral contraceptives, *JAMA,* 203, 980, 1968.
138. Chang, T. W., Cold urticaria and photosensitivity due to griseofulvin, *JAMA,* 193, 848, 1965.
139. Luton, E. F. and Finchum, R. N., Photosensitivity reaction to chlordiazepoxide, *Arch. Dermatol.,* 91, 362, 1965.
140. Schreiber, M. M. and Naylor, L. Z., Antihistamine photosensitivity, *Arch. Dermatol.,* 86, 58, 1962.
141. Kasuistik, I. and Jung, E. G., Photoallergic durch Triacetydiphenolisatin (TDI), *Arch. Klin. Exp. Dermatol.,* 229, 170, 1967.
142. Kobori, T. and Araki, H., Photoallergy in dermatology, *J. Asthma Res.,* 3, 213, 1966.
143. Lamberg, S. I., A new photosensitizer: the artificial cyclamate, *JAMA,* 201, 121, 1967.
144. Tatsuji, K. and Toshie, A., Photoallergic dermatitis probably due to artificial sweetening agents, *Med. Cult.,* 5, 795, 1963.
145. Van Weelden, H., Bolling, H. H., Baart de la Faille, H., and van der Leun, J. C., Photosensitivity caused by chloroquine, *Arch. Dermatol.,* 118, 290, 1982.
146. Lang, P. G., Jr., Quinidine-induced photodermatitis confirmed by photopatch testing, *J. Am. Acad. Dermatol.,* 91, 124, 1983.
147. Marx, J. L., Eisenstat, B. A., and Gladstein, A. H., Quinidine photosensitivity, *Arch. Dermatol.,* 119, 39, 1983.
148. Merot, Y., Harms, M., and Saurat, J. H., Photosensitivity associated with carprofen (Imadyl) a new non-steroidal anti-inflammatory drug, *Dermatologica,* 116, 310, 1983.

149. Beardmore, G. L., Recalcitrant sporotrichosis: a report of a patient treated with various therapies, including oral miconozole and 5-fluorocytosine, *Aust. J. Dermatol.*, 20, 10, 1979.
150. Shelley, W. B. and Sica, P. A., Disseminate sporotrichosis of skin and bone cured with 5-fluorocytosine: photosensitivity as a complication, *J. Am. Acad. Dermatol.*, 8, 229, 1983.

Chapter 8

PORPHYRIAS

Maureen B. Poh-Fitzpatrick

TABLE OF CONTENTS

I. INTRODUCTION

The porphyrias are a group of related clinical disorders that arise from several different enzymatic errors of heme biosynthesis. These errors are partial enzyme blocks that result in accumulation of abnormal amounts of intermediaries and by-products of the heme biosynthetic pathway in patterns that differ according to the locus of the defective enzyme in the sequence. Each unique porphyria has been associated with defective activity of a particular enzyme. They are listed in Table 1.

The porphyrias are usually classified into "erythropoietic" or "hepatic" categories based on whether the bulk of the total excess porphyrin production occurs in the heme-synthesizing cells of the erythron or in hepatocytes. More recent information about these disorders suggests that in some disorders (particularly protoporphyria) abnormal amounts of heme precursors may be produced in both organs of heme synthesis and to a lesser extent in other tissues as well. The clinical characteristics of each distinct porphyria are determined by the properties of the particular array of porphyrins or porphyrin precursors that accumulate in the tissues of origin, are liberated into the blood and disseminate into other tissues, and are excreted by renal or hepatobiliary mechanisms.

II. ENZYME DEFECTS IN PORPHYRIAS

An outline of heme biosynthesis is shown in Figure 1. In normal individuals, heme synthesis is closely regulated so that very few of the intermediaries escape conversion into heme. The rate-limiting enzyme for the pathway is δ-aminolevulinic acid synthase (ALAS). The control of overall pathway activity is exerted by negative feedback repression of either ALAS synthesis or of its activity by the end-product heme. When heme supplies are adequate, ALAS activity is geared to maintain the level constant. Heme depletion or deficiency results in induction of new enzyme synthesis or in direct derepression of ALAS activity, thus driving the production of increased amounts of precursors to supply new heme.

In hepatic heme synthesis, ALAS regulation is affected by numerous agents including many drugs, selected steroid hormones, and other compounds that rapidly stimulate new ALAS synthesis by several different mechanisms having the common result of reducing available free heme.[1-3] Repletion of heme or heme analogues from exogenous sources can abort or prevent this effect.[4] High concentrations of dietary glucose also appear to retard induction of ALAS in clinical settings.[5,6]

Erythropoietic heme synthesis appears to have a different set of factors that stimulate ALAS function, and the mechanism of heme feedback repression appears to be directly on enzyme activity rather than on rate of new enzyme synthesis.[7] Factors that promote or inhibit ALAS activity in in vitro experimental systems may have clinical relevance in preventive and interventive management of patients.

A specific enzyme defect for each of the porphyrias has been determined. Accumulation of the substrates for the partially blocked enzymes results in the biochemical abnormalities that characterize each distinct porphyric entity. Since the array of clinical manifestations demonstrated by each of these disorders is related to the types of porphyrin precursors accumulated, knowledge of the site of the defect associated with each porphyria aids greatly in the understanding of both the biochemical and clinical features of each syndrome.

The partial enzyme defect associated with a unique porphyria that occurs earliest in the pathway is in uroporphyrinogen synthase (US), otherwise termed porphobilinogen deaminase. Deficient activity of this enzyme is linked with acute intermittent porphyria

Table 1
CLASSIFICATION OF PORPHYRIAS AND THEIR
ENZYMATIC DEFECTS

Disorder	Defective enzyme
Erythropoietic	
Congenital erythropoietic porphyria	Uroporphyrinogen cosynthase
Protoporphyria	Heme synthase
Hepatic	
Porphyria cutanea tarda	Uroporphyrinogen decarboxylase
Acute intermittent porphyria[a]	Uroporphyrinogen synthase
Variegate porphyria[a]	Protoporphyrinogen oxidase
Hereditary coproporphyria[a]	Coproporphyrinogen oxidase

[a]   Acute attack forms of porphyria.

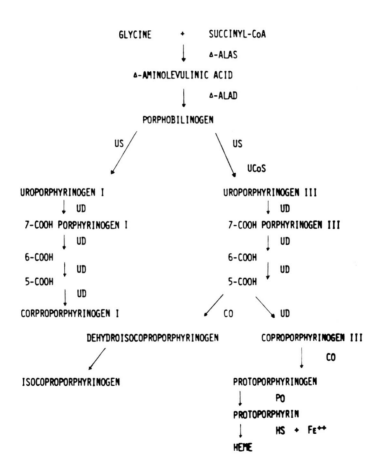

FIGURE 1.   Heme biosynthetic pathway. Δ-ALAS = delta-aminolevulinic acid synthase; Δ-ALAD = delta-aminolevulinic acid dehydrase; US = uroporphyrinogen synthase (porphobilinogen deaminase); UCoS = uroporphyrinogen cosynthase; UD = uroporphyrinogen decarboxylase; CO = coproporphyrinogen oxidase; PO = protoporphyrinogen oxidase; HS = heme synthase (ferrochelatase).

(AIP).[8] US utilizes porphobilinogen as substrate; thus this precursor (and its predecessor aminolevulinic acid) accumulate and are subsequently excreted in abnormal amounts. None of the subsequent intermediaries or photosensitizing by-products of heme synthesis are accumulated in AIP.

Partial deficiency of the next enzyme in the sequence, uroporphyrinogen cosynthase (UCoS) results in the ineficent conversion of the product of the uroporphyrinogen synthase reaction to uroporphyrinogen of the isomer III configuration. Only series III isomers can undergo complete conversion into heme. The accumulated substrate of this UCoS deficiency undergoes spontaneous (nonenzymic) conversion to the series I isomer of uroporphyrin. Series I precursors can be further utilized as substrates only by one additional pathway enzyme, thereby being metabolized through the 7-, 6-, 5-, and 4-carboxylic series I porphyrinogens, resulting in accumulation of their corresponding spontaneously oxidized, photoactive series I porphyrin by-products of the pathway. Accumulation and excretion of large amounts of the isomeric series I porphyrins are the major biochemical indicators of congenital erythropoietic porphyria, the disorder linked to a defect in UCoS activity.[9]

Uroporphyrinogen decarboxylase (UD) is the next enzyme in the sequence, and is responsible for the stepwise removal of 4-carboxyl groups from the uroporphyrinogen I or III substrate. Decreased UD activity has been established as the enzymic abnormality in all forms of porphyria cutanea tarda.[10] Partial deficiency of UD results in accumulation of all of the 8-, 7-, 6-, and 5-carboxylic porphyrinogens of both III and I isomeric series and their corresponding spontaneously oxidized photosensitizing porphyrins. The excess accumulation of the 5-carboxylic porphyrinogen, however, can serve as substrate for another enzyme, coproporphyrinogen oxidase (CO). CO converts this 5-carboxyl compound to dehydroisocoproporphyrinogen, a by-product of the pathway occurring in large amounts only in the presence of deficient UD activity. Spontaneous oxidation of this tetracarboxylic porphyrinogen yields isocoproporphyrin, a marker molecule for UD deficiency disorders that is readily detectable in both urine and feces when present in large amounts.[11]

Deficient activity of CO levels leads to accumulation of its substrate coproporphyrinogen III. Defective CO and overproduction and excretion of coproporphyrin III are associated with hereditary coproporphyria.[12,13]

The next enzyme in the sequence is protoporphyrinogen oxidase (PO). Deficient conversion of protoporphyrinogen to protoporphyrin is the result of this partial block. This defect is associated with variegate porphyria (VP).[14] The array of heme precursors that accumulate and are excreted in abnormal amounts in VP includes not only oxidized protoporphyrin, considered to be the nonenzymatic oxidation product of accumulated protoporphyrinogen rather than the protoporphyrin normally formed by enzymatic conversion,[14] but also lesser amounts of coproporphyrin and hydrophilic porphyrinpeptide complexes.[15] The accumulation of coproporphyrin could be explained by the observation that protoporphyrinogen is an effective competitive inhibitor of CO,[16] leading to a secondary backup of the CO substrate, coproporphyrinogen III. Some investigators have also given evidence that at least in some cases, a defect in heme synthase activity may also be associated with this disorder.[17,18]

The last enzyme, heme synthase (or ferrochelatase), is responsible for incorporation of a ferrous iron molecule at the central position of the tetrapyrrole ring structure of protoporphyrin. This results in heme, a nonphotoactive compound. Partial deficiency of heme synthase results in accumulation of the dicarboxylic, hydrophobic protoporphyrin, the only photosensitizing molecule serving as a substrate in the pathway. Excess protoporphyrin and defective heme synthase are linked with the disorder photoporphyria.[19,20]

The solubility properties of the intermediaries and porphyrin by-products of heme synthesis determine the route of their excretion. The more water-soluble group — aminolevulinic acid (ALA), porphobilinogen (PBG), uroporphyrin, and heptacarboxylic porphyrins — are primarily excreted into the urine, while the dicarboxylic hydrophobic protoporphyrin molecule is excreted by biliary secretion into the feces. Coproporphyrin and isocoproporphyrin with 4-carboxyl side groups and the penta- and hexacarboxylic porphyrins have intermediate solubility properties, and can be found in both urine and feces.

Whether patients with different forms of porphyria exhibit cutaneous photosensitivity and the different types of photocutaneous lesions that occur appear to be determined by the physiochemical properties of the particular metabolites accumulated and transported to the skin in each disorder. All forms of porphyria, except AIP, may have light-induced skin lesions as part of the clinical symptom complex. The explanation for the exclusion of AIP appears to be that the porphyrin precursors that accumulate in AIP (e.g., ALA and PBG) are not photosensitizing molecules. Patients with all of the other porphyrias do accumulate molecules that can absorb light radiation in the visible spectrum, and re-emit this energy by several mechanisms including fluorescence and performance of photochemistry.

The reduced tetrapyrrolic porphyrinogens that are the true intermediaries of the pathway are not photoactive molecules. However, as these molecules accumulate, nonenzymatic oxidation converts them irreversibly to the corresponding photosensitizing porphyrins. Oxidized porphyrins are purple pigments, and discolor the tissues or fluids in which they are heavily deposited.

III. CLINICAL PATTERNS IN PORPHYRIAS

Patients with any of the porphyrias that are biochemically characterized by accumulation and excretion of the more water-soluble porphyrins exhibit similar cutaneous lesions. The skin of these patients is so fragile in sun-exposed areas that the epidermis shears away from the underlying dermis with minimal mechanical trauma. Blisters or bullae form spontaneously, with the fluid-filled cavity between the epidermis and dermis (Figure 2). These lesions are slow to heal, and form heavy crusts and residual scars (Figure 3). Hypertrichosis, pigmentary disturbances (Figure 4), sclerodermoid changes with loss of dermal appendages and calcification, and scarring of potentially mutilating severity are the major chronic manifestations of this type of porphyric phototoxicity. Although the chronic changes may be severely deforming, very often there is little or no acute discomfort in the skin at the time of light exposure, and some patients remain unaware of the association of skin lesions and light.

In contrast, patients with protoporphyria who have accumulated hydrophobic protoporphyrin exhibit a different acute and chronic phototoxicity response pattern. Within minutes of sunlight exposure, patients with protoporphyria experience sensations of stinging, tingling, or burning deep within their skin. With sufficient exposure, the skin becomes massively edematous within several hours and then develops petechial erythema (Figure 5). The skin remains very painful during the 2 to 3 days of evolution of these lesions. However, after the petechiae resolve, the residual scarring is usually limited to shallow, pitted depressions of the skin of the face, and a roughened or leathery texture of the dorsum of the hands, and occasionally of the forehead, nose, and malar skin (Figure 6).

Three of the hepatic porphyrias are clinically similar in the occurrence of acute attack episodes which may be of life-threatening severity. These three are AIP, VP, and hereditary coproporphyria (HCP). Each of these hepatic porphyrias is characterized

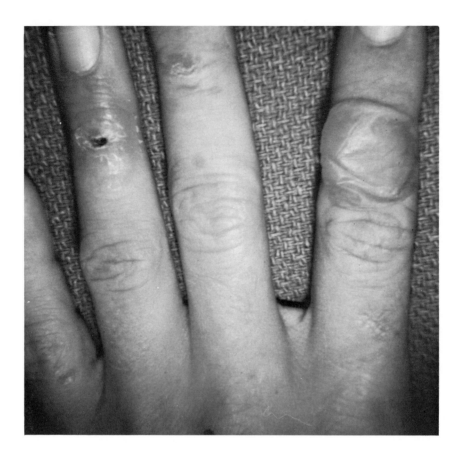

FIGURE 2.   Large bulla on the index finger of a patient with porphyria cutanea tarda. Note also a crusted erosion over the middle knuckle and the healing site of a previous bulla on the fourth finger.

by the excretion of large amounts of ALA and PBG, either constantly (AIP), or primarily during the episode (VP and HCP). The same factors are responsible for triggering onset of the attacks in all of these disorders, and the treatment of such attacks is also the same for all.

A. Congenital Erythropoietic Porphyria (CEP)

CEP is the least-common porphyria, and the only one inherited as an autosomal recessive defect. The onset of signs and symptoms may occur at birth or shortly thereafter. Copious excretion of porphyrins of the more water-soluble classes into the urine causes pink discoloration of urine and diapers.

As described earlier, reduced activity of UCoS results in accumulation of series I isomers of the porphyrinogens and the corresponding spontaneously oxidized porphyrin molecules with 8- to 4-carboxylic side groups. Only series III porphyrinogen isomers can be fully processed to complete the heme sequence beyond coproporphyrin formation. Reduction in heme synthesized is often profound and reflected clinically as an anemia detectable at birth. Heme deficiency also results in derepression of the rate-controlling enzyme of the pathway, ALAS, so that the sequence is driven to produce more intermediaries. In addition to the characteristically heavy accumulation of the series I porphyrin by-products, the corresponding series III isomers may be found in increased amounts as well.

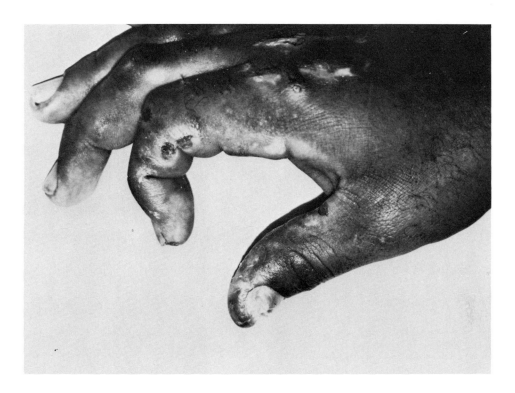

FIGURE 3. Crusted erosions and depigmented scars forming on the hand of a patient with porphyria cutanea tarda.

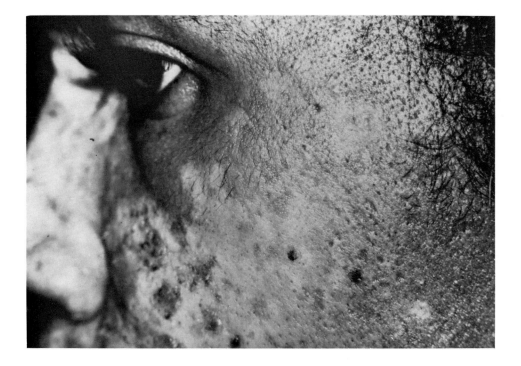

FIGURE 4. Crusted facial erosions and marked depigmentation in a patient with porphyria cutanea tarda. Several coarse hairs are present over the zygomatic arch.

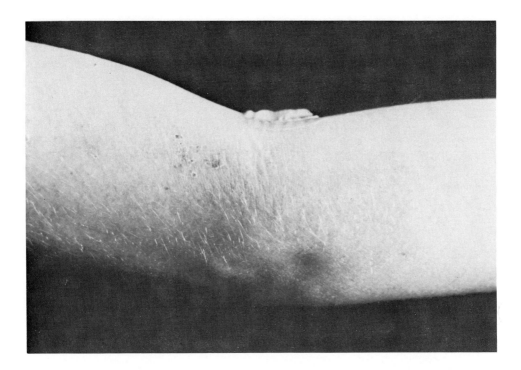

FIGURE 5.   Petechial erythema in a patient with protoporphyria.

Photosensitivity is severe, and may be present at birth. Infants exposed to sunlight will form blisters. If not protected rigorously from light exposure, the chronic sequelae of CEP can be terribly deforming. Deep scars, destruction of cartilage of ala nasi and auricular pinnae, scarring alopecia, pigmentary changes, ectropion, eclabium, resorption of distal phalanges, and teeth stained brown-red by deposited porphyrin pigment all contribute to a clinical morbidity of potentially horrific proportions. The associated anemia may be severe, with secondary splenomegaly and stunting of growth. The hyperactive bone marrow, attempting to compensate the anemia and shortened erythrocyte life span, may encroach on the bony cortices causing retarded growth and thinned bones that may fracture easily.

Treatment for these patients includes measures to physically protect the skin from offensive wavelengths of light, oral β-carotene photoprotection (see Section III.B), splenectomy in selected cases to reduce premature destruction of circulating erythrocytes, and transfusion to provide adequate heme in circulation to reduce erythropoiesis. Recent clinical trials of hypertransfusion have had good success, combined with vigorous cutaneous photoprotection, in limiting the usual clinical morbidity associated with CEP.[22,23]

B. Protoporphyria (EPP)

Inherited in an autosomal dominant mode, human protoporphyria is one of the more common disorders of porphyrin metabolism. A partial block of the enzyme heme synthase (ferrochelatase) reduces conversion of protoporphyrin to heme, resulting in accumulation of the photoactive, hydrophobic protoporphyrin molecule. In the majority of cases, this defect appears to be expressed chiefly in the erythropoietic bone marrow tissue.[24,25] Thus, this disorder is often referred to as "erythropoietic protoporphyria". In selected cases, an important contribution to the total excess of protopor-

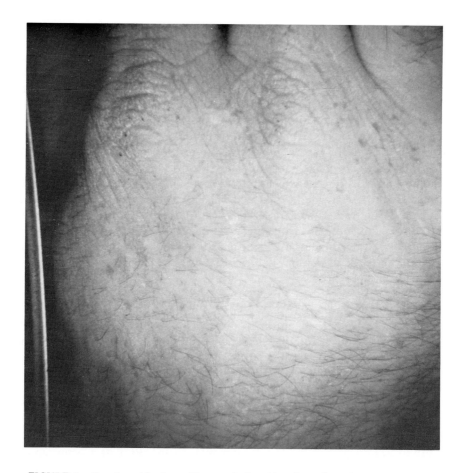

FIGURE 6.   Roughened leathery skin over the knuckles of a patient with protoprophyria.

phyrin may also derive from hepatocytic protoporphyrin production.[25,26] Therefore, many investigators now refer to this syndrome simply as "protoporphyria".

Despite the defective enzyme activity, sufficient heme is usually formed, so that clinically detectable anemia is typically mild or may be absent. The most frequent clinical manifestations are the cutaneous symptoms that typically appear sometime during childhood. Apart from painful acute phototoxicity, patients with EPP have an increased incidence of early-onset cholelithiasis.[27] This appears related to the very large excesses of protoporphyrin cleared from the blood by the liver and secreted into the bile. Fecal protoporphyrin excretion rates are affected by the enterohepatic reabsorption of some fraction of the secreted protoporphyrin.[28]

The livers of patients with EPP are characterized by the presence of pigmented protoporphyrin deposits in hepatocytes, macrophages, and biliary canaliculi. Crystals of protoporphyrin and abnormal mitochondria can be seen in hepatocytes with electron microscopy.[29,31] and with polarizing lenses, the porphyrin deposits are seen as doubly refractile "Maltese cross" bodies.[32] Although liver biopsy specimens from virtually all patients show these abnormalities to a variable extent, in a minority of unknown percentage, protoporphyrin deposition is heavy and associated with inflammatory changes, fibrosis, and even cirrhosis. Some patients with EPP will develop signs and symptoms of hepatic dysfunction, and some 20 cases of progressive liver failure and death from dysfunction or hemorrhage from esophageal varices have been recorded in the medical literature.

Treatment for the cutaneous phototoxicity includes avoidance of sunlight exposure and ingestion of β-carotene. The naturally occurring yellow pigment, β-carotene, was noted to have photoprotective effects in bacterial and animal model systems.[33,34] Subsequently, this provitamin was administered to human volunteers with EPP and was found to increase cutaneous tolerance to light exposure.[35,36] Ingestion of synthetic β-carotene in amounts sufficient to raise serum carotene levels to the 400 to 800 μg/dl range produces clinical carotenoderma. As the skin yellows, patients note decreasing symptom levels compared with pretreatment exposures. Synthetic β-carotene has now been available for use for several years without recognition of serious side effects. Safety for use in pregnancy has not been determined.

The mechanism of action by which the β-carotene molecule provides photoprotection is considered to reside chiefly in its avid singlet-oxygen quenching and free-radical scavenging properties rather than from a physical filter effect of the yellow pigment.[37] However, all of these mechanisms may contribute to the total effect. The efficacy of carotene in EPP has suggested its use in the porphyrias in which the more water-soluble porphyrin molecules are the major photosensitizers. In these other disorders, benefit is less readily evident than in EPP.

C. Porphyria Cutanea Tarda (PCT)

Probably the most frequently occurring disorder of porphyrin metabolism is PCT. The disorder is an hepatic porphyria which may occur in familial or sporadic forms.

An autosomal dominant transmission of the genetic defect for deficiency in UD results in the familial form of PCT. Heterozygous inheritance results in the classical adult-onset form of PCT (only rarely seen in children), while homozygous inheritance of the same defect apparently causes a much more severe, childhood-onset disorder whose clinical picture resembles that of CEP. In addition to familial PCT, cases have been observed to occur in sporadic instances or epidemic outbreaks apparently related to exposure to hepatotoxic drugs or environmental toxins. PCT as a symptom of hepatic tumors has been well described,[38,39] and PCT-manifesting symptoms after institution of maintenance dialysis for chronic renal failure has also recently been recognized.[40,41]

UD mediates the sequential decarboxylation of 4-carboxyl groups from uroporphyrinogen I or III, yielding the hepta-, hexa-, and pentacarboxylic porphyrinogens and coproporphyrinogens. Partial deficiency of the enzyme (approximately 50% of normal activity in heterozygous inherited PCT) results in accumulation of 8-, 7-, 6-, and 5-carboxylic spontaneously oxidized porphyrin by-products. Although the normal conversion of pentacarboxylic porphyrinogen to coproporphyrinogen is compromised, the next enzyme in the pathway, CO, causes conversion of this substrate to dehydroisocoproporphyrinogen which oxidizes to isocoproporphyrin, a tetracarboxylic molecule that accumulates in large amounts characteristically in PCT.[42] Isocoproporphyrin appears, along with coproporphyrin, in feces as well as in urine. A fecal isocoproporphyrin to coprocoproporphyrin ratio >0.1 is associated with PCT.[43]

In familial PCT, the enzyme defect can be measured in erythrocytes as well as in hepatocytes, while in sporadic cases the defect appears to be present only in hepatocytes.[44,45] In cases of homozygous inheritance of the genetic defect for PCT, the enzyme activity is further reduced to approximately 10% of normal.[46]

Inheritance of the defect in the heterozygous mode is often insufficient to produce clinically, or even biochemically manifest disease. PCT may be silent, or clinically latent, until the predisposed individual encounters an additional factor that induces the unmasking of the disorder. Factors associated with clinical appearance of PCT include iron overload, alcohol, estrogenic hormones, or exposure to environmental hepatotoxins. In the last instance sufficient exposure appears able to produce PCT even in persons not genetically predisposed. The class of compounds that have produced epidemic PCT are the polychlorinated aromatic hydrocarbons. The classical example of hepatotoxin-induced nongenetic epidemic PCT occurred in Turkey.[47] Famished peoples there consumed seed wheat that had been treated with hexachlorobenzene as a fungicide. Large numbers of them subsequently developed cutaneous fragility, bullae, hyperpigmentation, and hypertrichosis, and urinary porphyrins were excreted in amounts and types similar to genetic PCT. Children breast fed by poisoned mothers developed skin lesions of a peculiar type. Short stature, shortened digits, increased pigmentation, and hypertrichosis have persisted for two decades after the acute events.[48] Occurrences of PCT have also been linked to exposure to polychlorinated biphenyls[49] and to dioxin.[50]

PCT has developed in association with benign and malignant liver tumors and with metastatic liver disease.[39] In addition to numerous individuals who have developed PCT-like blisters while receiving chronic hemodialysis treatment for renal failure, a situation associated with increased incidence of mildly elevated plasma porphyrin levels,[51,52] there are also numerous reports of similar patients with extraordinarily high levels of plasma porphyrins of the PCT type who had never had any cutaneous symptoms until after several months' dialysis.[53]

Patients with all of these types of PCT demonstrate similar skin lesions of the vesiculobullous, scarring pattern. Those with the largest accumulations (homozygous children or dialysis-related forms) have the most profound photosensitivity. Children with homozygous PCT may be as severely affected as children with CEP, and may exhibit erythrodontia. Homozygous PCT is also associated with anemia and with hepatosplenomegaly and abnormal liver function in some cases.[54]

Treatment of familial heterozygous or sporadic cases includes avoidance of sunlight exposure, removal of factors that are known inducers, and use of phlebotomy and/or chloroquine phosphate regimens to try to induce remission. In uncomplicated familial heterozygous PCT or in sporadic cases, removal of the inducer may have a beneficial effect even without additional treatment, but in most cases biochemical and clinical improvement is hastened by use of either or a combination of the two therapeutic approaches.

Patients with PCT often have associated increased body iron stores and a tendency toward polycythemia. Increased hepatic iron may play a role in facilitating the enzyme defect.[55,56] Removal of whole blood (several units over a period of several weeks to several months) often produces both biochemical and clinical improvement.[57-61] Although the rationale for this is usually considered to be the beneficial result of removing excess tissue iron,[57-60,62] it has also been suggested that removal of a plasma factor may play a role.[63] Supporting the role of iron mobilization is the observation that replacement of the iron is accompanied by worsening of the disease.[64,65] Supporting the role of the postulated plasma factor is the response of some patients to plasmapheresis.[66,67] Plasmapheresis has also been effective therapeutically for hemodialysis patients with PCT,[68] in whom anemia of chronic disease is a relative contraindication to phlebotomy as a method of treatment.

Chloroquine phosphate has been shown to complex with hepatocyte porphyrin stores in PCT, forming a water-soluble complex that is apparently discharged from the cells and excreted in the urine.[69] This appears to be a hepatotoxic event, for if large doses of the drug are given, patients with PCT may become quite ill, with markedly elevated serum liver enzymes, indicating liver-cell necrosis. Therefore, the dosages used for this indication are much smaller than the amounts used for lupus erythematosus or for malaria. It cannot be used in anephric patients, as dialysis does not remove the complex from the plasma, and patients are worsened.

Patients with PCT as a sequela of hepatic tumor may improve following resection of the lesion. There is no current experience with successful treatment of homozygous PCT.

β-Carotene oral photoprotection is not as obviously beneficial in PCT as in EPP, but may be used in cases in which other treatment is not possible or is ineffective.

Patients with PCT have an increased incidence of glucose intolerance and may have overt diabetes.[70] PCT has also been associated with systemic lupus erythematosus.[70]

D. Acute Intermittent Porphyria (AIP)

AIP is the only porphyria with solely systemic symptomatology. An autosomal-dominant disorder, AIP is characterized biochemically by the constant urinary excretion of increased levels of ALA and PBG.

ALA and PBG are colorless, nonphotosensitizing compounds that accumulate due to a partial block in US as discussed earlier. This defect is clinically significant in hepatocytes, where heme synthesis is active to provide the prosthetic heme for cytochromes, catalases, and peroxidases. Inheritance of the gene defect remains silent during childhood, becoming biochemically manifest after puberty. Clinical expression of the disease may remain latent in adulthood unless the affected individual encounters an inducing factor that triggers systemic symptoms. These symptoms are neurovisceral in nature, and are identical in AIP, VP, and HCP. These symptoms may include one or more chronic complaints (neurosis, psychosis, vague abdominal distress, constipation, neurological dysfunctions) or one or more of the more severe "acute attack" manifestations (coma, paralysis, seizures, psychosis, severe abdominal pain, hypertension, tachycardia, fluid and electrolyte disturbances) that may be life threatening in severity.

Acute attacks may be induced by several factors including dietary carbohydrate restriction, infections, hormonal fluctuations, stress, and an extensive list of drugs,[71,72] some commonly used (i.e., barbiturates, sulfonamides, griseofulvin). Patients subject to these attacks must be informed of their diagnosis and carefully counseled in avoidance of these factors.

Patients recognized to be suffering from an attack are often encountered in hospital intensive care settings. Early recognition of an acute attack is usually treated by infusion of glucose as well as general supportive measures dictated by the condition of the individual patient. High levels of glucose appear to inhibit the rate-controlling enzyme ALAS, thus slowing overproduction of ALA and PBG. The precise molecular mechanisms by which these precursors elicit the neurovisceral effects seen in AIP, VP, and HCP remain uncertain. High-dose propranolol has also been administered with beneficial effect during acute attack episodes,[73] but has significant side-effect potential and must be used with caution.[74] If the attack continues, intravenous infusion of hematin may be tried and may reverse the deregulation of heme synthesis.[75-78] Hematin appears to affect hepatic heme synthesis by providing an increased supply of a heme analogue that exerts negative feedback repression on the rate-limiting enzyme similar to that of heme. This repression slows production of ALA and PBG which then accumulate to a lesser extent at the partially blocked level of US.

Patients with AIP have no apparent defect in erythropoietic heme production. Nevertheless, deficient activity of the enzyme can be detected in erythrocytes as well as in other nonliver cell lines.

E. Variegate Porphyria (VP)

VP is another autosomal-dominant genetic defect resulting in an hepatic porphyria characterized by acute attack episodes.

As in AIP, symptoms are rarely apparent until after puberty, and may also remain latent in adulthood unless triggered by the same factors that are associated with AIP. The acute attacks and chronic systemic disorders are identical to those of AIP and are treated in the same manner.

In contrast to AIP, patients with VP may develop cutaneous photosensitivity, either alone, or in association with any of the systemic complaints. Some VP patients, however, have only systemic symptoms, and VP must be distinguished from AIP by laboratory analyses of porphyrins and precursors in urine, plasma, and stool. The enzyme defective appears to be PO, although in some cases heme synthase may be deficient as well.[17,18] The defect in PO, although demonstrable in several cell lines, is clinically manifested only in hepatocytes. Erythropoietic heme synthesis appears to be adequate, and there is no anemia or accumulation of erythrocyte porphyrins. Treatment for the acute attack and preventive measures are as outlined for AIP.

The cutaneous lesions, if present, are identical to those of PCT. Therapy of these lesions is difficult if the hepatic heme synthetic pathway is induced. Sun avoidance is the mainstay of treatment. β-carotene may be tried, but its efficacy in VP is unclear. Phlebotomy or chloroquine treatments are not helpful in VP.

F. Hereditary Coproporphyria (HCP)

HCP is encountered rarely, but is an autosomal-dominant, acute attack type hepatic porphyria with an occurrence of PCT-like skin lesions in occasional cases.[79]

As in AIP and VP, symptoms are absent in childhood, and are triggered in adult life by the set of agents noted for AIP. The attack symptoms, and treatment thereof, are identical to those of AIP and VP.

Cutaneous lesions are infrequent, but when observed, are similar to those of PCT. Phlebotomy and chloroquine are not effective. There is no associated anemia or accumulation of erythrocyte porphyrins.

REFERENCES

1. Granick, S., The induction in vitro of the synthesis of δ-aminolaevulinic acid synthetase in chemical porphyria: a response to certain drugs, sex hormones, and foreign chemicals, *J. Biol. Chem.,* 241, 1359, 1966.
2. Tschudy, D. P., Porphyrin metabolism and porphyrias, in *Metabolic Control and Disease,* Bondy, P. K. and Rosenbery, L. E., Eds., W. B. Saunders, Philadelphia, 1980, 939.
3. Giger, V. and Meyer, V. A., Role of haem in the induction of cytochrome P-450 by phenobarbitone, *Biochem. J.,* 198, 321, 1981.
4. Granick, S., Sinclair, P., Sassa, S., and Grieninger, G., Effects by heme, insulin, and serum albumin on heme and protein synthesis in chick embryo liver cells cultured in a chemically defined medium, and a spectrofluorometric assay for porphyrin composition, *J. Biol. Chem.,* 250, 9215, 1975.
5. Tschudy, D. P., The influence of hormonal and nutritional factors on the regulation of liver haem biosynthesis, in *Heme and Hemoproteins,* Springer-Verlag, Berlin, 1973, 255.
6. Redeker, A. G. and Sterling, R. E., The "glucose effect" in erythropoietic protoporphyria, *Arch. Intern. Med.,* 121, 466, 1968.
7. Elder, G. H., Haem synthesis and breakdown, in *Iron in Biochemistry and Medicine,* Vol. 2, Jacobs, A. J. and Worwood, M., Eds., Academic Press, New York, 1980.
8. Strand, L. J., Felsher, B. F., Redeker, A. G., and Marver, H. S., Heme biosynthesis in intermittent acute prophyria: decreased hepatic conversion of porphobilinogen to porphyrins and increased δ-aminolaevulinic acid synthetase activity, *Proc. Natl. Acad. Sci. U.S.A.,* 67, 1315, 1970.
9. Romeo, G. and Levin, E. Y., Uroporphyrinogen III cosynthetase in human congenital erythropoietic porphyria, *Proc. Natl. Acad. Sci. U.S.A.,* 63, 856, 1969.
10. Pimstone, N. R., Porphyria cutanea tarda, *Semin. Liver Dis.,* 2, 132, 1982.
11. Elder, G. H., Porphyrin metabolism in porphyria cutanea tarda, *Semin. Hematol.,* 14, 227, 1977.

12. Elder, G. H., Evans, J. O., Thomas, N., Cox, R., Brodie, M. J., Moore, M. R., Goldberg, A., and Nicholson, D. C., The primary enzyme defect in hereditary corproporphyria, *Lancet,* 2, 1217, 1976.
13. Grandchamp, B. and Nordmann, Y., Decreased lymphocyte coproporphyrinogen III oxidase in hereditary coproporphyria, *Biochem. Biophys. Res. Commun.,* 74, 1089, 1977.
14. Brenner, D. A. and Bloomer, J. R., The enzymatic defect in variegate porphyria, *N. Engl. J. Med.,* 302, 765, 1980.
15. Rimington, C., Lockwood, W. H., and Belcher, R. V., The excretion of porphyrin-peptide conjugates in porphyria variegata, *Clin. Sci.,* 35, 211, 1968.
16. Elder, G. H. and Evans, J. O., A radiochemical method for the measurement of coproporphyrinogen oxidase and the utilization of substrates other than coproporphyrinogen III by the enzyme from rat liver, *Biochem. J.,* 169, 205, 1978.
17. Becker, D. M., Viljoen, D. J., Katz, J., and Kramer, S., Reduced ferrochelatase activity: a defect common to porphyria variegata and protoporphyria, *Br. J. Haematol.,* 36, 171, 1977.
18. Viljoen, D. J., Cyanis, E., and Becker, D. M., Reduced ferrochelatase activity in fibroblasts from patients with porphyria variegata, *Am. J. Hematol.,* 6, 185, 1979.
19. Bottomley, S. S., Tanaka, M., and Everett, M. A., Diminished erythroid ferrochelatase activity in protoporphyria, *J. Lab. Clin. Med.,* 86, 126, 1975.
20. deGoeij, A. F. P. M., Christianse, K., and van Steveninck, J., Decreased haem synthetase activity in blood cells of patients with erythropoietic protoporphyria, *Eur. J. Clin. Invest.,* 5, 397, 1975.
21. Bloomer, J. R., Bonkowski, H. L., Ebert, P. S., and Mahoney, M. J., Inheritance in protoporphyria — comparison of heme synthetase activity in skin fibroblasts with clinical features, *Lancet,* 2, 226, 1976.
22. Haining, R. G., Cowger, M. L., Labbe, R. F., and Finch, C. A., Congenital erythropoietic porphyria. II. The effects of induced polycythemia, *Blood,* 36, 297, 1970.
23. Piomelli, S., Poh-Fitzpatrick, M., Skolnick, L., Graziano, J., Berdon, W., and Seaman, C., Supression of porphyrin production in congenital erythropoietic porphyria by hypertransfusion, *Blood,* 63(Abstr.), 49, 1983.
24. Schwartz, S., Johnson, J. A., Stephenson, B. D., Anderson, A. S., Edmondson, P. R., and Fusaro, R. M., Erythropoietic defects in protoporphyria: a study of factors involved in labelling of porphyrins and bile pigments from ALA-³H and glycine-¹⁴C, *J. Lab. Clin. Med.,* 78, 411, 1971.
25. Lamon, J. M., Poh-Fitzpatrick, M. B., and Lamola, A. A., Hepatic protoporphyrin production in human protoporphyria: alteration of protoporphyrin levels in blood and feces with intravenous hematin and analysis of red cell protoporphyrin distribution, *Gastroenterology,* 79, 115, 1980.
26. Scholnick, P., Marver, H. S., and Schmid, R., Erythropoietic protoporphyria: evidence for multiple sites of excess protoporphyrin formation, *J. Clin. Invest.,* 50, 203, 1971.
27. Cripps, D. J. and Scheuer, P. J., Hepatobiliary changes in erythropoietic protoporphyria, *Arch. Pathol.,* 80, 500, 1965.
28. Ibrahim, G. W. and Watson, C. J., Enterohepatic circulation and conversion of protoporphyrin to bile pigment in man, *Proc. Soc. Exp. Biol. Med.,* 127, 890, 1968.
29. Wolff, K., Wolff-Schreiner, E., and Gschnait, F., Liver inclusions in erythropoietic protoporphyria, *Eur. J. Clin. Invest.,* 5, 21, 1975.
30. Bruguera, M., Esquerda, J. E., Mascaro, J. M., and Pinol, J., Erythropoietic protoporphyria, *Arch. Pathol. Lab. Med.,* 100, 587, 1976.
31. MacDonald, D. M., Germain, D., and Perrot, H., The histopathology and ultrastructure of liver disease in erythropoietic protoporphyria, *Br. J. Dermatol.,* 104, 7, 1981.
32. Klaskin, G. and Bloomer, J., Birefringence of hepatic pigment deposits in erythropoietic protoporphyria. Specificity and sensitivity of polarization microscopy in the identification of hepatic protoporphyrin deposits, *Gastroenterology,* 67, 294, 1974.
33. Mathews, M. M. and Sistrom, W. R., Function of carotenoid pigments in non-photosynthetic bacteria, *Nature (London),* 184, 1892, 1959.
34. Mathews, M. M., Effect of beta-carotene against lethal photosensitization by hematoporphyrin, *Nature (London),* 203, 1092, 1964.
35. Mathews-Roth, M. M., Pathak, M. A., Fitzpatrick, T. B., Harber, L. C., and Kass, E. H., Beta-carotene as an oral photoprotective agent in erythropoietic protoporphyria, *JAMA,* 228, 104, 1974.
36. DeLeo, V. A., Poh-Fitzpatrick, M. B., Mathews-Roth, M. M., and Harber, L. C., Erythropoietic protoporphyria: ten years experience, *Am. J. Med.,* 60, 8, 1976.
37. Lamola, A. A. and Blumberg, W. E., The effectiveness of beta-carotene and phytoene as systemic sunscreens, in Program 4th Annu. Meet. American Society for Photobiology, 1976, 109.
38. Tio, T. H., Leijnse, B., Jarrett, A., and Rimington, C., Acquired porphyria from a liver tumor, *Clin. Sci.,* 16, 517, 1957.
39. Grossman, M. E. and Bickers, D. R., Porphyria cutanea tarda, a rare cutaneous manifestation of hepatic tumors, *Cutis,* 21, 782, 1978.

40. Poh-Fitzpatrick, M. B., Bellet, N., DeLeo, V. A., Grossman, M. E., and Bickers, D. R., Porphyria cutanea tarda in two patients treated with hemodialysis for chronic renal failure, *N. Engl. J. Med.,* 299, 292, 1978.

41. Poh-Fitzpatrick, M. B., Masullo, A. S., and Grossman, M. E., Porphyria cutanea tarda associated with chronic renal disease and hemodialysis, *Arch. Dermatol.,* 116, 191, 1980.

42. Elder, G. H., The metabolism of porphyrins of the isocaproporphyrin series, *Enzyme,* 17, 61, 1974.

43. Elder, G. H., Differentiation of porphyria cutanea tarda symptomatica from other types of porphyria by measurement of isocoproporphyrin in feces, *J. Clin. Pathol.,* 28, 601, 1975.

44. Kushner, J. P., Barbuto, A. J., and Lee, G. R., An inherited enzymatic defect in porphyria cutanea tarda: decreased uroporphyrinogen decarboxylase activity, *J. Clin. Invest.,* 58, 1089, 1976.

45. Elder, G. H., Lee, G. B., and Tovey, J. A., Decreased activity of hepatic uroporphyrinogen decarboxylase in sporadic porphyria cutanea tarda, *N. Engl. J. Med.,* 299, 274, 1978.

46. Elder, G. H., Smith, S. G., Herrero, C., Mascaro, J. M., Lecha, M., Muniesa, A. M., Czarnecki, D. B., Brenan, J., Poulos, V., and DeSalamanca, R. E., Hepatoerythropoietic porphyria: a new uroporphyrinogen decarboxylase defect or homozygous porphyria cutanea tarda?, *Lancet,* 1, 916, 1981.

47. Cam, C. and Nigogosyan, G., Acquired toxic porphyria due to hexachlorobenzene, *JAMA,* 183, 88, 1963.

48. Cripps, D. J., Gocmen, A., and Peters, H. A., Porphyria turcica. Twenty years after hexachlorobenzene intoxication, *Arch. Dermatol.,* 116, 46, 1980.

49. Bleiberg, J., Wallen, M., Brodkin, R., and Applebaum, I. L., Industrially acquired porphyria, *Arch. Dermatol.,* 89, 793, 1964.

50. Poland, A. P., Smith, D., Metter, G., and Possick, P., A health survey of workers in a 2,4-D and 2,4,5-T plant, *Arch. Environ. Health,* 22, 316, 1971.

51. Day, R. S. and Eales, L., Porphyrins in chronic renal failure, *Nephron,* 26, 90, 1980.

52. Poh-Fitzpatrick, M. B., Sossin, A. E., and Bemis, J., Porphyrin levels in plasma and erythrocytes of chronic hemodialysis patients, *J. Am. Acad. Dermatol.,* 7, 100, 1982.

53. Hannon, R. and Callen, J. P., Porphyria cutanea tarda as a cause of bullous dermatosis of hemodialysis. A case report and review of the literature, *Cutis,* 28, 261, 1981.

54. Czarnecki, D. B., Hepatoerythropoietic porphyria, *Arch. Dermatol.,* 116, 307, 1980.

55. Kushner, J. P., Lee, G. R., and Nacht, S., The role of iron in the pathogenesis of porphyria cutanea tarda. An in vitro model, *J. Clin. Invest.,* 51, 3044, 1972.

56. Kushner, J. P., Steinmuller, D. P., and Lee, G. H., The role of iron in the pathogenesis of porphyria cutanea tarda. II. Inhibition of uroporphyrinogen decarboxylase, *J. Clin. Invest.,* 56, 661, 1975.

57. Ippen, H., Allgemeinsymptome der spaten Hautporphyrie (porphyria cutanea tarda) als Hinweise für deren Behandlung, *Dtsch. Med. Wochenschr.,* 86, 127, 1961.

58. Epstein, J. H. and Redeker, A. G., Porphyria cutanea tarda, a study of the effect of phlebotomy, *N. Engl. J. Med.,* 279, 1301, 1968.

59. Kalivas, J. T., Pathak, M. A., and Fitzpatrick, T. B., Phlebotomy and iron-overload in porphyria cutanea tarda, *Lancet,* 1, 1184, 1969.

60. Walsh, J. R., Lobitz, W. C., Mahler, D. J., and Kingery, F. A. J., Phlebotomy therapy in cutaneous porphyria, *Arch. Dermatol.,* 101, 167, 1970.

61. Ippen, H., Treatment of porphyria cutanea tarda by phlebotomy, *Semin. Hematol.,* 14, 253, 1977.

62. Felsher, B. F. and Kushner, J. P., Hepatic siderosis and porphyria cutanea tarda: relation of iron excess to the metabolic defect, *Semin. Hematol.,* 14, 243, 1977.

63. Rifkind, A. B., Sassa, S., Merkatz, I. R., Winchester, R., Harber, L. C., and Kappas, A., Stimulators and inhibitors of hepatic porphyrin formation in human sera, *J. Clin. Invest.,* 53, 1167, 1974.

64. Lundvall, O., The effect of replenishment of iron stores after phlebotomy therapy in porphyria cutanea tarda, *Acta Med. Scand.,* 189, 51, 1971.

65. Felsher, B. J., Jones, M. L., and Redeker, A. G., Iron and hepatic uroporphyrin synthesis. Relation in porphyria cutanea tarda, *JAMA,* 226, 663, 1973.

66. Allen, B. R., Parker, S., Thompson, G. G., Moore, M. R., Darby, F. J., and Hunter, J. A. A., The effect of treatment on plasma uroporphyrin levels in cutaneous hepatic porphyria, *Br. J. Dermatol.,* 93, 37, 1975.

67. Miyachi, S., Shiraichi, S., and Miki, Y., Small volume plasmaphoresis in the management of porphyria cutanea tarda, *Arch. Dermatol.,* 119, 752, 1983.

68. Disler, P., Day, R., Burman, N., Blekkenhorst, G., and Eales, L., Treatment of hemodialysis-related porphyria cutanea tarda with plasma exchange, *Am. J. Med.,* 72, 989, 1982.

69. Scholnick, P. L., Epstein, J. H., and Marver, H. S., The molecular basis of chloroquine in porphyria cutanea tarda, *J. Invest. Dermatol.,* 61, 226, 1973.

70. Grossman, M. E., Bickers, D. R., Poh-Fitzpatrick, M. B., DeLeo, V. A., and Harber, L. C., Porphyria cutanea tarda: clinical features and laboratory findings in forty patients, *Am. J. Med.,* 67, 277, 1979.

71. Moore, M. R., International review of drugs in acute porphyria — 1980, *Int. J. Biochem.*, 12, 1089, 1980.
72. Disler, P. B., Blekkenhorst, G. H., Eales, L., Moore, M. R., and Straughan, J., Guidelines for drug prescription in patients with the acute porphyrias, *S. Afr. Med. J.*, 61, 656, 1982.
73. Atsmon, A., Blum, I., and Fischl, J., Treatment of an acute attack of porphyria variegata with propranolol, *S. Afr. Med. J.*, 46, 331, 1972.
74. Bonkowsky, H. H. and Tschudy, D. P., Hazards of propranolol in treatment of acute porphyria, *Br. Med. J.*, 4, 47, 1974.
75. Watson, C. J., Pierach, C. A., Bossenmaier, I., and Cardinal, R., Use of hematin in the acute attack of the ''inducible'' hepatic porphyrias, *Adv. Intern. Med.*, 23, 265, 1978.
76. Lamon, J. M., Frykholm, B. C., Bennett, M., and Tschudy, D. P., Prevention of acute porphyric attacks by hematin, *Lancet*, 2, 492, 1978.
77. Lamon, J. M., Frykholm, B. C., Hess, R. A., and Tschudy, D. P., Hematin therapy for acute porphyria, *Medicine (Baltimore)*, 58, 252, 1979.
78. Pierach, C. A., Hematin therapy for the porphyric attack, *Semin. Liver Dis.*, 2, 125, 1982.
79. Goldberg, A., Rimington, C., and Lochhead, A. C., Hereditary coproporphyria, *Lancet*, 1, 632, 1967.

INDEX